AUDIENCE EVOLUTION

AUDIENCE EVOLUTION

NEW TECHNOLOGIES AND THE TRANSFORMATION OF MEDIA AUDIENCES

PHILIP M. NAPOLI

COLUMBIA UNIVERSITY PRESS
NEW YORK

COLUMBIA UNIVERSITY PRESS

Publishers Since 1893

New York   Chichester, West Sussex

Copyright © 2011 Columbia University Press

All rights reserved

Library of Congress Cataloging-in-Publication Data
Napoli, Philip M.
Audience evolution : new technologies and the transformation of media audiences /
Philip M. Napoli.
p. cm.
Includes bibliographical references and index.
ISBN 978-0-231-15034-7 (cloth : alk. paper) — ISBN 978-0-231-15035-4 (pbk. : alk.
paper) — ISBN 978-0-231-52094-2 (ebook)
1. Mass media—Audiences. 2. Digital media—Technological innovations.   I. Title.

P96.A83N35   2010
302.23—dc22   2010023906

Columbia University Press books are printed on permanent and durable acid-free
paper.
This book is printed on paper with recycled content.

Printed in the United States of America

c 10 9 8 7 6 5 4 3
p 10 9 8

References to Internet Web sites (URLs) were accurate at the time of writing. Neither
the author nor Columbia University Press is responsible for URLs that may have
expired or changed since the manuscript was prepared.

TO BELLA, WHO MADE ME LAUGH EVERY DAY

CONTENTS

List of Illustrations   ix

Preface   xi

Introduction   1

1. Contextualizing Audience Evolution   25

2. The Transformation of Media Consumption   54

3. The Transformation of Audience Information Systems   88

4. Contesting Audiences   117

5. The Implications of Audience Evolution   149

Notes   175

References   193

Index   239

ILLUSTRATIONS

Figures

I.1. The Process of Audience Evolution 5

2.1. The Fragmentation of the Media Environment 57

2.2. The Long Tail of Media Consumption 59

2.3. New Audience Information Flows 87

3.1. Audience Dimensions 91

5.1. The Decline of Exposure and the Rise of Alternative
     Audience Conceptualizations 151

Tables

2.1. Components of Audience Autonomy 79

3.1. Definitions of Audience Engagement 97

PREFACE

It wasn't long after I completed my 2003 book, *Audience Economics,* that I realized that the final chapter of that book, which considered the impact of technological changes on the marketplace for media audiences, could very easily be expanded into an entire book in its own right. The seven years since the publication of *Audience Economics* have included some of the most dramatic technological and economic changes in the history of our media system: the rise of social networking sites, to the point where social networking has eclipsed email as the most common online activity; the development of increasingly sophisticated hand-held devices such as the iPod, iPad, iPhone, and Kindle; the explosion of blogging and other forms of user-generated content, as well as platforms (such as YouTube and Twitter) for disseminating it; the transition to digital audio and video broadcasting; the rise of DVRs; the recession and, of course, the associated dramatic economic hardships that confront traditional media sectors such as newspapers, magazines, and broadcast television. All of these developments are contributing to a dramatic reconfiguration of the relationship between the media and their audiences.

Less visible to the casual observer, however, is another layer of developments that are also contributing to these changes. These revolve around the systems that media organizations and advertisers utilize to learn about their audiences, to measure their behavior, to predict future behavior, and to assign value to different segments of the audience. These measurement systems are the lifeblood of ad-supported media. And they too are changing dramatically, with these changes driven in large part by many of the technological changes mentioned previously. And so in recent years we have seen the launch of new systems for measuring television and radio audiences, new approaches to the measurement of Internet audiences, and a flurry of ongoing efforts to effectively capture the flow of audiences across so many new platforms for consuming media.

Examining how media industries seek to understand their audiences has always struck me as an interesting and fruitful path of inquiry for gaining a deeper understanding of these industries and how they go about producing and distributing the content that flows through our media system. Engaging in this kind of inquiry during a period of intense transition (some would say crisis), such as is currently taking place, struck me as particularly interesting.

And so this book represents an effort to extend a line of inquiry that I began with *Audience Economics*—one that focuses this time entirely on the subject of how new technologies are affecting the audience marketplace and that therefore treats this subject in much greater depth than was the case in *Audience Economics.* It is important to emphasize, though, that the hope here is to provide an analysis that not only contributes to an understanding of the developments that are taking place today, but also creates a useful framework for understanding developments that have taken place in the past, as well as those that will take place in the future.

This project spent a fair bit of time gestating, and I am grateful to a number of colleagues who endured early, somewhat half-baked, presentations of the ideas contained in this book. The faculties of the Department of Communication at the University of Michigan and the Medill School of Journalism were early, receptive, though challenging audiences for these ideas. I am also thankful for the opportunity I was provided to present parts of this project to audiences of media professionals at the Office of the Consulate General of Finland in New York, as well as to academic audiences at the International Communication Association 2008 and 2009 conferences, the International Association for Media and Communications Research's 2008 conference, the Massachusetts Institute of Technology's Media in Transition 6 conference, and the University of Miami's Advances in Audience and Consumer Measurement conference. Thanks to Robert Picard of the Media Management and Transformation Centre and Walter McDowell of the University of Miami for including me in the latter.

Thanks are due to my Communications and Media Management Area chair, Everette Dennis, as well as to the dean of the Graduate School of Business, Howard Tuckman, and the Office of Academic Affairs of Fordham

University, for awarding me a Magis Professorship, which provided me with three years of a reduced teaching load and therefore allowed me to devote more time to this project and to finish it much sooner than would probably otherwise have been the case. Fordham continues to provide me with a very hospitable and supportive research environment that, in the heart of New York City, could not be better situated for conducting research for a project such as this one.

A number of graduate and undergraduate research assistants were tremendously helpful in the completion of this project. These include Kurt Andrews, Adrienne Shiffman, Jackie Jay, Sheea Sybblis, Anne Halligan, Jessica Crowell, Amanda Trokan, Advaitha Arunkumar, Hyun Kyung Oh, Jeremy Brotchner, Adrienne Harth, Taryn Bensky, Lee Rosenberg, and Lindsay Kaufman. I hope I'm not forgetting anyone.

Conversations with a number of colleagues, including Jim Webster of Northwestern University, Patricia Phalen of George Washington University, Joe Brown of Versus, Matthew Pagen of Nielsen IAG, David Gunzerath of the Media Ratings Council, Minna Aslama of the University of Helsinki, Gabriel Rossman of UCLA (who also emailed various useful bits of information over the past couple of years), and Paul Lavrakas (formerly of Nielsen), were all helpful in terms of fleshing out various parts of the book. I'm appreciative of the time these individuals all took to speak with me.

Thanks are also due to Philip Leventhal of Columbia University Press for taking an interest in this project and shepherding it through the publication process and to Kerri Cox Sullivan for her expert copyediting. Three anonymous reviewers provided useful feedback on the proposal that helped me to refine the project's focus, as well as to make sure that important issues were not neglected. The feedback of two anonymous reviewers on the completed manuscript also helped me to refine some points and improve some areas of ambiguity. The book is much better for these reviewers' input, though of course its remaining shortcomings are entirely my doing.

Thanks to my parents for always being supportive of my academic tendencies. And finally, thanks to Anne, my wife, for not getting too annoyed with me for spending nights working on this rather than being particularly engaging company.

AUDIENCE EVOLUTION

INTRODUCTION

Much has been made in recent years of the many ways in which the media environment is undergoing dramatic change. We know, for instance, that the explosion of Web sites, the proliferation of television channels, and the emergence of new content-delivery platforms—ranging from hand-held devices, to satellite radio, to on-demand and interactive television services— all are contributing to exponential increases in the fragmentation of the media environment. We also know that new media technologies are providing media audiences with unprecedented control over the media consumption process. From the time-shifting and commercial-skipping capabilities of the DVR, to the personalization of online news sites, to the unprecedented content portability offered by hand-held devices, individuals have ever-growing levels of control over when, how, and where they consume media. And, perhaps most dramatic of all, new media are increasingly putting the power to create and distribute content into the hands of the audience. User-generated content now competes with traditional media content for audience attention (Berman et al. 2007).

What has received less attention, however, is the question of what these changes in the media environment mean for how media organizations think about their audiences.[1] What can examining these environmental changes tell us about how media organizations' perceptions of their audiences change over time? What are the specific technological and institutional forces that can effect such change? How are such changes negotiated and resisted within the complex dynamics of the various stakeholders involved in attracting and monetizing media audiences? And, finally, what are the broader sociocultural implications of the changes taking place in the conceptualization of media audiences?

Answering these questions involves adopting a somewhat unusual analytical position. It requires focusing on the audience exclusively as conceptualized through the particular sets of practices, behavioral patterns, and analytical orientations and priorities that characterize the operation of media industries. This approach essentially involves focusing on what is perhaps best described as the *institutionalized audience,* or what Ettema and Whitney have called the "institutionally effective" audience (1994:5).

From a media research standpoint, the term *institutions* has had two interrelated meanings (Moe and Syvertsen 2007). The first involves the analysis of concrete organizations, be they media outlets (Gans 1979/2005; Gitlin 1983/2000), government agencies (Bimber 1996; Napoli 1998b), advertising agencies (Hackley 2002; Laird 1998), or audience research firms (Beville 1988; Buzzard 1990). The term *media organizations* will be used throughout this book as a simplifying catch-all for these various organizational categories that, in combination with the technologies they employ and the regulations under which they operate, comprise our media system.

The second meaning focuses on established norms, formal procedures, and practices (see, e.g., Leblebici, Slancik, Copy, and King 1991). This in many ways reflects the more traditional meaning of the term *institution,* as it applies to concepts as marriage, religion, or the law. Along these lines, the practice of journalism, for instance, can be seen as such an institution; and as such has been the focus of an extensive body of research (e.g., Cook 2005; Weaver et al. 2006; Winfield 2008). Similarly, "Hollywood" can be thought of as an institution, and has been analyzed from this perspective (Baumann 2007; Scott 2005). The audience also can be thought of as such an institution, particularly within the context of this analysis, which considers the audience primarily in terms of how it is constructed within the formal procedures and practices of media organizations (see Ang 1991; Bermejo 2007; DeWerth-Pallmeyer 1997; Ettema and Whitney 2004; Hagen 1999; Oswell 2002; Webster and Phalen 1997).

Moe and Syvertsen identify the first approach as focusing on institutions as "specific organizations" and the second approach as focusing on institutions as "spheres" (2007:150). What it is particularly important to emphasize, however, is the interrelatedness of these two analytical frames, as the examination of specific organizations is often a key method of understanding the broader spheres in which they operate, and vice versa. Thus, for instance, studying how new technologies are being employed by news outlets is a useful way to understand how new technologies are transforming the institution of journalism (e.g., Boczkowski 2004b). Conversely, understanding the broader sphere of journalism and how it is changing is vital to understanding the organizational dynamics within individual news outlets (e.g., Cook 2005).

This analysis employs such an integrated approach to the study of media institutions. It builds upon previous research that has illustrated how the concept of the audience is constructed and defined to reflect the economic and strategic imperatives of media organizations, and that has considered the broader social and political ramifications of these constructions. A common undercurrent of many of these analyses has been the contention that the institutionalized media audience is largely a socially constructed phenomenon (see, e.g., Ang 1991; Meehan 1984). As Peter Dahlgren has noted, "'audiences' are always *at least in part* discursive constructs, shaped by specific institutional needs and discursive domains" (1998:307; emphasis in original).[2] This point reflects the fact that media organizations define audiences in particular ways, using analytical tools and perspectives that reflect their needs and interests. This is what Ettema and Whitney meant with the term "institutionally *effective* audiences" (1994:5; emphasis added). *Effective* audiences are those that can be efficiently integrated into the economics of media industries.

Given this fundamental constraint, many significant dimensions of what it means to be part of the media audience tend to be neglected (see, e.g., Ang 1991). The institutionalized audience, it should be emphasized, represents just one of many possible perspectives on the concept of the audience, but one that has dramatic repercussions for the production, distribution, and exhibition of a wide range of entertainment and information products of substantial cultural and political influence.

This book is primarily concerned with the institutionalized audience; that is, the audience as socially constructed by media industries, advertisers, and associated audience measurement firms. This focus is adopted in an effort to develop a deeper understanding of how these social constructions of media audiences change over time, of how technological and institutional forces can effect such change, and how such changes are negotiated and resisted by the stakeholders involved in attracting and monetizing media audiences. And in the end, this book considers the broader sociocultural implications of the changes currently taking place in the social construction of media audiences.

FROM MEDIA EVOLUTION TO AUDIENCE EVOLUTION

It is the central contention of this book that we are in the midst of an evolution in the nature of media audiences. This use of a biological metaphor is not uncommon in the analysis of media institutions. For instance, a growing body of scholarship has demonstrated how media industries evolve in response to changing environmental conditions (see, e.g., Dimmick 2002, Lehman-Wilzig and Cohen-Avigdor 2004; Noll 2006). Media evolution research has shown how media industries respond to environmental changes, such as changes in socioeconomic conditions, the regulatory environment, or (most important to this analysis) technological changes such as the introduction of a new, competing media technology. This line of research has also examined how new media technologies evolve over time as they interact with, and become integrated into, the established media system (see, e.g., Cheong and Leckenby 2003). A recurrent theme within this line of research is how various institutional interests and pressures lead to various forms of resistance to new technologies that often affect the pace and/or the direction of the evolutionary process (see, e.g., Jackaway 1995; Winston 1999).

The same basic analytical framework is being applied in this analysis of media audiences. Just as media industries evolve in response to environmental changes, so too do the conceptualizations of the audience employed by media organizations evolve in response to environmental changes. Today, technological changes are compelling media industries to think differently about their audiences, undermining traditional conceptual and analytical approaches while at the same time opening up alternative approaches. Specifically, while in some ways technological changes are destabilizing traditional approaches to audiences, in other ways new media technologies, as well new technologies for measuring media audiences, gathering feedback from them, and anticipating their tastes and preferences, are making it possible for media industries to fundamentally redefine what media audiences mean to them and how they factor into the economics and strategy of their businesses. These dynamics are represented in figure I.1, and are detailed below.

THE EFFECTS OF MEDIA AND AUDIENCE FRAGMENTATION

The first key driver of contemporary audience evolution comprises the technological changes that are transforming how, when, and where audiences

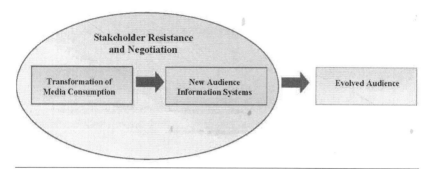

FIGURE I.1 The Process of Audience Evolution

consume media. The two key phenomena that these changes have produced, and thus the two key phenomena that media industries must integrate into their reconceptualization of their audiences, are media and audience *fragmentation* and *audience autonomy* (see Napoli 2003a).

Many observers have noted the ever-growing fragmentation of the media environment, in which an increased array of content options is provided across an increased array of distribution platforms (Neuman 1991; Turow 1997). New technologies such as hand-held devices and interactive television services build upon established technologies, providing ever-expanding means by which content can reach audiences. At the same time, within many of these distribution platforms the capacity for providing more choices continues to expand dramatically (see, e.g., Anderson 2006; Napoli 2003a). Individual technologies such as cable television and the Internet continue to expand their capacity to deliver content. These phenomena contribute to the continued disintegration of traditional "mass" audiences (Neuman 1991), and the increasing prominence of "long tail" scenarios, in which audience attention is clustered around a select few content options, followed by a long tail, in which the remaining multitude of content options each attract very small audiences that in the aggregate can exceed the audience for the "hits" (Anderson 2006).

The key implication of this process of media and audience fragmentation is the extent to which it is undermining traditional approaches to conceptualizing media audiences. These traditional approaches have been oriented around conceptualizing audiences primarily in terms of their exposure to media content. Traditionally, the holy grail of media strategy—particularly in the realm of advertising-supported media—has involved the acquisition of as many "eyeballs" as possible. More recently, the focus has reoriented around attracting only the most desirable "eyeballs"; i.e., those eyeballs attached to the kind of people highly valued by advertisers (Turow 1997). Typically, this has meant an emphasis on appealing to audiences in the 18–49-year-old range, to the relative neglect of younger and older audiences (Gabler 2003; Napoli 2003a). Still, however, the key concern has been with how many people were exposed to the content and/or exposed to the advertisements embedded within the content (Webster and Phalen 1997). As a result, the currencies employed in most sectors of the media industry have revolved around the basic question of how many people in various audience categories were exposed to a particular piece of content (Webster, Phalen, and Lichty 2006).

In contrast, questions of how audience members reacted to the content, either cognitively or behaviorally, have at best resided at the margins of the audience marketplace. This prioritization within media industries of maximizing *exposure* by the desired audience segments is reflected in discussions of the growth of an *attention economy*, in which the capturing of audience attention is the key criteria for success (Davenport and Beck 2002; Goldhaber 1997; Lanham 2006). Reflecting these priorities, the majority of the commercial systems used to measure media audiences across both newer and established media typically have focused entirely on the basic question of what type of, and how many, people were exposed to the content (see Webster, Phalen, and Lichty 2006).

Today, increased media and audience fragmentation is straining and undermining the traditional, exposure-based approaches to audiences that long have served as the foundation of the audience marketplace (see, e.g., Ephron and Philport 2005; Webster 2008). Such approaches typically rely upon data gathered from small, but presumably representative, samples of the audience, who take part in a systematic measurement process (Webster, Phalen, and Lichty 2006). From this sample of participants, data are gathered about their media consumption habits. These data form the basis of the ratings, circulation, and unique visitors figures that are the economic engine of advertiser-supported television, radio, print, and online media.

However, the extent that audiences today are spread across a much wider range of content options, and across a much wider range of delivery platforms, means that larger and larger samples of audiences are needed to accurately and reliably ascertain the distribution of audience attention (see, e.g., Napoli 2003a). It is difficult for the organizations that measure media audiences, whether online, on television, or on the radio, to keep up with these processes of fragmentation, due to both the costs and the methodological challenges involved. As a result, inaccuracy of basic exposure data increases, as do unpredictable fluctuations in the data (Kirkham 1996). This is particularly the case for content that attracts relatively small audiences (Napoli 2003a).[3] In the new, highly fragmented media environment, this characteristic applies to the majority of available content options, ranging from individual Web sites to individual television or radio programs (Anderson 2006). These patterns undermine both the descriptive and the analytical (i.e., for predicting future audience behavior) uses of traditional exposure data (Kirkham 1996).

One recent industry analysis claims that "the extent to which the media landscape has changed over the past 15 years [has placed] far more stress on audience measurement than ever before" (Harris and Chasin 2006:3). Another has announced "the fall of exposure" (Jaffe 2005:172). Approaching media audiences primarily in terms of their exposure to content is therefore becoming a much more difficult and ultimately potentially less viable proposition than it was in years past. This stress on traditional audience measurement systems has generated substantial concern and discontent among advertisers, media buyers, and content providers (Harris and Chasin 2006; Starkey 2002). This state of affairs is particularly significant given that, as Starkey has observed, "the media industries are accustomed to working with rather than against [audience] data. Usually they have no choice, because of the importance placed on the data by others" (2004:12).

What had been an institutionally effective audience is essentially losing its effectiveness. When we see a situation such as the one that is developing now, in which something approaching a consensus is emerging among various stakeholder groups that established exposure-based approaches to conceptualizing media audiences are inadequate (see, e.g., Kim 2006), then the institutional conditions are likely right for an evolutionary change to take place.

THE EFFECTS OF AUDIENCE AUTONOMY

Audience autonomy is the second shift in the dynamics of media consumption that is central to the ongoing process of audience evolution. The term *audience autonomy* in this case refers to how contemporary characteristics of the media environment, ranging from interactivity to mobility to on-demand functionality to the increased capacity for user-generated content, all serve to enhance the extent to which audiences have control over the process of media consumption.

This transition to a more interactive media environment, like the transition to an increasingly fragmented media environment, also has undermined traditional analytical approaches to media audiences. At the most basic level, an audience marketplace predicated primarily on the quantity of audience exposures to advertisements is being undermined by various technologies that empower audiences to block or skip advertisements, whether in terms of online pop-up blockers or the fast-forwarding features associated with digital video recorders (DVRs). More broadly, as one analysis has noted, "Traditional measures that were designed for passive media fail to capture the important and differentiating dimensions of response to interactive communication" (Stewart and Pavlou 2002:382). That is, traditional approaches to media audiences fail to capture all of the important dimensions of audience behavior that are exhibited when audiences' relationship with media becomes more interactive in nature. In an increasingly interactive media environment, the very concept of the audience becomes more robust, more multifaceted in nature. Exposure-focused analytical approaches ultimately fail to capture this. Instead, they emphasize only the more passive element of media consumption—basic exposure—to the neglect of more active elements that may have substantial economic and strategic value for media organizations.

However, as much as the autonomy facilitated by the new media environment undermines the utility of the more passive, exposure-focused conceptualization of audiences, it also is highlighting other, traditionally marginalized, aspects of media audiences. The new media environment is one in which there are substantial opportunities for audiences to interact with media, whether it be at the most basic level of searching for content, or at more advanced levels such as providing feedback, influencing outcomes, responding directly to advertising messages, or generating parallel content (see, e.g., Spurgeon 2008; Svoen 2007). These various interactive components of the new media environment illuminate previously concealed dimensions of audiences, many of which are being judged to have significant value.

THE RISE OF NEW AUDIENCE INFORMATION SYSTEMS

The interactive capacities of the new media environment facilitate the systematic gathering, aggregation, and analysis of information about these previously concealed dimensions of audience behavior. That is, these newly demonstrated aspects of the audience are both quantifiable and monetizable (Rohle 2007; Spurgeon 2008). New streams of data can be gathered and analyzed about audience members' media consumption habits, content preferences, degree of engagement, and levels of interest in, anticipation about, and appreciation of the content they consume. All of these dimensions of audience behavior are fundamentally different from the traditional exposure metric. Some, such as interest and anticipation, actually precede exposure. Others, such as engagement and appreciation, are essentially byproducts of exposure, though the relationship can be a complex one. For instance, it may not be the case that television programs with the largest audiences are necessarily those with the most engaged or appreciative audience; nor might those programs be the ones that exhibit the highest levels of audience appreciation (see, e.g., Gunter and Wober 1992; Menneer 1987; Mitgang 2002).

In the new media environment, various dimensions of participation, appreciation, and feedback are now expressed in very public forms online that are accessible to, and are being readily accessed and analyzed by, both commercial and academic audience researchers (Harris and Chasin 2006; Livingstone 2003; Lotz and Ross 2004). According to one participant in a recent industry study, "'Technology is . . . allowing us to measure just about anything'" (Harris and Chasin 2006:18). In the commercial context, systematic, syndicated research products using data gathered from online forums are being offered by audience research firms such as Nielsen, Simmons, and Optimedia for media ranging from television to magazines to Web sites (ARF 2006b; Vasquez 2008a).

As a result, media organizations can now look beyond the basic question of how many people watched, for example, a particular television program (be it via television, online, or via hand-held devices); they can also look at how much the audience enjoyed the program by analyzing the online "chatter" posted on Internet discussion boards and blogs afterward (Vasquez 2008a; see also Russell and Puto 1999). Such information can even be used to determine the level of anticipation for new media products before they are available. Television programmers, motion picture studios, and advertisers, for instance, have begun analyzing the online chatter for upcoming films and television programs in order to formulate estimates of their likely audience size.

The key here is that new data streams related to these alternative dimensions of audience behavior can then become the basis for audience information systems that offer gateways into entirely new dimensions of audience understanding (see Harris and Chasin 2006; Sen et al. 1998). The term *audience information systems* will be used throughout this book in reference to the broad array of data gathering and feedback mechanisms used by media industries and advertisers not only to measure audience exposure to media content, but also to predict content preferences and consumption patterns, target content to specialized audience segments, and gather information on audiences' reactions and behavioral responses to content. The term is intended as an extension beyond the more traditional, but more limited, term *audience measurement*, which traditionally has been used primarily in reference to systems for measuring audience *exposure* to content (Balnaves and O'Regan 2002). In total, these audience information systems serve as primary mechanisms via which media organizations form their perceptions of the markets in which they operate (Anand and Peterson 2000). They are, as described by Oswell, the mechanisms for the "institutional production of knowledge about audiences" (2002:11).

From the standpoint of gathering information about audiences, new media such as the Internet have been described by one marketer as making it "possible to record data about individual consumers at an unprecedented level of detail" (Mullarkey 2004:42). One industry analyst has even gone so far as to describe the Internet as "*too* measurable. . . . It is measurable in terms of audience delivery; it is measurable in terms of audience interaction; it is even measurable on the transactional/ROI front" (Jaffe 2005:113–114). This statement reflects the key point here—that aspects of the audience *other than exposure* are now capturable via the measurement techniques facilitated by the new, highly interactive media environment, in which most of the ways in which audiences interact with media leave some sort of measurable data trail that can be aggregated, analyzed, and in many cases monetized (see, e.g., Carlson 2006).

Understanding the nature of the analytical tools employed to develop audience understanding is of particular importance, as these tools serve as the lens through which participants in the system of cultural production observe their audiences and formulate the perceptions of them that in turn affect their decision-making (Anand and Peterson 2000).[4] Thus, understanding the contemporary dynamics of the institutionalized audiences requires not only considering the dramatically changing dynamics of how audiences consume media; it also requires considering the dynamics of how media organizations gather information about the audience. As in the realm of media technology, dramatic change is taking place in the mechanisms used by media organizations and advertisers to generate audience understanding. Importantly, as these tools for understanding audiences change, so too do the portraits of the audience that they provide (Anand and Peterson 2000; Napoli 2005). These changes can be dramatic, and can compel significant behavioral changes and strategic responses on the part of media organizations (Barnes and Thomson 1988 1994; Napoli 2003a; Peterson 1994).

All of these mechanisms for gathering and analyzing information about media audiences are reflective of a decision-making environment that has been characterized by a persistent *rationalization of audience understanding.* That is, over time media industries' perceptions of their audience have become increasingly scientific and increasingly data-driven, with more impressionistic or instinctive approaches to audience understanding increasingly falling by the wayside. The days of movie studio executives, or television or radio station programmers, or magazine or newspaper editors making decisions based on their own subjective assessments of what will succeed and what will fail have largely been replaced by a decision-making environment driven by a wide range of analyses of audience tastes, preferences, and historical behavioral patterns (see, e.g., Ahlkvist 2001; Andrews and Napoli 2006). Thus, this ongoing process of audience evolution fits squarely into a broader historical pattern of rationalization in relation to media audiences.

THE BLURRING OF THE CONTENT PROVIDER–AUDIENCE DIVIDE

Audience autonomy is also contributing to audience evolution via the same ways that the increased interactive capabilities of the new media environment are contributing to a blurring of the traditional boundaries that have separated content providers from their audiences (see, e.g., Stewart and Pavlou 2002; Svoen 2007). Roscoe has noted that "the idea of an audience presupposes a binary opposition between producers and consumers, between the creators, providers and purveyors of content, and the 'audience' itself, which views, browses and 'consumes' the content" (1999:678). Such clear-cut distinctions no longer can be made. Online, for instance, virtually anyone with the capacity to receive content also has the capacity to produce and distribute content (see Berman et al. 2007; Springel 1999). This is, of course, a fundamental change in the media–audience dynamic from, for example, broadcast television, which was almost a purely one-way medium. As Cover notes, "interactivity . . . has resulted in new tensions in the author-text-audience relationship, predominantly by blurring the distinction between author and audience" (2006:140). Similarly, audience researcher Sonia Livingstone contends that the result of this technological shift is a transformation of the audience from "passive observer to active participant in a virtual world" (2003:338; see also Svoen 2007). Livingstone (2003) goes on to suggest that the implications of this evolutionary process extend so far as to potentially mean the end of the concept of the audience. The contention here is not that the audience concept is dying, only that it is evolving.

What is particularly interesting about this aspect of the evolutionary process is that it represents in some ways a return to a conceptualization of the audience that was predominant in the pre–mass media era. The literature on the history of audiences has frequently demonstrated that early manifestations of the audience were very much participatory and interactive (Billings 1986; Butsch 2008; Harrison and Barthel 2009). Theater audiences, for example, once engaged in a wide array of activities, ranging from singing songs to yelling instructions and insults at the performers to yelling at (and fighting with) each other (Billings 1986; Butsch 2008). It was only with the development of electronic mass media such as motion pictures and radio (and later, of course, television) that the dynamic between content provider and audience became increasingly uni-directional. However, even in the early developmental days of some of these mass media, the remnants of a more engaged and active audience persisted (see Griffin-Foley 2004; Newman 2004). Ross (1999), for instance, chronicles the "worker film movement" in the early years of the twentieth century, in which members of various workers' organizations, frustrated with the anti-labor messages they perceived in motion pictures, set about creating and distributing their own self-produced films. In the early days of the radio industry, audiences (primarily via fan mail) played an integral role in the creation of radio programs, as producers and writers frequently incorporated suggestions received from audience members into their scripts (Razlogova 1995). However, the more familiar one-to-many, top-down audience-content provider dynamic within these media quickly became institutionalized (Butsch 2000; Razlogova 1995).[5] And, interestingly, this dynamic spread to the older audience contexts that previously had been more participatory in nature (Butsch 2008). For instance, yelling and throwing objects at theater performers and fellow theater-goers has largely gone out of style.

One could almost argue that the mass media contributed to a pacification of audiences, with this tendency toward passivity becoming almost a defining element of the idea of the audience (see Butsch 2008). As Angus argued, prior to the widespread diffusion of the Internet, the tendency of the most significant contemporary communications systems has been to produce audiences without the capacity to produce and circulate social knowledge (1994:233). Or it may be more accurate to say that the transition to traditional mass media made the observation of many aspects of audience-hood much more difficult, or that this transition simply made it easier for media institutions to embrace a much more passive conceptualization of their audience.[6] According to Livingstone, "With the shift away from visible and audible participation by live audiences, the activities of the new, mass mediated audiences became highly interiorized and hence inaccessible to the researcher" (2003:17). Livingstone's statement illustrates a fundamental aspect of the institutionalized media audience—namely, that its conceptualizations and applications in media industry practices are fundamentally tied to those aspects that are readily observable.[7]

As this book will illustrate, only now, via contemporary developments in the realm of media technologies, is the more uni-directional approach to the relationship between media and audiences that took hold during the growth of traditional mass media through the twentieth century being undone. According to Cover, new media technologies "effectively restore to the audience their capacity to participate in the same ways in which a contemporary culture views ancient Greek theatre and communicative forms as being driven by active and creative participation over transmission" (2006:150). In this way, a number of aspects of audience evolution can be seen as somewhat cyclical.[8]

ENVIRONMENTAL CONDITIONS THAT COMPEL CHANGE

A key aspect of the ongoing process of audience evolution that must be emphasized is that the technological changes taking place simultaneously undermine the traditional exposure model *and* enhance the ability to observe and assess alternative dimensions of audience behavior. That is, while the fragmentation of the contemporary media environment makes basic exposure metrics increasingly difficult to generate and increasingly unreliable in their interpretation, the autonomy and interactivity of the new media environment facilitate feedback mechanisms and data streams that can increasingly be fed into new audience information systems that provide portraits of other aspects of audience behavior that go well beyond basic exposure.

Media trade publications are increasingly providing stories of cable networks, magazines, or Web sites essentially seeking to move beyond their (often quite small) exposure metrics in order to succeed in the new audience marketplace, where criteria such as the extent to which the content affects attitudes toward advertised products, or the extent to which content has an established brand identity, serve as increasingly viable alternatives in an environment where the exposure metric is essentially on the wane (see, e.g., Crupi 2008a, 2008b; Story 2008a). Some researchers have argued for the value of systematic measures of constructs such as "connectedness," "engagement," or "experiences" within the commercial media sector, and suggest that such constructs be incorporated into the established repertoire of the syndicated audience research products and services used as currency by the various participants in the audience marketplace (see, e.g., Calder and Malthause 2005; Russell and Puto 1999). One recent analysis of the radio and television industries operated from the bold title, "Why Ratings No Longer Matter" (Pilotta 2008). Again, the key point here is that the pressures undermining the traditional exposure model, *combined* with the new audience information obtainable in the new media environment, are *together* propelling the current process of audience evolution.

The relationship being asserted here is essentially a causal one. That is, despite the opportunities that have now become available for media organizations and advertisers to look beyond exposure, migration away from the exposure model would not be taking place unless that model was suffering mightily at the same time. The history of the rationalization of audience understanding shows us that various technological and methodological opportunities making it possible to move beyond the exposure model have long been available, but simply were not embraced because of various forms of institutional resistance as well as reasonable levels of satisfaction with the status quo across relevant stakeholder groups. Only when opportunities for change are accompanied by developments that raise substantial questions about the viability of the status quo can the process of audience evolution take place.

This is the situation today, in which our media system is migrating toward a *post-exposure audience marketplace*. The new audience marketplace will be one in which traditional exposure metrics will lose their predominant position as the exclusive coin of exchange. Exposure is being supplanted by other dimensions of audience behavior that can now be better expressed, and better gathered, in the new media environment. The move to a post-exposure media environment may have dramatic implications for the process of cultural production, as the criteria for success for media products are likely to fundamentally change in step with the evolution of the institutionalized audience.

RESISTANCE AND CONSENSUS IN AUDIENCE EVOLUTION

As previously noted, both the process of media evolution and the process of the rationalization of audience understanding have been accompanied by various forms of resistance from relevant stakeholder groups. Stakeholder resistance therefore factors prominently in the process of audience evolution as well. The ongoing process of audience evolution essentially involves a redefinition of what is in many ways the currency upon which many media industry sectors operate. For such a redefinition to take place, a broad array of stakeholders need to support the transition to some degree. As with any currency, acceptance and efficient usage depend upon mutual agreement as to its value.

From this standpoint, the technological changes affecting audiences' media consumption and audience information systems need to be placed within their broader institutional context, where various stakeholder interests and pressures frequently are brought to bear in an effort to influence the evolutionary processes, or even to prevent them from taking place (see fig. I.1). It is important to recognize that dominant conceptualizations of audiences are, in fact, often negotiated outcomes between key institutional stakeholders, including media firms, advertisers, audience measurement firms, and even policymakers and advocacy groups (Napoli 2005; Oswell 2002).

Within the context of this analysis, the nature of the resistance at issue is focused on either the technological processes that are transforming the dynamics of media consumption or the new audience information systems. Resistance to the former is perhaps more pronounced at this point. We see this, for instance, in various attempts by media organizations to limit the reconfiguration of the audience-content provider relationship. Ongoing legal battles over fair use and copyright represent a focal point of this resistance. As Cover notes, tensions in the author-text-audience relationship "result in a struggle for control over the authorial 'purity' or 'authenticity' of the text through intellectual property management or digital programming protections, or limited, channeled or 'permitted' forms of interactivity" (2006:140). The blurring of the audience–content provider relationship has been resisted via mechanisms such as broadband access providers limiting online upload speeds relative to download speeds—a strategy that essentially seeks to preserve the traditional sender–receiver dynamic. Similar industry resistance has taken place in relation to technologies that simply enhance audience autonomy in respect to the consumption of traditional media content. Thus, for instance, various sectors of the media industry initially posed substantial resistance, via threats of litigation, to the digital video recorder. These efforts were in response to the capacity of DVR technology to undermine fundamental dynamics of the exposure model upon which advertising-supported media have been built by helping audiences to avoid exposure to commercials (see Carlson 2006).

In terms of resistance to new audience information systems, perhaps the most visible contemporary form can be found in the policymaking sector, where privacy issues surrounding new mechanisms for gathering data about media consumption, and about the demographic characteristics of the consumer, have increasingly come to the fore. An early example of this (relative to the current transition being discussed) involved a U.S. Federal Trade Commission (FTC) investigation into the privacy practices of DVR manufacturer TiVo, which was gathering a wide range of television viewing data that could be linked to personally identifiable information about TiVo subscribers (see Carlson 2006). More recently, the FTC has been investigating the nature of "behavioral advertising," which involves sophisticated forms of online data gathering, aggregation, and analysis of audiences' online media consumption, many of which facilitate exactly the kinds of expansions beyond the traditional exposure metric described above (see, e.g., Federal Trade Commission 2007). Not surprisingly, this issue has become a significant area of contention between various media industry trade groups and public interest and advocacy organizations (see, e.g., American Advertising Federation 2008; Consumer Federation of America 2008). As these examples illustrate, the process of resistance can be motivated by a variety of concerns, ranging from industry self-interest to the broader public interest, though these interests are sometimes difficult to disentangle.

Ultimately, for markets for audiences to function, there needs to be a reasonable degree of consensus surrounding how audiences are defined (Napoli 2003a). However, it is often the case that particular reconceptualizations of audiences can be beneficial to certain stakeholder interests while harmful to others. Thus, the power dynamics surrounding the key institutional actors play a central role in the determination of any reconceptualization of audiences. Understanding these dynamics involves establishing the basic contours of a political economy of audience evolution (see chapter 5).

In any case, the momentum toward a significantly reconceptualized notion of the media audience seems quite powerful at this point; and the predominance of the traditional exposure model seems very much in jeopardy. This is not to say that exposure will be eliminated as a currency in the marketplace for audiences; only that it will occupy a position of diminished importance alongside other dimensions of audience understanding. It remains to be seen exactly what kinds of constraints on the process of audience evolution emerge out of this process of resistance and negotiation between the various stakeholders. Media history tells us that stakeholders seeking to preserve the status quo generally are unable to do so, but that processes of resistance and negotiation do tend to suppress the extent to which innovations can radically reconfigure existing institutional structures and processes (see Winston 1999). Witness, for instance, the fact that DVRs today have the capacity—but do not offer the functionality—to allow audiences to skip television commercials in their entirety, but instead require audiences to fast-forward through the ads while of course paying at least some attention to the accelerated images in order to be able to quit fast-forwarding at the appropriate time (Donaton 2004; Notkin 2006; Piccalo 2004). DVRs also had the capacity, for a brief time, to allow subscribers to the same DVR service to share recorded programs among themselves; this functionality is also now gone (Carlson 2006).

THE BROADER IMPLICATIONS OF AUDIENCE EVOLUTION

Understanding this institutionalized perspective on audiences, the evolutionary processes at work, and the factors that affect it is important for a number of reasons. First, it is this perspective on audiences that is fundamental to the process of cultural production. How media organizations and advertisers perceive their audiences naturally feeds into their decision-making about what kinds of content to produce and the choice of media outlets on which to advertise. An extensive literature on the organizational processes associated with the production of culture has developed,[9] and a significant subcomponent of this literature has examined the important role that audience perceptions play in decision-making related to the production, distribution, and exhibition of a wide array of cultural products, ranging from music (Ahlkvist 2001; Anand and Peterson 2000) to books (Andrews and Napoli 2006), to television programs (Ang 1991; Eaman 1994), to motion pictures (Austin 1989; Handel 1950), to art exhibits and live performances (DiMaggio and Useem 1979; O'Regan 2002). The perceptions that producers of culture have about their audience (be they informed or uninformed, narrow or well-rounded) naturally feed into judgments as to what kinds of content will succeed and what kinds of content will fail, as well as into assessments of which audience interests are being well served and which are not.

And, of course, media content—which we can define broadly in terms of the full range of news, information, and entertainment media available to audiences—is a product with a distinctive capacity for cultural and political influence. A wide-ranging literature has developed around the issue of media effects, and this literature has at various times demonstrated significant effects in areas ranging from political attitudes and beliefs to cultural values to perceptions of social problems and even other social groups (see, e.g., Bryant 2008). The profound nature of this influence further underscores the importance of understanding the processes by which content production, distribution, and exhibition decisions are made, as well as the inputs that go into these decisions.

A key question, therefore, is whether the types of media products that succeed under the new success criteria being established in this post-exposure media environment will be the same or different from those that performed well under the old criteria. Might these new success criteria better encourage the production of higher-"quality" content? Might they contribute to the serving of a wider range of audience interests? Or might they in some way limit the range of content produced, or promote an overemphasis on certain content dimensions? Will the media system—and media audiences—be better off as a result of this process of audience evolution? We are at a point in time where we can begin to develop some informed speculations on these questions.

This ongoing process of audience evolution also raises a number of media policy questions. For instance, do any of the social and cultural issues raised by this process of audience evolution justify closer government scrutiny of those organizations involved in the construction of the institutionalized media audience? Or is any such government intervention precluded by the First Amendment rights of these organizations to construct and disseminate their representations of the media audience? These questions remain very much open for debate. Also, the blurring of the distinction between institutional communicator and individual speaker would seem to compel a complete reconfiguration of the analytical criteria and normative goals that underlie media policymaking, as traditional media organizations no longer reflect the exclusive focal point of concern. At the same time, however, these altered dynamics between media industries and their audiences are being interpreted by some as fundamentally threatening to the continued viability of valued media institutions such as journalism (see Starr 2009). Such concerns raise the question of whether media policy needs to focus on mechanisms for preserving traditional media organizations.

And finally, this ongoing process of audience evolution may have implications for media scholarship—particularly those areas of scholarship that focus on media audiences. What does the changing nature of the institutionalized media audience mean for academic audience researchers, and for their relationship with their media industry counterparts? The process of audience evolution may represent the decline of certain lines of inquiry, the revitalization of others, and, perhaps most interesting of all, an opportunity for bridging gulfs that have developed between academic traditions and between academic and industry researchers.

DATA AND METHOD

In addressing all of these issues, this book draws upon a wide range of primary sources. Participant observation was conducted at a variety of media and advertising industry conferences and symposia, including—but not limited to—the 2006 through 2009 annual conferences on audience measurement sponsored by the Advertising Research Foundation (ARF); the 2007 and 2008 ARF annual conventions; and the ARF's 2009 360 Measurement Day Workshop; the 2008 Digital Media Forum; the 2010 Online Media, Marketing, and Advertising Measurement and Metrics Conference; online seminars offered by Nielsen; and conferences organized by the Interactive Advertising Bureau, including the MIXX 2008 conference. These events provide useful insights into how various media and advertising industry stakeholders are coping with the changes taking place in their industries. These events represent an important context in which the redefinition of the institutionalized audience is being discussed and negotiated by the various interested stakeholders. At many of these events, I conducted informal interviews with attendees in order to develop a deeper understanding of the issues, questions, and concerns being confronted by professionals in these fields. The various promotional, marketing, and research materials distributed at these events also provided a large trove of valuable material for analysis. The media and advertising industry trade press served as another important primary data source for understanding the dynamics of the ongoing evolution of media audiences. Publications of interest for this analysis included *Media Week, Adweek, Media Life Magazine, Broadcasting and Cable, Advertising Age,* and *Media Daily News.*

Also vital to this analysis was the steady flow of media, advertising, and audience measurement industry white papers and research reports, many of which were obtained via regular surveillance of the Web sites of relevant commercial firms (such as Nielsen, Arbitron, and comScore) as well as those of industry associations such as the Interactive Advertising Bureau, the National Cable and Telecommunications Association, and the National Association of Broadcasters. Of particular value were the complete proceedings for the 2006 through 2009 annual audience measurement conferences held by the World Association for Opinion and Marketing Research Professionals (ESOMAR). The papers presented at these meetings represent the cutting edge in audience measurement and provided a vital roadmap to the technological changes taking place in the media sector and how the audience measurement sector is working to keep pace.

Finally, given the extent to which the process of audience evolution is raising a variety of public policy concerns, this analysis also draws heavily from a wide range of primary government sources, including congressional hearings and testimony, regulatory agency and court decisions, and correspondence between members of Congress, industry representatives, and government agencies such as the Federal Trade Commission and the Federal Communications Commission (FCC). Also useful in addressing these issues were the relevant research and position papers produced by industry associations and public interest and advocacy organizations.

Secondary sources consulted for this analysis included the academic literature on audience behavior and audience measurement that is widely scattered across the fields of marketing, advertising, communication and media studies, and cultural studies, as well as the literature on new media technologies, particularly the literature focusing on institutional responses to new media technologies. The study of media and audiences is an inherently interdisciplinary enterprise, as will be clear from the diverse range of disciplinary perspectives that are brought to bear on this analysis.

PLAN OF THE BOOK

Chapter 1 contextualizes the process of audience evolution that is the focus of this book within the related processes of media evolution and the rationalization of audience understanding. The discussion and analysis of these related phenomena is intended to provide both historical and theoretical context for the analyses that follow. As this chapter illustrates, the literature on media evolution provides a useful jumping off point for developing the concept of audience evolution. This chapter also documents the process of the rationalization of audience understanding, including the critiques and concerns that have been raised in various quarters about this process, in order to contextualize ongoing developments in audience evolution within the historical progression of how media organizations have conceptualized their audiences.

Chapter 2 delves in detail into the technological changes affecting the dynamics of media consumption, and their implications for the process of audience evolution. This chapter pays particular attention both to the fragmentation of the media environment that has taken place, and to how this fragmentation has undermined the traditional approaches to media audiences that have long characterized the audience marketplace. A point of focus for this analysis is the frequently discussed "long tail" phenomenon

(Anderson 2006), given that most discussions of the long tail have focused on its implications for those involved in the retail sale or rental of media content (e.g., online retailers such as Amazon and Netflix) to the neglect of detailed discussions of its implications for advertising-supported media. This chapter also details how the increased autonomy of the new media environment—particularly in terms of the increased interactivity it facilitates—serves to both undermine traditional approaches to media audiences and to facilitate the rise of alternative approaches. In addressing this issue, this chapter pays particular attention to the blurring of the traditional separation between content provider and audience member.

Chapter 3 follows the discussion of the changes taking place in media technology with a discussion of the changes taking place in the realm of audience information systems. This chapter considers the wide range of new audience information systems that have arisen in response to an increasingly interactive media environment. As this chapter makes clear, these new audience information systems help to illuminate dimensions of audience behavior that were previously, to a large extent, unmeasurable. This chapter also illustrates the ways in which economic value is being assigned to these newly excavated dimensions of audience behavior, as the assignment of value to this information is fundamental to its ability to contribute to the process of audience evolution.

Chapter 4 places the changes in media technologies and audience information systems within their broader institutional context, where various stakeholder interests and pressures frequently are brought to bear in an effort to influence, or even to prevent, evolutionary processes from place. By focusing on the role and impact of institutional pressures and interests in this evolutionary process, this chapter illustrates how dominant conceptualizations of audiences are negotiated outcomes between key institutional stakeholders, including media firms, advertisers, audience measurement firms, and even policymakers and advocacy groups. This chapter pays particular attention to instances in which policymakers have been drawn into the institutional dynamics surrounding new media technologies and new audience information systems.

Chapter 5 considers the wide-ranging implications of the process of audience evolution presented here, and developed in chapters 2 through 4, within the broader contexts of media evolution and the rationalization of audience understanding discussed in chapter 1. This chapter also situates the issues related to both the transformation of media consumption and the transformation of audience information systems within the broader context related to the production of culture, with an eye toward how cultural production is likely to be affected by the evolution of the institutionalized media audience. In addition, this chapter explores the media policy implications of the issues addressed in this book—particularly in terms of ongoing debates over the appropriateness of government regulation of the audience measurement industry and in terms of the broader policy implications of a media environment in which the line between media producer and media consumer is becoming increasingly blurred. These discussions also touch upon important First Amendment concerns that are inextricably intertwined with these policy issues. Finally, this chapter considers the implications of this process of audience evolution for media scholarship, particularly in terms of the divides that have grown between academic and industry audience researchers and in terms of the organization of audience research as an academic field.

CHAPTER 1

CONTEXTUALIZING AUDIENCE EVOLUTION

Although this book focuses on the contemporary dynamics surrounding the evolution of media audiences, it is important to recognize that audience evolution is an ongoing process that is likely to persist into the future (when appropriate conditions are present) and that extends back into the past. This chapter looks backwards, aiming to provide both theoretical and historical contexts for contemporary developments in the evolution of media audiences.

Addressing these goals involves integrating two distinct bodies of literature, which have seldom been brought together. The first of these is the literature on media evolution. *Media evolution* in this case refers to the idea that media industry sectors essentially evolve over time in response to changing environmental conditions; these may be technological, economic, cultural, or regulatory. A growing body of literature has charted these evolutionary patterns and identified the key environmental changes that have triggered evolutionary responses. For the purposes of this book, this theoretical construct of media evolution is useful for providing an analytical starting point for the closely related concept of audience evolution being developed here. Indeed, a primary contention of this book is that a similar analytical framework can be applied to media audiences. That is, there is a wide range of changing environmental conditions that can affect how media industries conceptualize their audiences. As a result, old conceptualizations of audiences can gradually be replaced by new ones.

This relationship between the concepts of media evolution and audience evolution begins to make itself clear when we take into account the second body of literature being used to contextualize this analysis—involving what is termed here the *rationalization of audience understanding.* This work addresses the processes via which media industries seek to understand their audiences. Examining the totality of this literature (which dates back at least to the 1930s) provides a strong sense of how media industries' conceptualizations of their audiences have evolved over time. As the label suggests, the process has been one of increased rationalization, in which efforts to understand media audiences have become increasingly scientific and data driven. This literature essentially provides the historical and theoretical foundation on which the present study's model of audience evolution rests.

MEDIA EVOLUTION

As various analyses of media institutions and technologies have illustrated, it is useful to examine media systems and media industries through an evolutionary analytical lens (Napoli 1998a; Noll 2006; Stober 2004). From this perspective we see that media industry sectors tend to follow specific evolutionary patterns in response to changes in their external environment (Dimmick 2002). This applies to established media—in terms of how they respond to environmental changes (e.g., Boczkowski 2004b) such as the introduction of new, competing technologies—as well as to new media, as they navigate, and become integrated into, the established media system (Bolter and Grusin 2000; Cheong and Leckenby 2003; Greenberg 2008).

Thus, for instance, researchers have illustrated that changing sociocultural conditions, such as increased literacy or increased per capita income, can alter the environmental conditions for media in ways that not only affect the extent to which a particular medium is utilized, but also how it is utilized and even the nature of the content it provides. Increased literacy, for instance, helped book publishing change from an industry that served only the highly educated—and publishing only content appealing to such an audience—to one serving a much wider range of audience interests. The Internet similarly evolved from serving primarily the needs of the government and academic research communities to being embraced by—and serving the needs and interests of—a much broader spectrum of the population (Abbate 2000). Such patterns, which have been exhibited in other media as well, such as radio and television, represent what has been termed the "elite to popular/mass" stage of media evolution (Merrill and Lowenstein 1971).

Technological changes—particularly changes in available media technologies—have also been a fundamental driver of media evolution. Most often such changes have been instrumental in moving media from the popular/mass stage to what has been termed the "specialized" stage, in which more mature media technologies often find themselves struggling to remain viable in the face of competition from new media (see Lehman-Wilzig and Cohen-Avigdor 2004; Napoli 1998a). Thus, for instance, the arrival of television forced fundamental changes to the motion picture industry, leading the industry to focus much more intently on the adolescent and young adult audience (the audience segment exhibiting the greatest continued interest in leaving the house to watch a movie). The widespread adoption of television also compelled the motion picture industry to alter its content in ways that would better differentiate it from what could be found on television at that time. Consequently, the motion picture industry came to increasingly emphasize content characteristics such as special effects, sex, violence, and foul language, as these content elements were either unavailable via broadcast television due to regulatory restrictions, or did not transfer well to the small, black-and-white screens of the early television era (Napoli 1998a).

The pattern here is typically one of differentiation or adaptation, as established media industry sectors seek to maintain their viability in the face of a new competitive threat that is coopting much of the old medium's audience and/or revenue streams (Stober 2004). Dimmick (2002) has termed this process "competitive displacement." Today, for instance, there is much discussion about the challenging future facing the printed newspaper in the face of seemingly insurmountable competition from various online news sources (e.g., Carr 2008a, 2008b; Kinsley 2006; Kuttner 2007). These discussions tend to focus on possible ways that the traditional newspaper can effectively differentiate itself from its online competition, whether in terms of cultivating new categories of readers, or in terms of broadly rethinking the role and function of the printed paper and altering content accordingly. Thus, for instance, many newspapers at this point are ceding the provision of traditional content categories such as stock quotes, classified ads, and even foreign news, and instead are focusing more on the provision of consumer and entertainment-oriented information (e.g., Project for Excellence in Journalism 2008; Saphir 2008). Other papers have cut back or eliminated their film, television, art, and food critics, in part under the presumption the Web provides an effective substitute via the many easily accessible opinion aggregation sites that not only provide audiences with access to a much wider range of opinions, but also allow these same audiences to contribute their opinions as well (Carr 2008a).

One aspect of media evolution that is particularly relevant to this book involves the ways in which changes in the nature of information about media audiences have contributed to the process. Thus, for instance, Barnes and Thomson (1988, 1994) illustrate how increased, more afford-able, and more widely available computing power played a fundamental role in transforming magazines from a traditional "mass" medium into a medium in which stakeholders became much more focused on attracting and monetizing more narrowly defined niche audiences. Essentially, the ability to gather and analyze more granular data about media audiences allowed for more targeted approaches to identifying desirable audiences for advertisers, and thus provided an important impetus for magazines to reorient themselves in ways that served more narrowly targeted audiences (see also Wehner 2002). It would seem, however, that these new analytical tools were an important, though likely not a sufficient, condition for the conceptualization of the magazine audience to change in ways that funda-mentally altered the dynamics of magazine publishing. During the period these new analytical tools were being developed it was also the case that the rapid diffusion of television was enabling this new medium to effec-tively supplant mass-appeal magazines as the primary mechanism via which advertisers reached large, undifferentiated audiences (Barnes and Thomson 1988, 1994). The key point here—and one that will recur through-out this discussion of the process of audience evolution—is that *both* improvements in the available analytical tools *and* technological changes that undermined the status quo were necessary conditions for the process of media evolution to take place.

Finally, it is important to recognize that the process of media evolution does not occur without substantial institutional resistance, as industry sec-tors engage in various efforts to preserve their established position, whether by attacking the emerging media through legal or economic means, or by attempting to adopt the characteristics of the new, threatening medium (Lehman-Wilzig and Cohen-Avigdor 2004). Thus new media technolo-gies—ranging from radio to cable television, to the VCR, to file-sharing and online video aggregation services. to digital video recorders and search engines—have been attacked in various ways by established media seeking to curb or eliminate emerging competitive threats. In some instances these resistance efforts have taken the form of legal actions, whether it be the Hollywood movie studios going all the way to the Supreme Court in pursuit of the outright ban of the VCR (Greenberg 2008; Lardner 1987), or the record labels suing not only the creators of various music file-sharing services but also the most egregious users of these services (Bhattacharjee et al. 2006; Waterman, Ji, and Rochet 2007).

In other instances, this resistance has taken the form of concerted efforts to deny the new, threatening medium access to desired resources—most often content. Thus, for instance, the newspaper industry went to great lengths to prevent the nascent radio industry from conveying newspaper stories over the air (see Chester 1949; Jackaway 1995). The motion picture industry for a time refused to license its films to the emerging television industry (Napoli 1998a). And, more recently, multimedia content providers such as Viacom have been very aggressive in preventing their content from being accessible via services such as YouTube (*Viacom v. YouTube* 2007). Such resistance strategies often accompany simultaneous efforts by the established media to diversify into the new media. Thus, newspapers very quickly became purchasers of radio stations; the motion picture industry eventually became the primary supplier of programming to the television industry; and television programmers and the motion picture studios have been aggressively developing and rolling out online distribution platforms for their content.

As Winston (1999) illustrates, these strategies of resistance and diversification can substantially reduce the destabilizing effects of new media. As a result, the effects of new media tend to be incremental and evolutionary as opposed to dramatic and revolutionary, as the established media are able to exert influence over the development of new media both externally (via resistance) and internally (via diversification). Winston (1999) goes so far as to propose a "law of the suppression of radical potential" in relation to new media. He convincingly demonstrates that established institutional interests and structures serve to limit the extent to which any new media technology is able to fully realize its revolutionary potential, not only in terms of how the technology itself is used by audiences and content providers, but also in terms of how dramatically it affects the established behavioral patterns and competitive dynamics within the broader media system. Thus, for instance, despite early rhetoric surrounding its revolutionary potential (see, e.g.,

Smith 1972), cable television evolved in a manner quite similar to established broadcast television and became well integrated into the established dynamics of the commercial television industry (Mullen 2003). Similarly, the VCR evolved primarily into an extension of the Hollywood studios (Greenberg 2008). We may be seeing similar patterns at work within new media contexts such as the DVR and YouTube (see chapter 4).

As will become clear, these dynamics of resistance, which have proven to be an integral component of the process of media evolution, also play a central role in the process of audience evolution (see chapter 4), where once again we see how institutional interests in favor of the status quo can serve to limit the transformative effects that new technologies can potentially facilitate.

THE RATIONALIZATION OF AUDIENCE UNDERSTANDING

The concept of rationalization has been interpreted in a variety of ways and has been applied both theoretically and empirically in a wide range of contexts. It is most commonly associated with the work of sociologist Max Weber. Broadly, Weber (1978) defined the process of rationalization as a historical process involving the migration away from tradition. More concretely, it has been associated with processes such as increased reliance on bureaucratic organization, an increased emphasis on calculation, and the generation and utilization of specialized knowledge (Weber 1978). Subsequent explorations of the concept have identified four central components of the process of rationalization: (a) the refinement of techniques of calculation; (b) the enhancement of specialized knowledge; (c) the extension of technically rational control over natural and social processes; and (d) the depersonalization of social relationships (Brubaker 1984). These processes of rationalization have been associated with a variety of spheres of endeavor, including management (Beniger 1987) and public policymaking (Stone 2001), as well as communications-related areas such as public opinion assessment (Herbst 1995; Herbst and Beniger 1994; Igo 2007), marketing (Turow 2006), and advertising (Laird 1998).

As will become clear, all of these elements of the process of rationalization are prominent in the history of media organizations' approaches to audience understanding. Indeed, to the extent that rationalization has been described as "a central element of institutional theories of organization"

(Townely, Cooper, and Oakes 1999:3), it is particularly well-suited to enhancing our understanding of how media organizations conceptualize their audiences. This connection was recognized as early as 1957 by market researcher Leo Bogart, who observed that tendencies toward rationalization in the media sector "seem to have emerged as part of the same wave of rationalization that has produced, since Frederick Taylor, several generations of industrial efficiency experts" (1957:133; see also Bogart 1986b).

Within the context of media organizations and media audiences, the notion of the rationalization of audience understanding has involved efforts to bring greater empirical rigor and (primarily) quantitative methods to the processes of understanding a range of dimensions of audience behavior (Bogart 1957; Carey 1980; Maxwell 2000), under the presumption that these analyses facilitate greater predictability and greater control of audience behavior (see, e.g., Ahlkvist 2001; Rossman 2008). These efforts have been pursued via the integration of various forms of analytical specialists, the gathering of various forms of (typically quantitative) data, as well as the development of increasingly specialized skill sets (Rossman 2008; Turow 2006).

These efforts to enhance knowledge, predictability, and control in relation to the audience have, however, been accompanied by the kinds of analytical simplifications that historically have been associated with the process of rationalization. As Beniger (1987) notes, the increased information processing that is at the core of the process of rationalization generally can be achieved only by structuring systems of data gathering and processing that are highly selective in terms of the nature of the material gathered, in order to avoid information overload. This of course limits possible perceptions or analytical orientations toward the particular social phenomenon under observation.

Also of particular importance to this analysis is the extent to which the process of rationalization is reliant on mechanisms for two-way communication between the observer and the observed (Beniger 1987). Such reciprocal communication is essential for the gathering of information about those under study (in this case, the audience) in order to facilitate efforts at analysis and prediction. Thus any developments that facilitate greater reciprocity in communication between media organization and audience have the potential to intensify the rationalization of audience understanding.

THE EARLY INTUITIVE MODEL OF AUDIENCE UNDERSTANDING

Most historical accounts of the evolution of audience understanding within various sectors of the media industry emphasize the early reliance on what is perhaps best termed the *intuitive model.* Under this approach, the subjective, often instinctive, judgments of content producers, distributors, and exhibitors regarding audience tastes, preferences, and reactions were the primary mechanisms via which organizational decisions were made. Historical accounts of early mass media, such as motion pictures, books, and newspapers, frequently highlight this analytical approach (see, e.g., Eaman 1994; Hagen 1999; Handel 1950; Powell 1978; Silvey 1974). Austin, for instance, presents the story of Harry Cohn, president of Columbia Pictures in the 1930s and 40s, "who claimed he had a 'foolproof' method for predicting the success of a movie: 'If my fanny squirms, it's bad. If my fanny doesn't squirm, it's good'" (1989:1). Similarly, accounts of the newspaper industry emphasize how decision-making regarding news content has historically been driven largely via the application of the news values and editorial judgment cultivated within the journalistic profession, with the audience existing as a somewhat distant abstraction from the standpoint of journalists and editors (see DeWerth-Pallmeyer 1997; Min 2004; de Sola Pool and Shulman 1959; Sumpter 2000).

This approach frequently resulted in information vacuums regarding the nature of the interaction between content and audience. For instance, one account of this time period notes the observation of a 1920s-era motion picture director, who complained that "production departments of the major companies 'have not the slightest idea what happens to our pictures,' and a director had no way of finding out 'why his picture didn't do well in the South, why his picture didn't do well in England, why his picture could not be shown in Germany'" (Maltby 1999:23).

Some analysts have suggested that the fact that the economic conditions for these early mass media were relatively favorable created little demand for more rigorous empirical analyses to guide strategic decision-making (see, e.g., Austin 1989; Bakker 2003). For instance, according to early film audience researcher Leo Handel, "The young industry, which could readily finance research projects, found little motivation to do so because the new, expanding market was active enough to provide a highly satisfactory volume of business for the leading firms. Most motion picture executives were content to let product improvement and sales policies rest on their intuitive insight of what the public wanted, rather than on direct contact with the consumer" (1950:3–4).

EARLY STEPS BEYOND THE INTUITIVE MODEL

The description above is not intended to suggest that early media organizations were *completely* lacking in information about their audiences, or that the relationship between media organizations and their audiences has ever been a pure one-way, one-to-many model. Basic data such as box office grosses, sales, and circulation figures were available for analysis, although the analytical limitations of such data were for the most part readily apparent. Early motion picture audience researchers, for instance, were well aware that box office figures could not be interpreted purely as an indicator of a film's audience appeal, as these figures could be a function of other factors, such as advertising and promotional strategies (see, e.g., Handel 1950). This consequently undermined the analytical utility of box office figures as a tool for explicitly gauging audience preferences, and thus as a tool for guiding future production decisions. In addition, at the time box office figures were completely dependent upon distributor and exhibitor cooperation (in terms of the reporting of box office grosses), raising questions about their accuracy, and thereby further limiting their analytical value (Fiske and Handel 1946).

Other feedback mechanisms, such as audience correspondence with the content provider, have a long history (see, e.g., Lenthall 2007; Newman 2004; Razlogova 1995; Turow 1977–78). Such correspondence was utilized in audience assessment and strategic decision-making across early mass media such as motion pictures, newspapers, magazines, and eventually broadcasting (see Ohmer 2006; Silvey 1974). Movie studios, for instance, would measure and weigh the amount of fan mail received by their performers and "deduce from its increase or decrease the rise or fall in the popularity of the recipient" (Handel 1950:10). Most of the studios had dedicated fan mail departments engaged in such tasks, even going so far as to organize the mail according to the writer's estimated age, gender, and geographic location (Bakker 2003).

Early efforts to more rigorously assess audiences were perhaps most pronounced in the nascent broadcasting sector. The introduction of broadcasting as a primarily ad-supported medium in countries such as the United States represented a somewhat different context from established media such as motion pictures and newspapers, in that the economic model provided an immediate, powerful incentive for more rationalized approaches to audience understanding—at least in terms of quantifying the size of the audience being reached by radio programming and its embedded advertising messages (Silvey 1974). Adding to this dynamic the more ephemeral nature of broadcast audiences, which are inherently more challenging to make concrete than print or motion picture audiences—whose behaviors can at least be represented by tangible actions such as purchasing a publication or a ticket—the imperative to develop new systems of audience understanding became more pronounced (see, e.g., Socolow 2004).

Consequently, in the early days of radio, stations utilized a variety of approaches to provide advertisers with audience estimates. One method involved mapping the station's coverage area against the area's population size and demographic data (Chappell and Hooper 1944; Kingson 1953); another involved gathering data on the number of radios sold in a listening area (Chappell and Hooper 1944; Kingson 1953). Of course, such approaches provided neither the station nor the advertiser with any concrete information about the size or composition of the *actual* listening audience; rather, they simply provided a rough estimate of the *potential* audience for any radio program. Nonetheless, the economic model of advertiser-supported broadcasting was able to take sufficiently firm hold in an environment of such imprecision.

As was the case with motion pictures and newspapers, letters to the stations figured prominently in early efforts to understand radio audiences (see, e.g., Chappell and Hooper 1944), and often played an influential role in programmers' decision-making (Razlogova 1995). British audience researcher Robert Silvey (1974) provides one of the more detailed discussions of how early broadcasters dealt with audience mail as a feedback mechanism in his history of audience research at the BBC. Silvey notes that, within the BBC, "seeds of doubt" about the analytical value of audience letters were quickly sown "when it became quite apparent that the overwhelming majority of letters came from middle-class writers; that some issues . . . provoked far more letters than others . . . that while many letters began 'I have never written to the BBC before,' others came from people who wrote so often that they might be called BBC pen friends. . . . In a word, no one knows what any letter or bunch of letters is a sample of" (1974:28–29). In 1955 the BBC went so far in its assessment of audience letters as to conduct a survey in the wake of a broadcast of George Orwell's *1984,* in which the distribution of opinions in the letters received was compared to the distribution of opinions of a broader sample of the viewing audience. The results indicated that, across groups, the ratio of approving versus disapproving audience members was similar; however, only the viewer survey sample captured the perspective of the large majority of viewers, who did not have a strong opinion about the broadcast in either direction (Silvey 1974).[1]

EARLY STAGES OF RATIONALIZATION

The period of the 1930s frequently emerges in the literature as a key starting point in the progression to more rationalized approaches to audience understanding (see, e.g., Hurwitz 1984; Ohmer 1999). There are a number of key developments during this time period that are worth noting. The economic hardships of the Depression have been identified in many historical accounts as a key driver in the development of marketing, advertising, and audience research, as marketers, advertisers, and, ultimately, media organizations found themselves under more intense pressure to maximize the efficiency of their resource allocations and to provide "tangible" evidence that money was being spent logically and effectively (Kreshel 1993; Lenthall 2007; Ohmer 2006). As NBC executive E. P. H. James noted in 1937, "when the depression descended upon us, advertisers and their agencies immediately began to check over their advertising expenditures and sought justification for every dollar spent. In so far as it was possible, sales were traced to the mediums [*sic*] being used, or other strong evidence was accumulated to justify the continuance of the use of each advertising medium" (p. 141).

Looking beyond the Depression, another important cultural shift taking place during this time period involved the transition from a *production culture* to a *consumption culture* that many scholars assert began to take place during the early part of the twentieth century (see Lenthall 2007; Strasser 1989). This transition brought with it the need for goods manufacturers to know much more about their potential consumers, how best to identify and reach them, and how best to appeal to them (Buzzard 1990; Ward 1996). It is worth noting that both the *Journal of Marketing* and the journal *Public Opinion Quarterly* were established in this decade (both were launched in 1936)—

an indicator of the extent to which the intellectual infrastructure underlying these more rationalized analytical approaches to understanding the public, both as citizens and as consumers, was becoming institutionalized (see Bogart 1957).

A number of historical analyses have identified industry-specific factors that also were drivers toward greater rationalization of audience understanding. For instance, one analysis of the motion picture industry points to such factors as rising production costs, extended contract terms with stars, and the transition from fixed fee to percentage-based rental contracts as key motivators within Hollywood to more enthusiastically embrace audience research (Bakker 2003). Later, the rise of television dramatically altered the competitive landscape for motion pictures, and further compelled the utilization of audience research in an effort to maximize box office grosses, as studios sought information to help them retain their shrinking audience (Austin 1989). Moreover, the (at that time) relatively short product life-cycle for a single motion picture was seen as compelling studios to closely track changes in consumer preferences (Bakker 2003).

As noted above, the widespread commercialization of radio that took place in the United States in the aftermath of the passage of the Radio Act of 1927 (see McChesney 1993) provided a particularly powerful impetus for radio programmers and advertisers to aggressively invest in, support, and utilize systematic ratings services that could bring the desired objectivity and empirical rigor to the processes of buying and selling audience attention that had been established as the commercial model under which the industry would operate. The fact that other potential funding systems that were considered, such as a subscription-based approach, were rejected in favor of an advertising-supported model (see McChesney 1993) created an impetus for approaching audience understanding in a particular way, one that would take into very strong account the needs and interests of the advertisers supporting the radio programming.

THE INTEGRATION OF SPECIALIZED KNOWLEDGE AND SKILLS

The rationalization of audience understanding involved the integration of new types of professionals into the operation of media organizations—obviously those with strong research backgrounds and/or quantitative analytical skills.[2] Newman has described these new professionals as "audience intellectuals," and links their emergence to the birth of the commercial radio industry in the 1930s (2004:8). Psychology, for instance, became increasingly integrated into the work of advertising agencies (Balnaves and O'Regan 2008; Kreshel 1993; Socolow 2004; Turow 2006). Renowned public opinion pollster George Gallup (a psychologist by training) spent the early part of his career conducting newspaper audience research (Chaffee 2000; Wood 1962). This work grew from his doctoral dissertation, which was titled *A New Technique for Objective Methods for Measuring Reader Interest in Newspapers* (Gallup 1928). Gallup later moved on to motion picture audience research and became a pioneering figure in that field as well (Handel 1950; Ohmer 1999, 2006). A number of scholars from the famed "Chicago School" of sociology, such as Lloyd Warner and Ira Glick, played an integral role in the establishment of the field of news consulting—which relies very heavily on various forms of audience research (Allen 2005).

Perhaps most influential was sociologist Paul Lazarsfeld (1939) (in actuality a mathematician by training). Lazarsfeld played an integral role in the development of many areas of commercial audience research, via his survey research work as well as his work with the Lazarsfeld-Stanton Program Analyzer, which was a device used to gather and aggregate data on audience appreciation for media products ranging from radio and television programs to motion pictures (Levy 1982). Lazarsfeld also proved tremendously influential to the development of commercial audience research via the wide-ranging radio audience research projects conducted by his Bureau of Applied Social Research during the 1930s and 1940s (Morrison 1978; Lenthall 2007; Newman 2004; see also Lazarsfeld and Field 1946).

METHODOLOGICAL DEVELOPMENTS

During this period we see the development of a number of advancements in the systematic empirical assessment of audiences.[3] For instance, in magazine publishing, we see the beginnings of detailed readership reports that went beyond basic circulation statistics to also include demographic and behavioral characteristics of magazine readers (Ward 1996). It is also during this time period that we see the beginnings of the systematic charting and reporting of the popularity of recorded music (Hesbacher, Downing, and Berger 1975).

Perhaps most important, we also see the beginnings of syndicated ratings services in radio (Beville 1940; Buzzard 1990; Karol 1938). As one early account noted, "Fan mail was once the measure of a broadcaster's popularity. . . . These happy, innocent days came to an abrupt end when [radio audience measurement pioneer] Archibald Crossley announced a scientific audience-measurement system which would count the non-letter writing part of the audience, too" (Kingson 1953:291). Early methodological approaches to measuring radio audiences included "telephone coincidentals" (in which homes were called and asked what programs they were currently listening to), meters (electronic devices attached to radios), and paper listening diaries. It is this last method that ultimately emerged as the standard approach to the measurement of radio audiences (see Beville 1988; Buzzard 1990), and that continues to be a prominent, if no longer the primary, approach to radio audience measurement to this day.[4]

As media researcher Leo Bogart noted within the context of radio, the move to ratings systems "consisted of estimating an intangible—'the listening experience'—rather than making a count of tangible objects—radio sets or letters to the station" (1966:48). Efforts such as these were central to establishing the fundamental exposure metrics that eventually were transferred to television (see Hurwitz 1983; Banks 1981) and that to this day reside at the center of how most media organizations, advertisers, and marketers conceptualize their audience.[5]

The greater demand for rigorous audience data in ad-supported broadcasting meant that the rationalization of audience understanding in this sector advanced more rapidly than in others. As Lazarsfeld noted in an early analysis comparing the state of motion picture and radio audience research:

In movie research, the situation is somewhat different for two reasons. First, the movie industry has its box office returns as an index to work with. . . . Its very existence makes it understandable that mere descriptive audience research has not developed so much with movies as with other media. Furthermore, the motion picture industry does not sell advertising. While the analysis of box office returns should be very important for the understanding of its own business, it does not need to account to anyone for the size of its audience. (1947:162)

Thus, despite its being the newer medium, radio's audience research strategies and techniques soon influenced the strategies and techniques employed in older media such as motion pictures (Bakker 2003).[6] In the preface to his

1950 book on motion picture audiences, Leo Handel credits Paul Lazarsfeld, "who's trailblazing work in radio research inspired [him] to study motion picture audiences along similar lines" (p. vii). The techniques of radio audience research proved instrumental in film audience research on a number of fronts (Bakker 2003), perhaps most notably in terms of the motion picture industry's adoption of the Lazarsfeld-Stanton Program Analyzer, which quickly became a key tool used in the pre-testing of motion pictures (Fiske and Handel 1947b). The program analyzer was used within the motion picture industry to re-edit films, as well as to determine general likes and dislikes of various audience segments in order to guide future production decisions (Fiske and Handel 1947b). Ultimately, extensions of the Lazarsfeld-Stanton program analyzer, such as the Cirlin Reactograph (Cirlin and Peterman 1947), were employed by a number of motion picture industry research organizations, including the Motion Picture Research Bureau and Audience Research, Inc. (see Bakker 2003; Ohmer 2006).

By the 1940s, "a new research-mindedness . . . permeat[ed] all branches of the industry," along with "an emphasis on scientific, objective analysis" (Chambers 1947:170), as the motion picture industry employed a wide range of methodological approaches to audience understanding. These included the pre-testing of completed films, the pre-testing of film titles and concepts, survey research examining the popularity of individual stars, and survey research measuring audience awareness and anticipation of upcoming films (see, e.g., Adams 1953; Barker 1998; Fiske and Handel 1946, 1947a, 1947b; Handel 1950; Ohmer 2006).

STAGE TWO IN THE RATIONALIZATION OF AUDIENCE UNDERSTANDING

If the 1930s can be identified as essentially the starting point in the process of the rationalization of audience understanding, then it appears that the 1970s represent the second major period of advancement. Many historical analyses of media industries point to the 1970s as a pivotal point, when a pronounced push took place (see, e.g., Balnaves and O'Regan 2002; Hesmondhalgh 2007; Schultz 1979). Motion picture industry historians have identified the 1970s as the time in which Hollywood *fully* embraced a wide range of audience information systems, after first embracing them in the 1930s and 40s (e.g., Austin 1989). Analyses of the recorded music industry also identify the 1970s as the period when strategic decision-making moved away from more intuitive approaches and began to rely heavily on various audience data sources, ranging from sales monitoring systems to radio ratings data (Negus 1999).

Assessments of this analytical transition often point to enabling factors such as the reduction in cost and rise in power of computer systems, which brought with them an increased capacity to gather and analyze large quantities of statistical data (Buzzard 2003a; Goss 1995; Hesmondhalgh 2007; Starr and Corson 1987; Wehner 2002). Not only were large quantities of data now able to be gathered, tabulated, and analyzed in a timely manner, but (with the diffusion of the personal computer and data analysis software) the tools for analyzing such information were more widely distributed (Balnaves and O'Regan 2002; Barnes and Thomson 1994; McKenna 1988). These developments both facilitated and encouraged the adoption of more quantitatively oriented "scientific" approaches to organizational management and decision-making (Bogart 1986b; Starr and Corson 1987).

In television, audience measurement was being further rationalized via the introduction of set-top meters that provided not only a daily flow of audience data (as opposed to the much slower and intermittent data flow provided by paper diaries), but also detailed demographic information about the composition of the audiences for individual programs (see, e.g., Buck 1987; Buzzard 2003a; Wilcox 2000). News consulting also became a firmly institutionalized practice during this time (Allen 2007), as television news outlets came to increasingly rely on various forms of quantitative audience research in order to calibrate their news content and on-air news staffs in an effort to attract larger audiences. These consultants proved enormously influential in altering the form and structure of television newscasts (Allen 2007). Entertainment programs also began to undergo much more rigorous pre-testing in an effort by programmers to predict the audience appeal of the programs they were considering airing (Gitlin 1983/2000).

As James Carey (1980) has noted within the context of the evolution of the newspaper industry, the process of rationalization that characterized that industry (as well as other media sectors) was one in which it was necessary first to be able to construct the audience into a tangible, measurable mass; and then to effectively segment that mass into discrete, homogeneous subunits in order to best satisfy the needs of marketers and advertisers, who have historically demanded ever greater-levels of granularity and compre-hensiveness in relation to certain dimensions of audience information—particularly exposure (see, e.g., Bogart 1956; Dimling 1985; Ehrenberg 1968; Keller 1966; Politz 1943; Sen et al. 1998; Smythe 1986; Turow 2006).

A key aspect of this process was the move away from "households" as the primary unit of analysis toward the more detailed level of individuals, who could then of course be sorted into various demographic groupings. For this to happen, there needed to be both a change in the dynamics of media con-sumption and an increase in the availability of audience information sys-tems capable of capturing this more granular audience data. Technological developments such as the portable transistor radio and the growth of multi–television set households have been identified as key mechanisms for the necessary changes in the dynamics of media consumption that undermined more traditional household-level approaches to media consumption (Bal-naves and O'Regan 2008). These developments were then accompanied by advancements such as set-top meters capable of capturing individual-level data and computing systems capable of analyzing the greater volume of data that resulted when the individual, rather than the household, was the unit of analysis (Buzzard 2003a).

It is important to recognize that the increased technological fragmentation that has characterized the evolution of media (Neuman 1991), and that began its dramatic increase in the 1970s (with the arrival of technologies such as satellite and cable television)—and that would become dramatically more pronounced in the decades to follow in large part because of the dif-fusion of the Internet (Bermejo 2007)—is another important contributor to the increased rationalization of audience understanding that took place dur-ing this time period. This fragmentation facilitated the greater granularity in audience composition (and audience data) that many advertisers (and thus, by association, content providers) desired (Rubens 1984; Sen et al. 1998; Turow 1997).

Also, in the online realm we have seen a pattern at work that is similar to what took place in the traditional media, in which the embracing of ad-supported models provided much more powerful incentives for more ratio-nalized approaches to audience understanding. For instance, early on in the development and popularization of the Internet, there was minimal demand for audience research, given that the predominant business model was focused around subscription-driven online services (such as Prodigy, CompuServe, and earlier incarnations of AOL). With the growth of the Web, the lowering of the "walled gardens" employed by Internet service providers (ISPs), and the influx of content providers relying upon advertising support, the demand for data on audience exposure blossomed (see Coffey 2001). This growth in demand then led to an explosion in the number of firms involved in online audience measurement and the development of a variety of methodological approaches (Bermejo 2007; Mullarkey 2004; Wenthe and Wenthe 2001).[7]

In this regard, then, the process of the rationalization of audience understanding continues apace, extending into the realms of new media. What is becoming increasingly clear at this point is that within the new media environment, there is a wider array of analytical tools for media organizations to employ in their efforts to understand audiences (Davenport and Harris 2009). According to a report by consulting firm Booz Allen Hamilton, the increased accessibility, usability, and affordability of large quantities of data has been one of the biggest changes affecting the media landscape (Rasmussen et al. 2007). Research has suggested that the processes of media buying and planning are becoming increasingly specialized as a result of the fragmentation of the media environment and the increasing flow of complex audience data (see, e.g., Ferrier 2002).

These latest developments in the ongoing process of the rationalization of audience understanding also are due in large part to the highly interactive nature of the medium, which offers a wider range of information-gathering opportunities (see chap. 3). The increased interactivity that is at the core of these developments feeds directly into the ways that enhanced mechanisms for two-way communication between the observer and the observed can further facilitate the process of rationalization (Beniger 1987).

RESISTANCE

This process of the rationalization of audience understanding has not proceeded smoothly. At various points in the process, resistance has been intense. Studies across a variety of organizational contexts—including newsrooms (Berkowitz and Allen 1996; Gans 1979/2005), arts organizations (DiMaggio and Useem 1979; O'Regan 2002), motion picture studios (Handel

1953), publishing houses (Andrews and Napoli 2006), and advertising agencies (Kreshel 1993)—have identified a tendency among some stakeholders to be hostile toward efforts to further rationalize the process of audience understanding.

Often this resistance has broken down along professional lines, with those in more creative positions resisting the process and those in more analytical positions embracing and promoting it. In advertising, for instance, the influx of research in the early part of the twentieth century was resisted by creative staff such as copywriters, while being embraced by those involved in media buying activities (Kreshel 1993). Such resistance typically involved the prioritization of traits such as "experience, intuition, and common sense" (Kreshel 1993:61). In his assessment of early resistance in Hollywood to audience research, Leo Handel recalls that "Hollywood, by and large, resisted the development of high-level audience research. In the race between intuition and the IBM machine the latter came in a poor second. The reasons for the reluctance to use reliable audience research in the film industry are manifold. Most frequently, we hear that movie making is basically an artistic endeavor" (1953:304). During the 1940s, as audience research first grew in prominence and influence in the motion picture industry, creative personnel such as actors and writers came to the conclusion that such research "muzzled innovation" (Ohmer 2006:10). Other objections included the viability of making any kind of organizational decisions based on what one motion picture executive described as the "whimsies of public opinion" and the stifling of risk-taking likely to result from more research-driven decision-making (Ohmer 2006:152).

This tension within the motion picture industry in terms of the positioning of motion picture production, distribution, and exhibition as art versus science persisted throughout the 1940s and 1950s (Ohmer 2006). Within the context of this industry, resistance was effective enough that, by the late 1940s, the studios had begun to move away from the research being conducted by Gallup's Audience Research, Inc., and the other firms that had established a foothold in this area (Garrison 1972; Handel 1953; Ohmer 2006), only to return to such analytical strategies in the 1970s (see above).

Debates about the appropriateness of relying upon systematic audience data have historically been particularly pronounced within the journalistic community, where concerns about the proper dividing line between "church" and "state" also have a long history (see, e.g., Hujanen 2008; McManus 1994).

Questions related to the utilization of audience research have mapped onto this persistent tension in such a way that journalists and editors have often expressed concern that reliance upon audience research in the production of news inevitably undermines established news values, as well as the subjective news judgments of journalists (see Beam 1995; DeWerth-Pallmeyer 1997; MacGregor 2007). One study posited that journalists' resistance to audience research has stemmed from four factors: (a) the liberal arts education background (and associated discomfort with statistics) that typifies most journalists; (b) insufficient evidence, from journalists' perspective, that such data are useful; (c) the doubts that such research may cast on journalists' news judgments and professional autonomy; and (d) the fact that audience research frequently is conducted by nonjournalists (see Gans 1979/2005). A study of Australian newsrooms similarly found a "defensive culture resistant to readership and audience research" (Green 2002).

Another important point of delineation as it relates to resistance involves the divide between commercial and public service media. A number of accounts of the operation of public service media (e.g., public broadcasting) have highlighted the extent to which professionals within such organizations have resisted—although in most cases, eventually succumbed to—the pressures to conduct and rely upon sophisticated audience research (Stavitsky 1993, 1995).[8] As Robert Silvey notes in his history of audience research at the BBC, "the BBC did not set about studying its public systematically until ten years after it had become a public corporation" (1974:28). Once, however, the transition toward rationalized audience understanding was initiated at the BBC, the shift in that direction was dramatic. Some observers saw this as antithetical to the BBC's mission. Born, for instance, chronicles the changing organizational culture of the BBC, in which the rise of what she terms the "new managerialism" (2002:69) in the 1980s and 1990s led to a heavy reliance on audience research in programming decisions and, consequently, less creative autonomy for individual production departments—a transition that caused substantial tension within the organization.

And not surprisingly, as public service media sectors have become privatized and commercialized in various nations, their demand for, and utilization of, audience data has increased (Hagen 1999). As BBC audience researcher Robert Silvey noted, "The demand for audience measurement was, of course, far less claimant in countries served by non-commercial broadcasting. They had no advertisers to satisfy or persuade to buy time.

There was also far less demand for moment-to-moment audience measurement for this mainly derived from the need to know how many people heard the commercials. In the context of public service broadcasting the need for audience measurement came mainly from the programme planners' concern to assess the effect, in terms of consumption, of the pattern of broadcasting they had devised" (1974:77). Armand Mattelart (1991) documents this pattern across a number of different nations, including the U.K., Canada, France, Brazil, and Venezuela.

U.S. public broadcasters also initially exhibited resistance to audience research on the grounds that such research represented the encroachment of commercial imperatives onto their public service mission (Stavitsky 1993). However, declines in federal funding contributed to a willingness among public broadcasters to adopt such techniques in an effort to better understand their audiences, who were becoming an increasingly significant source of operating funds, and in order to better document public broadcasting's relevance (as reflected in the size of its audience) to Congress and other potential funders such as charitable foundations (Stavitsky 1995, 1998). At the end of 2009, PBS finally began subscribing to full-time Nielsen ratings (rather than basic monthly reports), a move that a PBS executive described as being "about the growing need for data" (Stelter 2009c: 1).

CRITIQUES

Many of these instances of resistance reflect broader critiques that have emerged over the years from within both academic and industry sectors in regard to the rationalization of audience understanding and/or the particular directions it has taken (see, e.g., Buck 1987; Doscher 1947; Eaman 1994; Meehan 1984; Savage 2006; Schiavone 1988). Pioneering market researcher Leo Bogart criticized what he described as "formula thinking," which he sees as "demand[ing] ever greater amounts of marketing and media information extracted from single samples of overloaded respondents in the form of syndicated research" (1986a:102). Such an approach, he argues,

> tends to deflect advertising research from a confrontation with significant issues in communication. Instead, it favors bovine mastication of transient data that are already obsolete by the time they are published. Formula thinking also increases the pressure for proof of performance, as

though the advertiser could put in dollars at one end of the sausage grinder, with proven evaluation of effects emerging at the other end. And formula thinking resists the argument that real life is complicated and that things don't work that way.   (Bogart 1986a:102)

As these critiques suggest, it is important to emphasize that this rationalization of audience understanding evolved in very specific directions, to the neglect of other potential paths (Wehner 2002), particularly within the context of advertising-supported media. This pattern is reflective of the process of simplification of observable phenomena that is central to the process of rationalization (Beniger 1987). The overwhelming tendency within the context of media organizations has been one of the quantification of audience size and (later) composition, to the neglect of other dimensions of the audience. As Paul Lazarsfeld noted as early as 1947, "Questions of preference in radio research have been almost discarded in favor of actual listening figures. But this is not necessarily the best solution. It may be just as important to know that a person likes a certain program, although it happens to be on the air at a time when he or she cannot listen" (pp. 165–166).[9] Much of the early audience research conducted by Lazarsfeld's Radio Research Project reflected his concern with understanding audience appreciation of radio programming (see, e.g., Wiebe 1939),[10] although broadcast industry approaches to audiences ultimately went in a very different direction. We find such critiques even earlier in the history of audience research. As one analysis pointed out in 1936, "We have lost sight of our primary purpose for measuring radio programs. What we really want to know is not how many persons are listening . . . the real information that we desire is just how much influence the program in question is exerting on sales" (Likert 1936:175).

More public interest–oriented concerns frequently underlie this critique of media industries' traditional emphasis on exposure. Typically, these critiques emphasize the very limited conceptualization of the audience that is reflected in an exposure-oriented analytical approach, and the fact that such an analytical approach is much more reflective of the needs and interests of the content providers and advertisers than it is of the needs and interests of the audience (Ang 1991; Meehan 1984).[11] These concerns become particularly pronounced within media policy–related contexts, such as the funding and organizational mandates for public service media, or other contexts where an understanding of the public's media usage can usefully inform policymaking (see, e.g., Napoli and Gillis 2006; Raboy, Abramson, Proulx, and Welters 2001). Here the fact that audience research often is used as a mechanism for essentially gauging the public interest and making decisions accordingly means that any analytical approach that oversimplifies the nature of the public (as audience) and its needs and interests will lead to poor policy decisions (see, e.g., Eaman 1994).

Such concerns have prompted an extensive dialogue addressing the important distinctions between the audience as citizen and the audience as consumer (Butsch 2000; Couldry 2004; Livingstone, Lunt, and Miller 2007a, 2007b; Raboy et al. 2001; Syvertsen 2004; Webster and Phalen 1997). Some analyses of the media-audience relationship, for instance, have concluded that the early mass media exhibited a much stronger tendency to approach their audiences as citizens rather than consumers, and offered programming options more reflective of the needs of citizens rather than those of consumers and the advertisers seeking to reach them (Butsch 2008). Others have concluded that a consumer-oriented analytical frame is eclipsing a citizen-oriented analytical frame within policy discourse (Livingstone, Lunt, and Miller 2007a, 2007b) as policymakers grapple with how to address new media technologies (see Gandy 2002). Broader conceptualizations of the audience that not only account for the basic elements of media usage and exposure, but also approach audiences as "individuals with complex socio-economic positionings" have been advocated as essential to better media policymaking and to media that better serve the public interest (Raboy et al. 2001:101).[12]

As this discussion suggests, at many points in the history of the rationalization of audience understanding there have been calls, from within both academic and industry sectors, for audience information systems that move beyond exposure and consider other dimensions of the audience, such as appreciation or impact (see, e.g., Hoffman and Batra 1991; Philport 1993). Efforts to respond to such calls in the development of audience information systems have, however, historically failed to take hold, particularly in the realm of ad-supported media. Kingson (1953) describes an early radio audience measurement service launched by the Schewerin Research Corporation, which employed an audience panel and a program analyzer–type of device to measure not only the size of the audience, but also audience reactions to individual radio programs. This service was subsequently expanded to television, but in neither context did it displace established exposure-based systems. In the 1980s similar efforts within the context of television by a Markle Foundation–funded enterprise, Television Audience Assessment, Inc., similarly failed to take hold (Mitgang 2002).[13] Advertising researcher Joseph Philport describes his efforts at developing "qualitative ratings systems" for a variety of constituents in the television and radio industries, though "each of these efforts failed to evolve into a sound commercial application" (1993:RC-5).

The failure of such initiatives also serves to highlight the common critique with the "ratings" terminology, which has been described as "implicitly and misleadingly conveying the impression of an evaluative response to programmes . . . when all they represent is a measure of presence" (Gunter and Wober 1992:101). Leo Bogart summed up the situation as follows: "Variations in the intensity and character of the reading experience (as of the radio listening experience) have conventionally been ignored by both buyers and sellers of advertising. The advent and growth of television only added to the emphasis on 'boxcar' figures that showed the largest possible potential *exposure*" (1976:110; emphasis added). A more recent assessment led to a similar conclusion: that the history of audience measurement has been one in which "other forms of knowledge were invented, but discarded" (Oswell 2002:115).

Efforts to think about and analyze the audience in ways that extend beyond basic exposure have been meaningfully embraced only in certain contexts. We see this in the realm of noncommercial broadcasting, for instance, where the organizational mission is often less about maximizing audience size and more about maximizing audience satisfaction (Emmett 1968; Jeffrey 1994; Keegan 1980; Silvey 1944, 1951, 1974). Jeffrey (1994) documents such efforts within the context of the Canadian Broadcasting Corporation, where systematic measurements of program *quality* (as perceived by audience members) have been utilized. One approach involved the creation of an "enjoyment index," which asked television viewers to rate their level of enjoyment of the programs they watched on a five-point scale (Eaman 1994). This index was employed for more granular analyses, including the assessment of individual characters, as well as program elements such as the story, dialogue, and settings (Eaman 1994).

The BBC has similarly undertaken systematic efforts to determine the extent to which its programming is effectively serving the needs and wants of its audience (see, e.g., Emmett 1968). BBC audience researcher Robert Silvey, for instance, chronicles his realization in the 1940s that "in a properly balanced audience research service the continuous measurement of the quantity of listening—the estimation of the size of each programme's audience—should be supplemented by a continuous assessment of audience reaction—what listeners felt about the programmes they were listening to" (1974:113). From this perspective, the BBC went on to develop an "appreciation index," which was derived from questions gauging the extent to which audiences enjoyed individual broadcasts (Silvey 1974).

It is also interesting to note that early on the BBC decided not to publish a list of its top twenty programs, based on the conviction that "Top Twenties encouraged an entirely fallacious impression of the real significance of audience size: that every broadcast had the same target—the entire population—and that they were therefore all to be judged by the extent to which their audiences approached that goal. . . . There was no virtue in size per se, all that mattered was whether a broadcast attracted the audience which it was reasonable to expect of it" (Silvey 1974:185).[14] To a certain extent, this decision can be seen as reflective of the BBC's research findings at the time related to television viewership, which indicated little meaningful relationship between audience size and the intensity of audience appreciation for the content consumed (Silvey 1951).

In the realm of some consumer-supported media (e.g., motion pictures) there also has been, and continues to be, greater emphasis on probing the more "qualitative" aspects of an audience's interaction with content. Thus, for instance, motion picture audience research has traditionally devoted a substantial amount of attention to the extent to which audience members enjoy particular films, the reasons they enjoy the films, and changes that could be made to increase their enjoyment of the films (see, e.g., Doscher 1947; Handel 1950; Hayes and Bing 2006).

In the extreme, such approaches to audience understanding are practiced in such a way as to explicitly avoid any subjective assessments of content or its likely audience appeal, reflecting the depersonalization that has historically been a part of the process of rationalization. In a study of radio programmers and the process by which they gauge audience song preferences, Ahlkvist found that, for those programmers employing a research-oriented programming philosophy, "The lynch pin of this programming philosophy is not to listen to the music. Programmers should be far more concerned with 'the numbers' provided by audience research than they are with determining the viability of a song on their own by listening to how it sounds"

(2001:349; see also Ahlkvist and Faulkner 2002). The assumption here of course is that the audience data provide a far more objective, and thus consistently more accurate, assessment of the likely appeal of individual songs.

A broader, and very common, critique involves concerns that more rationalized approaches to audience understanding might stifle innovation, risk-taking, and diversity in the production of media content, and instead promote imitation, repetition, and homogenization (e.g., McCourt and Rothenbuhler 1997). In her study of George Gallup and his role in the development of motion picture research, Ohmer (2006) describes how the research conducted by Gallup's Audience Research Institute (ARI) factored prominently into movie studio RKO's decision to abandon efforts at producing "prestige films and artistic features," and focus instead purely on more commercially oriented films. Ohmer (2006) also notes that ARI's surveys researching the roles audiences would like to see stars appear in tended to conclude that the stars should perform in parts that were highly consistent with their established screen personas. According to Ohmer, "This result can be explained in part by ARI's methods: since the institute gave people a list of projects from which to choose, with only a short synopsis for each, film-goers would be inclined to select stories that resembled a star's previous roles" (2006:143).[15] Seldes has described such pre-testing methods as simply "providing justification for repeating . . . formulas"; as a result, he asserts, "the sheer mass of duplicated material will increase" (1950:223).

Similar findings have emerged in analyses of other sectors of the media industry. As noted previously, Born's analysis of the impact that an increased reliance on audience data had on decision-making within the BBC concluded that creativity was stifled, and that the broadcaster's "capacity for difference" was consequently eroded (2002:86). Similarly, Ahlkvist and Fisher's (2000) analysis of the radio industry demonstrated an empirical connection between a station's reliance upon research and consultants and its tendency toward standardization in its programming practices.

EXPLANATIONS

At the core of this process toward greater rationalization of audience understanding is the notion that there is a tremendous amount of uncertainty involved in assessing both the demand for, and the consumption of, most forms of media content (Hagen 1999; Napoli 2003a). Audiences across all media are notoriously unpredictable in terms of their preferences, making the forecasting of successes and failures incredibly difficult (Bernt et al. 2000; Caves 2000; McQuail 1969). Screenwriter William Goldman's famous adage about the motion picture industry's understanding of its audience— "Nobody knows anything" (1983:39)—has received empirical support not only within the context of film (De Vany 2004), but within other media industry sectors as well (Bielby and Bielby 1994; Caves 2000; Gitlin 1983/2000). Nonetheless, organizations that deal with audiences must try to anticipate audience preferences and make decisions accordingly (Gitlin 1983/2000; Maltby 1999; Pekurny 1982). When these predictions are inaccurate (in terms of overestimating audience demand), the economic consequences for a media firm can be disastrous, with the firm unable to recoup the large upfront costs associated with producing a media product (De Vany 2004; Gitlin 1983/2000).

Research traditionally has been seen as a key mechanism for reducing this uncertainty, and thus facilitating better-informed decision-making (Anand and Peterson 2000). Ideally audience data can reduce uncertainty, facilitate more effective predicting of audience behavior, and consequently enable more effective strategic decision-making. The process here is one of bringing something (media consumption) that traditionally has been, to varying degrees, somewhat intangible into more tangible relief, thereby facilitating a greater array of historical, strategic, and predictive analyses (see, e.g., Napoli 2003a). Historical trends in audience behavior are commonly used to try to anticipate audience preferences (Bielby and Bielby 1994; Hirsch 1972), despite the fact that evidence suggests that this technique is not particularly effective at identifying future successes (Bielby and Bielby 1994; Eastman 1998; Knee, Greenwald, and Seave 2009).[16]

Nonetheless, control (be it real or perceived) has often been seen as a key underlying motivation for this process of rationalization (Ang 1991; Beniger 1987; Kreshel 1990; McCourt and Rothenbuhler 1997; Wehner 2002). Within the context of media audiences, it has been argued that the increased predictability that comes from the rigorous gathering and analysis of audience data leads to increased control over what can be a very unruly and unpredictable audience (Carlson 2006; Rohle 2007). The presumption here is that such knowledge can be used in ways to influence behaviors, or at least make them more predictable. Critics of this presumption, however, have questioned whether greater knowledge truly facilitates greater control.[17] In his analysis of the construction of the children's television audience in the U.K., Oswell argues that "truths about audiences" actually exacerbate insecurity rather than contribute to greater confidence and control over the audience–content provider relationship (2002:116).

Some analyses have suggested that this process of rationalization of audience understanding may have been (and continues to be) as much about establishing and maintaining symbolic indicators of professionalism and legitimization as it has been about uncertainty reduction or control (Kreshel 1990, 1993; Schwoch 1990). Austin (1989), for instance, sees the motion picture industry's desire to improve its image in the eyes of the investment community as a key motivator for the industry's adoption of systematic audience information systems. As Starr and Corson have speculated in relation to the broader trend favoring data-driven decision-making across a variety of organizational contexts, "It is difficult to say how much of the new demand for data stems from a rational need for exact information to improve organizational performance and how much comes from the symbolic value of numbers in the competition for influence within organizations" (1987:422). From this standpoint, the symbolic value of data as "ritualistic assurance that appropriate attitudes about decision making exist" can generate powerful incentives to gather more data than are needed or than can be effectively analyzed (Feldman and March 1981:177). Some critics have been more blunt, arguing that the reliance on more rationalized approaches to audience understanding is less about the *formulation* of decisions and more about the *justification* of decisions (Bielby and Bielby 1994; Bogart 1986b; Seldes 1950). From this standpoint, in today's decision-making environment it is much easier to convince others that a particular course of action is appropriate when that course of action is supported by systematic analysis of the relevant audience data. By the same token, decisions that prove wrong can be much more easily defended if they are shown to have relied upon such analyses.

More narrowly, we can also try to explain why the rationalization of audience understanding proceeded down the particular path that it did. Why were certain elements of audience behavior the focus of this process, while others resided at the margins? In particular, why did exposure become the overwhelming focus of audience conceptualizations within the ad-supported media? In an early effort at addressing these questions, Bogart argues that more complex aspects of audiences' interaction with content have been neglected largely because they are "difficult, expensive and time-consuming to disentangle from other forces" (1969:5). As a result, "advertisers rely on the same data sources, simply because of the economy of syndicated research ... over customized research. The same numbers, applied by the same formulas, produce similar strategies and decisions" (Bogart 1976:109).[18]

Hurwitz (1988) argues that an early conflation of quality and popularity took place in audience research, a conflation that Buxton (1994) illustrates was central to the fissure that quickly grew between early academic and industry audience research. Drawing upon 1930s-era correspondence of audience researcher Hadley Cantril, Buxton (1994) illustrates that even in the formative years of broadcasting commercial broadcasters were reluctant to engage in or support audience research that extended beyond a very narrow band of audience dimensions, as the findings of such research might not, for a variety of reasons, be in their best interests. Instead, a very strong early connection was forged between the industry's audience research and market research. As a result, the priorities of market researchers largely eclipsed the somewhat different priorities that characterized early audience researchers (Hurwitz 1988). By many accounts, this "convergence" of market research with audience research (at least as it is practiced by media industries) has persisted (e.g., Wehner 2002).

A key aspect of this critique is the extent to which it suggests that institutionalized approaches to audience understanding reflect a tendency to travel the path of least resistance, particularly in terms of the expense involved with developing more holistic approaches to audience. This tendency represents a fundamental element of the process of audience evolution, which, it will be shown, takes place only when a particular set of circumstances are in place that reconfigure the path of least resistance in a way that reflects a fundamental departure from the status quo.

CHAPTER 2

THE TRANSFORMATION OF MEDIA CONSUMPTION

It is fairly well known at this point that the media environment is changing dramatically; that new technologies are providing audiences with more choice and control in terms of when, where, and how they consume their media; that these new technologies are providing increasing opportunities for audiences to interact with their media, to provide feedback, and to influence outcomes; and of course that today's media consumers are becoming much more than consumers—they are producers and distributors of content as well. This chapter begins by laying out the basic contours of these technological changes and how they are affecting the dynamics of media consumption.

However, the primary goal here is to move beyond these observations and to examine what these developments mean for how media industries conceptualize their audiences. How do these changing dynamics of media consumption affect what audiences mean to content producers and distributors, advertisers, and media buyers? What strains are these changes in media consumption placing on institutionalized conceptualizations of the audience? What opportunities for reconceptualizing the institutionalized media audience do these evolutionary changes provide? These are the questions that are the focus of this chapter.

This discussion is organized around the two fairly broad overarching concepts that capture the key changes taking place in the contemporary media environment: fragmentation and audience autonomy (see Napoli 2003a). Fragmentation involves the extent to which the media environment contains an increasing array of content delivery platforms, the extent to which the transmission capacity of these different delivery platforms is expanding, the extent to which media content is itself disaggregating, and the extent to which audience attention is increasingly spread out across a growing array of available content options. *Audience autonomy* refers to the extent to which the contemporary media environment provides audiences with unprecedented levels of control over not only what media they consume, but also when, where, and how they consume it; and also, increasingly, the extent to which audiences have the power to be more than mere media consumers, becoming contributors to the media environment as well.

Each of these concepts and their implications for how media organizations understand their audiences will be discussed in the sections that follow. As this chapter will make clear, the fragmentation and autonomy of the new media environment simultaneously undermine traditional approaches to audience understanding, while also opening up opportunities for alternative approaches. It is the pursuit of these alternative approaches that is the focus of the next chapter.

FRAGMENTATION

As has been outlined previously (see Napoli 2003a), the concept of fragmentation as it relates to the media environment can be broken down into two interrelated components, media fragmentation and audience fragmentation. These components, and their relationship, are illustrated in figure 2.1. Media fragmentation in this case refers to the technological processes that increase the range of content options available to media consumers. This, in turn, can be broken down further. First we need to consider *inter-media* fragmentation, which involves the growth of new delivery platforms. These new delivery platforms not only facilitate the delivery of additional content options, but also multiply the platforms in which any one piece of content can be accessed. Think, for instance, of the variety of options—broadcast network, cable network rerun, Internet stream, iPod download, DVR, cable system on-demand service, etc.—available for consuming a particular episode of a first-run, broadcast network television program today (see Lotz 2007). Similarly, consider all of the possible mechanisms by which one can read the *New York Times* (printed copy, online, delivered to an electronic book reader such as Amazon's Kindle, or via one's cell phone). We could similarly rattle off a litany of platforms on which one can now listen to a hit song. The same piece of content can be consumed across so many different media platforms that it is, of course, becoming difficult to draw firm boundaries around industry sectors. Defining any sector of the media industry in terms of a particular delivery platform (i.e., the "television" industry or the "newspaper" industry) no longer makes any sense, since individual content types have broken well beyond the confines of the delivery platforms that initially defined them.

Intra-media fragmentation refers to the processes that subdivide choices *within* particular media technologies. At the most obvious level this includes increases in bandwidth and channel capacity that we see not only in broadcast television and radio (via digitization), but also in cable, satellite, and online. For instance, the most recent count of the total number of cable television networks available in the United States is 585, according to the National Cable and Telecommunications Association (2008). Obtaining an accurate count of the number of Web sites in operation is hardly possible today, given the worldwide growth in Web sites—though one recent estimate puts the number at almost 187 million as of December 2008 (Netcraft 2009).

Equally important, if less discussed, is the phenomenon wherein individual content options are disaggregated into smaller, discrete components. Examples of this include the ability to watch television clips, rather than entire episodes, online,[1] or the return of the singles model to the recorded music industry as a result of the advent of music downloads. And, of course, the notion of purchasing an entire newspaper, with its many sections, many of which might be of no interest at all, seems increasingly archaic when one can focus exclusively on favorite sections (or even favorite journalists) online. These too are forms of intra-media fragmentation, as the content unit itself becomes fragmented into discrete units and the more traditional unified whole breaks down.

Content is also disaggregating from the advertisements that have traditionally been embedded within it. This is essentially the problem that has befallen the newspaper industry, where entire advertising segments, such as classifieds, have completely decoupled from the daily news and migrated online in the form of freestanding classified services such as Craigslist and Monster. And, unlike with most other media, the advertisements contained within newspapers were valued by audiences. That is, newspaper readers tend to prefer to see more ads in their newspapers rather than less, according to analyses of the relationship between ad pages and circulation figures.[2] This helps explain why many of the types of advertisements that traditionally have been prominent in newspapers (classifieds/employment ads, auto-

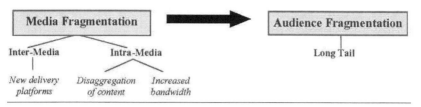

FIGURE 2.1 The Fragmentation of the Media Environment

mobile ads) can support stand-alone Web sites. The loss of these types of advertisements means not only lower ad revenues for individual papers, but also circulation declines, as the newspaper becomes a less appealing product for some readers, given its diminished advertising content.

These forms of disaggregation of traditional media content units in many ways represent the core crisis affecting the production of media content today, as this kind of disaggregation undermines the aggregation and support systems that long have been central to media content production. One or two hit songs support the production of twelve other songs on an album. The many people who may have bought a newspaper primarily for the sports or business section provide funds that support the production of less popular sections. Cable and direct-broadcast satellite (DBS) service subscribers support the operation of many cable networks that they never actually watch. Disaggregation of content into more discrete consumable units undermines these aggregation and support mechanisms and puts the less popular and/or more expensive content in peril (hence the concern, for example, about the future of investigative journalism as the newspaper business migrates online; see Starr 2009).

As media technologies continue to facilitate the increasing fragmentation of content options, the distribution of audience attention to a certain degree follows suit—which brings us to the notion of audience fragmentation. Audience attention can now be dispersed across an unprecedented array of content options. This fragmentation process has been aptly described by one Internet audience measurement firm executive as involving "millions of audiences of hundreds instead of hundreds of audiences of millions."[3] The term "slivercasting" has been coined to reflect the extension of audience fragmentation well beyond the notion of "narrowcasting" (Hansell 2006; see also Smith-Shomade 2004).

The most well-known examination of the dynamics, and implications, of this process has been provided by *Wired* magazine editor Chris Anderson's (2006) "long tail" analysis. First presented as a magazine article (Anderson 2004) and subsequently expanded into a book (Anderson 2006), the long tail concept builds upon the persistent pattern that we see in the highly fragmented distribution of audience attention across available content options. This pattern is illustrated in figure 2.2, in which we see audience attention clustered around a select few "hits," but then quickly spread out across a wide array of niche-content options (the tail).[4] This pattern often has been referred to as the 80/20 rule, in which 80 percent of revenues are derived from 20 percent of the available product offerings (also commonly referred to as the Pareto Principle; see Brynjolfsson, Hu, and Simester 2007)

As Anderson (2006) emphasizes, the highly fragmented media environment of today is one in which the tail is continuing to lengthen, so much so that the aggregated audience attention contained within the tail can begin to rival—and even exceed—the aggregated audience attention captured by the "hits" (i.e., the "head"). Anderson goes beyond this basic observation, however, to argue that the dynamics of the new media environment enhance the importance, and even the revenue potential, of niche content relative to hits.

First, because so much media content can today be stored and distributed digitally, this dramatically reduces the costs associated with making a wide range of content options available to consumers, and thereby increases the incentives for providing such material (Anderson 2006). From an economic standpoint, this trend represents the transition of many media products to a "pure public good" model. Media content is a classic example of what economists call a "public good" in that once it is produced it remains available to be sold and resold without incurring significant additional costs (Owen and Wildman 1992). A motion picture or television program or book can earn revenues for decades after its initial creation for relatively little cost beyond the additional production costs.

Historically, the only additional costs associated with the distribution and sale of public goods such as media products have been the costs associated with embedding these public goods in "private goods" to facilitate their distribution. Thus, movies have been embedded in discs and videotapes, songs have been embedded in tapes and CDs, the news has been embedded in printed papers. Utilizing these private goods to distribute public goods means incurring production, distribution, warehousing, and exhibition

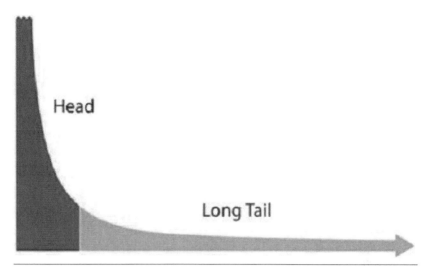

FIGURE 2.2 The Long Tail of Media Consumption

costs, ranging from the costs of printing newspapers and distributing them around the city to the costs of operating music, video, or book stores. In an environment in which this content can be stored and distributed online in digital formats, many of these costs go away or are significantly reduced, making the business of offering tremendous quantities of content potentially much more viable than in years past. Even the traditional processes of selling public goods embedded in private goods are affected by this transition, as online shopping facilitates a centralization of storage and distribution that can dramatically reduce costs relative to traditional models (think, for example, of Amazon versus traditional bookstores).

As a result, we find ourselves in an environment of unprecedented abundance, with the constraints associated with the storage and exhibition capacity limits of traditional bookstores, record stores, movie theaters, and cable systems replaced with the expansive menus of Amazon, iTunes, Netflix, digital cable, and the Web. While most of the content available through these sources attracts a very small audience, when these small audiences are aggregated, they are quite significant.

Their significance is further enhanced, according to Anderson (2006), by another key characteristic of the contemporary media environment—the extent to which it provides audiences with a variety of tools for navigating this landscape of increased choice. Tools such as peer recommendations, site-generated recommendations, and robust, multidimensional search features all make it easier for audiences to find content that appeals to them, thereby making it easier and more rewarding for them to take advantage of this environment of increased content abundance (Helft 2009). Such functionality is central to the operation of online content providers such as Amazon, iTunes, YouTube, and Netflix.

Anderson (2006) focuses on the online environment for his analysis, but we can also look to media contexts such as television to see the development of similar tools for navigating the long tail. Consider, for instance, the recommendation features of advanced digital video recorders such as TiVo. A TiVo can be programmed to learn from the user's demonstrated viewing behaviors and make program recommendations—and even record programs—based on the user's prior viewing patterns. In this way, TiVo subscribers can find themselves watching an obscure movie or television program that they hadn't even known existed. Similarly, the enhanced functionality of today's electronic program guides makes it possible to engage in reasonably thorough searches of available program offerings (using criteria such as program type, genre, star, etc.). Obviously, if today's television viewers had to engage in old-fashioned "channel surfing" to determine what programs were airing on the 200+ channels they typically receive, the likelihood of viewers ever venturing all the way to the niche channels placed at the high end of the channel spectrum would be greatly diminished.

Features as simple as being able to search for television program options while being able to stay on the channel currently being viewed, or to peruse the songs playing on other satellite radio channels while still listening to a particular channel, fundamentally affect the value associated with an increasingly fragmented media environment. In this regard, fragmentation and searchability essentially must go hand-in-hand for all new media. For the typical media consumer to see the value in an ever-expanding array of content options, that consumer must also feel reasonably confident that the necessary tools are available for efficiently and effectively navigating this complex media environment, so that any extra expense associated with receiving these additional content options provides genuine value. And, as this statement suggests, this is one of the key ways in which the processes of fragmentation and audience autonomy (see below) are fundamentally intertwined.

According to Anderson (2006), the greatly expanded content storage capacity of a digitized space such as the Internet, combined with the enhanced, highly interactive search tools such a space can provide, contributes to a media environment in which the traditional "power law distribution" of audience attention can become more lucrative than was possible in the offline world (Anderson 2006). That is, a consumption dynamic in which 20 percent of the content generates 80 percent of the revenue (and in which nobody knows what that popular 20 percent is going to be—see Napoli 2003a) can be more lucrative in an environment in which "shelf-space" is much less scarce and less expensive, distribution is inexpensive, and the consumer's ability to effectively and satisfactorily navigate this expansive shelf-space is enhanced via a wide range of search tools and linking systems. As Anderson summarizes, "Our culture and economy are increasingly shifting away from a focus on a relatively small number of hits (mainstream products and markets) at the head of the demand curve, and moving toward a huge number of niches in the tail. In an era without the constraints of physical shelf space and other bottlenecks of distribution, narrowly targeted goods and services can be as economically attractive as mainstream fare" (2006:52).[5]

In such an environment the content provider can make all available content accessible, and not have to make editorial judgments about which content to carry and which content not to carry based upon (often wrong) predictions regarding consumer tastes. The content provider can also be reasonably sure that all of the content will generate at least some revenue, even if the bulk of the revenues continue to be generated by only 20 percent of it. Under this model success is increased via the facts that: (a) the content provider never has to worry about not having any of the 20 percent of content options that prove to be enormously successful; and (b) the remaining content (the long tail) can be stored and exhibited cheaply enough—and can be located and accessed easily enough by the consumer—that it too will become a meaningful contributor to profits.

Perhaps the most controversial aspect of the long tail concept involves the extent to which the storage capacity and navigability of the new media environment can facilitate an actual *change* in how audience attention is distributed, not just an alteration in the underlying economics of this pattern in the distribution of audience attention. That is, does the availability of a greater range of content options, combined with the availability of navigation tools such as search functions and recommendation systems, shift consumption away from the head and into the tail? Are audiences less likely to focus their attention on a select few hits in an environment in which it is easier to locate and access a much broader range of choices? Anderson (2006) argues in the affirmative, asserting not only that the availability of more content options will essentially lengthen the tail, but that the greater ability to access this content will "fatten" the tail and simultaneously shorten the head.

As was noted above, the long tail phenomenon has characterized traditional media to some extent for many years. The difference now is that the tail has the potential to be much, much longer, given the efficiencies of digital storage and distribution. This lengthening can potentially come from: (a) audience attention that has migrated from the head or other parts of the tail to the further extremities of the tail; and (b) additional audience attention captured as a result of the fact that the available content options are more numerous now than was previously the case. Point (b) reflects the fact that in this migration to a media environment of greater storage capacity, cheaper distribution capacity, and greater navigability, we need to acknowledge the possibility that overall consumer welfare will be enhanced and that greater overall media consumption will result. The idea here, for instance, is that people will watch more DVDs when offered the easily searchable cornucopia of Netflix than when confronted with the more limited, and more difficult to navigate, selection at a video store.

Inherent in point (a) is the assumption that at least some parts of the long tail have the potential to fatten. Such a fattening would reflect the idea that a media environment in which search and recommendation systems make it easier to locate obscure content of interest would allow some content to attract a larger audience than was possible in years past. Using home video as an example: imagine, for instance, the DVD for an obscure 80s sci-fi action movie called *The Hidden* (a personal favorite of mine) gathering dust on the shelf at the back end of a video store—and most likely not even being available in most video stores. According to Anderson's logic, the availability of *The Hidden* on Netflix or iTunes could increase the size of the audience for it, as action movie aficionados are better able to discover the film thanks to the various search and recommendation systems available on the Netflix and iTunes Web sites. Presumably, then, if the total amount of audience attention remains constant between the old and new media scenarios, then the head would have to shrink in order to facilitate this migration of audience attention into the tail. Of course, it is also possible that for every *new* viewer attracted to *The Hidden* thanks to NetFlix's and iTunes search and recommendation systems, one or more of the viewers who *would have* watched *The Hidden* in the traditional media environment is led further away to other *even more obscure* sci-fi action movies, thanks to these same search and recommendation systems. From this standpoint, the overall effect of the new media environment on any one piece of content is difficult to determine.

Now, let's set aside the assumption that the total amount of audience attention is constant across the two scenarios. Instead, let's assume that—thanks to the greater variety and the satisfaction derived from using search and recommendation systems—the new media environment contributes to an overall increase in audience attention. That is, once I subscribe to Netflix I find myself watching more movies in a typical month than I did when I rented movies from Blockbuster. Under this model, the total space under the curve increases. The question then becomes: how does the overall shape of the curve change? According to Anderson's (2006) logic, most of this new audience attention will be directed at content in the tail. And the tail will certainly lengthen as audiences now gain access to content options that were inaccessible under the Blockbuster model. But will the tail (or at least parts of it) fatten as well? Returning to the case of *The Hidden*: under this scenario *The Hidden*'s potential to increase its audience is greater than under the scenario in which we held the quantity of audience attention constant. Now *The Hidden* can draw viewers not only from the head, but also from among those who were previously not actively renting movies. The potential to lose viewers to the increased content options available under the longer tail persists, but now that we're not talking about a zero-sum game, *The Hidden*'s potential to benefit from Anderson's long tail scenario is greater. And when we project this scenario for *The Hidden* to the full aggregation of niche content, then we can see how the long tail scenario can potentially enhance the prospects for niche content.

The unanswered question, however, remains whether the dramatic increase in choices that has accompanied the transition to the new media environment is of a magnitude sufficient to overwhelm any positive effects for individual niche-content options that arise from enhanced search and navigation systems.[6] Answering this question depends in large part on whether greater choice and searchability truly contribute to an increase in overall consumption. According to Anderson, evidence to date suggests that the answer to this question "depends on the [industry] sector" (2006:137). At this point, however, it seems safe to say that what is good for niche content in the aggregate is not necessarily what is good for any individual piece of niche content. The bottom line is that if the tail doesn't fatten, but only lengthens, then content options that were obscure in the old media environment will remain equally obscure in the new media environment (perhaps even more so)—there will just be more of them.

Some critics of the long tail argument have asserted that the greater choice, navigability, and searchability characteristic of the new media environment will not strengthen the position of niche content relative to "hits" and instead may ultimately strengthen the position of the hits relative to the niche products, in fact making for a head that is even more pronounced relative to the tail. Research by Elberse (2008; see also Elberse and Oberholzer-Gee 2008), which draws from data on music and movie consumption, suggests that the tail is becoming longer and flatter, rather than thickening. In addition, her research indicates that although the head is shrinking, a diminishing number of different content options are accounting for the top 10 percent of sales.[7] From these results, she concludes that "the importance of individual best sellers is not diminishing over time. It is growing" (Elberse 2008:92). This perspective receives support from research examining the distribution of audience attention across videos posted on YouTube, which determined that "counterintuitively, requests on YouTube seem to be highly skewed towards popular files" (Cha et al. 2007:4; see also Bughin 2007).

Why are tools such as search functionality and recommendations systems potentially unable to contribute to a thickening of the long tail? One reason, beyond the countervailing fragmenting effects of the availability of more choices, may be related to how recommendation systems operate. Many search and recommendation systems provide the user with indicators of each media product's popularity (in terms of sales rank, number of downloads, etc.). Some research suggests that this kind of information may contribute to the well-known "bandwagon effect," in which consumers gravitate to content that they know is popular (Fleder and Hosanagar 2009; Salganik and Watts 2008; Thorson 2008; Tucker and Zhang 2007). Moreover, the algorithms that underlie the operation of many online search tools display results in an order that is often based, at least in part, on demonstrated popularity (see, e.g., Finkelstein 2008). Thus the most popular items are shown first, and therefore are the most likely to be accessed—a pattern that can contribute to the popular options becoming even more popular and that further undermines the prospects for niche content to find an audience.

Another common search and recommendation tool involves consumer-generated review systems, such as those utilized by Amazon and Netflix. With these systems, individual audience members have the capacity to give ratings and write detailed reviews for the media products they have consumed. This information is then used to guide others, under the logic that audiences who liked product A also tended to like product B. Research indicates that "consumer populations exhibit a disproportionately higher propensity to contribute product reviews for successful ('hit') movies they have watched at the expense of obscure movies they have also watched during the same period" (Dellarocas and Narayan 2007:24). Thus there appears to be something of a bandwagon effect toward reviewing popular content. When this tendency is combined with research indicating that audiences, on average, tend to give higher ratings to "hits" than to niche media products (Elberse 2008), then the overall effect is likely to be one that inhibits, rather than promotes, the thickening of the long tail. In the end, the notion that this dramatically changed technological environment may ultimately do relatively little to alter the fundamental distribution patterns of audience attention is in many ways as remarkable, if not more remarkable, than the ways this changed technological environment can alter the economics of content distribution and exhibition.

As should be clear at this point, the bulk of the discussion and analysis that has surrounded the long tail concept has focused on consumer-supported media. And, for that matter, these discussions have tended to focus almost exclusively on the *exhibition* component of consumer-supported media. That is, the long tail discussions have made it very clear how the new media environment has altered the dynamics of *selling* content to customers. It is now both feasible and advisable to carry every available content option. The traditional notion of the retailer as gatekeeper is in decline. The bookstores capable of carrying only one hundred thousand titles or the music stores capable of carrying only five thousand CDs seem increasingly anachronistic in the era of Amazon and iTunes.

However, as much as this dynamic emphasizes that retailers increasingly need to be in the business of providing audiences with access not only to hits but to flops (or, to put it more kindly, niche content) as well, it does not necessarily mean that being in the business of *producing* niche content is any more appealing a financial proposition today than it was in the old media environment, particularly given the implications of the above analysis of what the long tail scenario means for any individual piece of content. From the standpoint of the individual content producer, perhaps the most important question posed by the long tail scenario is not how to make money from the long tail, but rather how to infiltrate the fat head. This has always been the question that bedevils media industries and this will remain a fundamental quest even in the media world of the long tail, unless the head flattens to a point at which it disappears.

THE LONG TAIL OF THE AUDIENCE MARKETPLACE

More directly relevant to the topic of audience evolution is the question of what this long tail dynamic means for media contexts in which audiences *are* the product (i.e., ad-supported media), rather than those in which audiences are *purchasing* the product. This is an issue that has received surprisingly little discussion amid all the attention that has been directed at the implications of the long tail phenomenon for media industries. This imbalance is surprising, given that the implications for ad-supported media are likely to be far more dramatic than they are for consumer-supported media.

Simply put, the long tail phenomenon has been nearly devastating to most media enterprises involved in the production and sale of audiences. An increasingly fragmented media environment allows the tail of audience attention to continue to lengthen, diminishing the audience for each individual content option. Equally important, as Elberse's (2008) research suggests, audience interfaces that include advanced search and recommendation functionality (see, e.g., Rowson, Gossweiler, and MacDonald 2005) do not seem likely to be able to meaningfully affect the distribution of audience attention in ways that would fatten the tail, but only lengthen and flatten it. The end result, then, is a process of persistent cannibalization and ever-greater fragmentation that is at the core of what is taking place on many media platforms. One marketing executive of one of the world's most popular Web sites described the current situation as "The Tyranny of More," which certainly provides an indication of how those within the industry perceive today's media environment of abundance—even those within the online realm, where search and recommendation systems have been put forth as the bearers of unprecedented opportunity.[8]

In the television context, we see this scenario playing out in the rise of digital cable and direct-broadcast satellite. Today, the average television household in the United States receives over 120 channels (Nielsen Media Research 2008) and 90 percent of all television channels have audience shares that are under one percent.[9] The digitization, and associated greater transmission capacity, of today's multichannel video programming delivery services drives the creation of ever more networks, even if the long-term value of these additional networks (both to audiences and to the content providers) is unclear. This dynamic forces individual media properties to continuously subdivide, amoeba-like. For example, sports programmer ESPN has expanded to eight cable networks. Other programmers have followed suit. At an industry panel I attended, a cable programming executive was asked whether this strategy of continually expanding network offerings, and essentially cannibalizing one's core networks with the launch of additional, related networks, was good strategy. "If we don't do it, someone else will," was the executive's response—an answer that highlights the fact that the technologies of content abundance are driving strategic decisions that are fundamentally defensive in nature, and are about trying to protect and preserve shrinking shares of audience attention in an environment in which outlets for this attention are ever-expanding.[10]

Ad-supported media are essentially buckling under the weight of audience fragmentation (Garfield 2009). Many of them may ultimately collapse—particularly if audience exposure remains the fundamental criterion for audience exchange. It is important to recognize, however, that the indicators of such an implosion are not necessarily what we might think. We're not likely, for instance, to see the number of cable networks shrink dramatically, or the number of Web sites contract substantially, anytime soon. The damage being inflicted can be seen only when we look beyond the "channels" to examine the underlying content—or lack thereof—being produced and disseminated. Using television as an example, industry data indicate that as the potential audience for a cable network shrinks, the amount of money spent on programming shrinks even more. Thus, for instance, networks such as Discovery, Nickelodeon, and MTV, which have more than 90 million subscribers, spend roughly 250 million dollars annually on programming. When we consider cable networks with roughly half that many subscribers (networks such as

Bloomberg, Nicktoons, and National Geographic), the annual programming budget drops to roughly 35 million dollars. And when we cut the potential audience in half yet again (for networks such as Boomerang or the Anime Network, which have only 20 to 25 million subscribers), annual programming budgets drop to roughly 12 million dollars (see Goolsbee 2007).

The key point here is that smaller audiences seem to demand a disproportionately larger reduction in production budgets. These networks can apparently exist under these conditions. However, their existence takes the form of very low budget programming and, perhaps more important, an overwhelming tendency to repeat each individual piece of programming over and over again, in order to extract the most possible mileage (in terms of programming hours) out of each dollar invested in programming.

Audience researcher James G. Webster (2006) has conducted research that looks, as he puts it, "beneath the veneer of fragmentation," within the context of the distribution of audience attention. If we adopt that same analytical orientation, and seek to look beneath the veneer of fragmentation in relation to content, what we will find is that, while on one level there is a tremendous amount of choice (in terms of the number of television channels, or the number of Web sites, or the number of radio stations), when we dig beneath surface, the amount of content being distributed across all of these available choices is comparatively limited. This is not to say that there is not a substantial amount of content variety available, only that using available "channels" as the unit of analysis dramatically overstates the extent to which media fragmentation has brought with it content abundance.[11]

"Repurposing," as it is referred to in industry terminology (see Caldwell 2006; Reynolds 2000), is fundamental to media organizations being able to effectively navigate today's highly fragmented media environment (see Chris 2006). This strategy tends to be taken to such an extreme that much of what we tend to generally consider "niche" content is quite often content that was never produced with the intention of reaching only a niche audience. Only in its repurposing is it essentially being repositioned as niche content. For example, I recently found myself aimlessly flipping through my available TV channels and stumbling upon the 1970s remake of *King Kong*. I had never seen the movie in its entirety, so I decided to watch it. This film was a *very* big budget Hollywood production when it was made (and a flop, as it turned out)—certainly not something we consider to have been produced for a niche audience. It struck me as surprising and ironic, therefore, when at the commercial break I learned that I, a man in his 30s, had been watching King Kong on the WE (Women's Entertainment) Network, a network whose movie programming tends to lean heavily toward romances and relationship dramas. King Kong had been repurposed into the niche that in movie industry terminology is typically referred to as a "chick flick."

The King Kong example illustrates a couple of things: First, in the highly fragmented media environment of today, even old and unsuccessful content continues to have a shelf life, given the enormous content hole that needs to be cheaply filled. Second, we need to be careful not to exaggerate the extent to which the highly fragmented media environment of today has promoted the production and distribution of true niche content. Regarding this second point, the economics of fragmentation simply have not allowed this to happen to the extent that was expected or that is commonly assumed.

It is important to recognize that as the stress that fragmentation places on content-production budgets intensifies, the effects not only take the form of recycling and repurposing, but also are reflected in media organizations' increasing reliance on various forms of user-generated content (see, e.g., Cohen 2008; Thurman 2008). For instance, today we see television and online news outlets increasingly relying on the reporting of the audience, in terms of hosting blogs on their Web sites and utilizing video delivered by camera phones. User-generated content will be discussed in greater detail in the next section, which deals with the notion of audience autonomy. It is important at this point, however, to emphasize that fragmentation and the integration of user-generated content into the activities of media organizations are related phenomena, that in addition to promoting repurposing and recycling, the fragmentation of the media environment is also compelling media organizations to rely increasingly on consumers to essentially supply their content. This is an important point of connection between the concepts of fragmentation and audience autonomy.

The process of fragmentation has been particularly challenging for advertiser-supported media in large part because the greater presumed efficiencies and the enhanced capacity to target specific audience segments that are natural byproducts of a more fragmented media environment have never translated into the kind of added value in the audience marketplace necessary to support such a system, let alone to allow it to flourish in ways that would truly lead to the development of a wide array of new and original content options targeting a truly diverse array of audience interests. As media economist David Waterman notes, "Although Internet technology . . . promises more efficient advertising-based business models to support broadband programming, history suggests formidable practical limits. First, although multichannel cable television has brought forth billions in total advertising, including many new advertisers, the 'magazine model' of higher rates for sharper segmentation has not materialized" (2004:67). As Waterman notes, relatively few cable networks have successfully cultivated true niche audiences (for example, MTV).

As he also notes, cable network cost-per-thousand (CPM) advertising rates are, on average, still below those of the major broadcast networks. A recent estimate places broadcast network CPMs at an average of $30 compared to an average of $11 for cable networks (Mermigas 2008).[12] Larger audiences seem to be worth more per capita than smaller audiences. As a result, cable networks capture a share of television advertising dollars that is less than their share of the television audience. The same pattern has established itself online, where the top Web sites capture a share of online advertising dollars that significantly exceeds their share of online audience attention in a way that some analysts have compared to the pattern that has characterized television (see Klaassen 2006b). One study estimated that the top ten Web sites captured roughly 70 percent of net online advertising revenues (Klaasen 2007), while another found that the top ten Web sites captured 26 percent of Web traffic (Hindman 2009).[13] These patterns fly in the face of the commonsense notion that the more narrowly defined, homogeneous niche audiences represent efficient targeting opportunities for which most advertisers would most likely pay a premium. Returning to the long tail terminology, these patterns suggest that the audience attention that is clustered in the head can be more effectively monetized than the audience attention that is found in the tail. The head of advertising revenues is even more pronounced than the head of audience attention, and the tail is even thinner.

The point here is that in the realm of ad-supported media, the "hits" typically are capable of attracting a disproportionately high share of the available advertising dollars, leaving the multitude of niche-content options to battle it out over the remaining ad dollars. And so, as much as the niche content may, in the aggregate, represent a substantial proportion of total audience attention, this content has not yet been able to translate its share of audience attention into a proportional share of advertising dollars.

As this discussion suggests, any excitement or opportunity that the long tail scenario may create for media industries will be, in all likelihood, largely confined to consumer-supported media. The scenario is much less promising, to say the least, for media that rely heavily on the sale of audiences to advertisers. The prospects might be different if the exhibition component of ad-supported media were to operate under the same centralized one-stop shopping model that is increasingly characterizing the exhibition component of consumer-supported media—that is, if advertisers' access to virtually all available audiences were possible via a single source, the same way that consumers' access to virtually all available movies is possible via Netflix, or to virtually all available books via Amazon.

The development of online ad networks is in many ways reflective of this perspective. With online ad networks, groups of content providers essentially aggregate their traffic for sale to advertisers. According to a recent study, the use of such networks grew from accounting for 5 percent of ad impressions sold in 2006 to 30 percent of ad impressions sold in 2007 (IAB 2008b). As one consulting report noted, online ad networks are "an essential vehicle for monetizing the Long Tail of the Internet. By aggregating traffic that was previously too difficult to buy or which was otherwise undesirable, ad networks provide small and mid-sized online publishers with significantly more advertising revenues than would otherwise be possible" (Desilva and Phillips 2008:2).

This passage points toward the key problem that fragmentation has posed for advertising-supported media. Specifically, it is much more difficult for the traditional exposure-focused approach to audience understanding to provide a satisfactory basis for "currency" in the audience marketplace when audience attention becomes increasingly fragmented. In many highly fragmented contexts, the purchasing of audience attention has essentially become too difficult, or the audience attention that is available to advertisers and media buyers has become unappealing.

Why does the fragmentation of audience attention seem to diminish its value in this way? What has happened is that audience information systems that have traditionally provided the currency in the audience marketplace are running up against their practical limits in terms of their ability to reliably represent the distribution of audience attention across the full range of available content options. Essentially, measuring the long tail of audience attention is becoming much more difficult in such a highly fragmented media environment. The fragmentation of media and audiences is straining and undermining the traditional, exposure-based audience information systems that long have served as the core of the audience marketplace (see, e.g., Ang 1991; Ross and Nightingale 2003; Webster 2008). As a result, the "quality" of the available representations of audience exposure diminishes the further one travels down the long tail.[14]

In particular, the extent to which audiences today are able to be spread across a much wider range of content options, and across a much wider range of delivery platforms, undermines traditional panel-based measurement approaches that rely on the creation, and systematic measurement of, a sufficiently large and representative sample of the audience (see, e.g., Faasse 2007). The viability of sample-based approaches to media audiences is increasingly questionable in media environments in which audience attention can be so widely distributed (see McDonald 2008). Providing representative and reliable samples has always been a challenge in the audience measurement industry (see, e.g., Starkey 2004). However, we may be approaching a point where it is simply impossible for measurement firms to recruit and maintain representative audience panels that are large enough to capture the true distribution of audience attention across the wealth of available content options and across all of the platforms on which that content can be consumed. Consider, as an extreme example, that while Internet audience measurement firm comScore has a panel of more than two million people, there are more than 187 million Web sites. This dynamic limits the utility of panel-based data to the select few Web sites that attract enough panelists to achieve minimum levels of statistical validity and reliability.

When samples are inadequate, the results are increased inaccuracy of basic exposure data, as well as unpredictable fluctuations in the data (Kirkham 1996). These patterns undermine both the descriptive and the analytical (i.e., for predicting future audience behavior) uses of such data. Research has, for instance, documented substantial discrepancies between various Web audience measurement firms in terms of the rankings of just the ten most popular Web sites. The magnitude of this discrepancy increases dramatically when the frame is expanded to include the top one hundred Web sites; here there is on average only 40 percent agreement between measurement services (Lo and Sedhain 2006).

Most cable networks and most Web sites have audiences that are too small to even be reported by established, panel-based audience measurement systems such as those operated by Nielsen and comScore. Nielsen is able to provide audience ratings for only about 80 of the more than 500 cable networks in operation in the U.S. The more than 400 remaining networks have audiences that are, on average, simply too small to be accurately captured by the roughly thirteen thousand households that are currently included in Nielsen's national television audience measurement sample;[15] yet in the aggregate these unmeasured networks can represent as much as 25 percent of television viewing (McClellan 2008b).[16] Radio audience measurement firm Arbitron provides audience ratings for only half of the more than thirteen thousand radio stations in operation in the United States (Gunzerath 2001). Magazine audience measurement firm MRI measures the audiences of only 232 of the more than five thousand magazines in print.[17] Newspaper audience measurement firm Scarborough, in its effort to quantify newspaper readers across both print and online platforms, reports data only on those readers within the paper's geographic market that are consuming the paper either in print or online, leaving all out-of-market readers who access these papers via the Web unreported.[18] And, at the most extreme end of the continuum, Internet audience measurement firms such as Nielsen NetRatings and comScore provide detailed audience estimates for roughly fifteen to thirty thousand[19] of the estimated 187 million available Web sites. The bottom line, as one media executive recently noted, is that "traditional audience measurement is geared toward the head, rather than the tail, of the long tail curve."[20] Another media executive described survey data as "woefully inadequate for the fragmented media environment of today."[21] The end result is a growing amount of what we can term "dark matter" of audience exposure—audience exposure that we know is taking place but that we can not meaningfully categorize.[22]

And as the traditional measurement systems associated with the various media struggle under the weight of fragmentation, the challenges associated with monetizing the audience for any individual piece of media content are compounded. Consider, for instance, that the size of the audience exposed to a single broadcast network television program must now be cobbled together from estimates not only from traditional broadcast and cable platforms, but also from on-demand services, DVRs, Web streaming, and handheld devices such as iPods. As the audience for this program fragments across different media, it is essentially migrating away from the traditional platform (broadcast television), where the limitations associated with traditional panel-based audience measurement systems are less pronounced, to newer platforms, where these limitations are much more pronounced and where sufficiently accurate and reliable alternate audience information systems have yet to be fully developed (Friedman 2009b). One study of television viewing estimated that 13 percent of television viewing time takes place via unmeasured viewing platforms (Brill et al. 2007). As audiences for any individual piece of content migrate into newer delivery platforms, the ability of content providers to monetize them has been diminishing.

One industry analysis claimed that "the extent to which the media landscape has changed over the past 15 years [has placed] far more stress on audience measurement than ever before" (Harris and Chasin 2006:3). Another analysis announced "the fall of exposure" (Jaffe 2005:172). As these statements indicate, the traditional institutionalized approach to media audiences primarily in terms of their exposure to content is becoming a much more difficult—and ultimately potentially less viable—proposition than it was in years past.

There are, it should be noted, a wide range of initiatives currently underway to combat the strain that the new media environment is imposing on traditional exposure-oriented approaches to media audiences. Efforts such as Nielsen's Local People Meter initiative are attempting to introduce advanced set-top meter technologies into local television markets in response to the inability of the paper diary to effectively gather audience exposure data in a highly fragmented television environment (Buzzard 2002). Arbitron's Portable People Meter initiative is a similar effort to combat the growing inadequacies of paper diaries with the introduction of portable electronic meters in a more fragmented radio environment characterized by additions such as low-power FM radio, digital audio broadcasting, and satellite radio (Napoli 2009).[23] Efforts are even underway to bring electronic measurement (using Portable People Meters and radio frequency identification technology) to the print media (Mattlin 2008; Pelligrini and Gluck 2007). Online audience measurement services are also working to enhance their sample sizes and develop alternative mechanisms for capturing accurate and reliable measures of online media exposure (Bermejo 2007).

Many current efforts online are focused on melding panel-based methodologies with site-centric approaches (Callius, Lithner, and Svanfeldt 2005; "ComScore announces," 2009; Goosey 2005; McDonald and Collins 2007; Pellegrini 2009). Site-centric methods focus on gathering data from the server logs of individual Web sites, and are appealing to content providers and advertises in the sense that they offer the ability to essentially analyze a census—rather than a sample—of all of a Web site's visitors (see, e.g., Quantcast 2008). It should be noted, however, that it is more difficult to obtain audience demographic information from server log data, though some firms have developed systems of projecting audience demographics from such information (see, e.g., Quantcast 2008), and that in general, panel-based and site-based measurement systems tend to produce significantly different results regarding the overall popularity of individual Web sites.[24]

Nielsen Online, for instance, provides an online video measurement service called VideoCensus, which it describes as "the first and only syndicated service to blend panel and server-based metrics in streaming media measurement."[25] In the television context, upstart measurement firms such as TNS Media Research (2008) and Rentrak have taken the lead in trying to implement measurement systems that obtain data directly from television set-top boxes, which are already installed in roughly 85 percent of television households (see Learmonth 2007).[26] Gathering data via set-top boxes provides the measurement firm with the potential to gather data from a sample of households that is much larger than can be economically generated and maintained via traditional panel-based measurement systems (see, e.g., Schley 2007). In the case of TNS, the company is developing a sample of one hundred thousand homes with direct-broadcast satellite set-top boxes. This DBS sample alone would be more than seven times larger than Nielsen's current (at the time of writing) national sample (see Kang 2008a). Nielsen also is working toward gathering and reporting set-top box data in response to these competitive threats (James 2008). There remains, however, substantial disagreement across various stakeholder groups as to whether set-top box data represent a legitimately viable improvement over traditional panel-based measurement systems (Oscar 2008).[27] Nonetheless, in some countries (such as South Africa) set top-box data are being used as the currency data for the buying and selling of television audiences.[28]

And of course, measurement firms are working to expand their analytical reach, and bolster their analytical rigor, in newer media contexts such as mobile phones, personal video recorders, Web download and streaming services, and social networking sites, as the range of platforms through which any form of media content can be consumed multiplies, further fragmenting the audience and imposing new, and often unique, challenges upon the measurement of audience exposure (see, e.g., Hackenbruch 2009; Pappachen and Manatt 2008; Shields 2008; Webster 2008). For instance, Nielsen has initiated an "Anytime Anywhere Media Measurement" program that seeks to measure television viewing "regardless of the platform on which it is viewed" (2006b:1; see also Fitzgerald 2007), as well as a "convergence panel" designed to extract data about television and Internet use from the same panel (Erichson 2009; Mandese 2008a; Steinberg 2007b). Along similar lines, NBC Universal has implemented what it calls its "total audience measurement index" (TAMI), which is a measure of viewers across multiple venues, including network and cable TV, online, video on demand, and mobile (Steinberg 2008b; see also Steinberg 2008a). Upstart firms such as Integrated Media Measurement (IMMI) (2008) have focused on trying to capture audience exposure to content across multiple platforms (television, radio, Web, phones, movie theaters) using a single measurement device—in IMMI's case a cell phone enhanced with the necessary measurement technology (Kang 2008b).

Despite these efforts, this stress on traditional audience information systems is generating substantial concern and discontent among advertisers, media buyers, and content providers (Council for Research Excellence 2006). Many within the industry remain pessimistic that such efforts can successfully counter the forces working against traditional exposure metrics. As one industry researcher noted, "Even the most ambitious and agile audience measurement company is likely to be hard pressed to measure and capture such diverse activities at the level of precision currently associated with the 'media currency'" (McDonald 2008:316). There is a growing consensus that traditional systems of audience measurement are essentially breaking down (Garfield 2005, 2007; Harris and Chassin 2006), so much so that assertions of a "crisis in confidence" are commonplace (e.g., Starkey 2002:56). This is particularly significant given that, as Starkey has observed, "the media industries are accustomed to working with, rather than against, [audience] data. Usually they have no choice, because of the importance placed on the data by others" (2004:12). This statement reflects the importance of mutual agreement among all participants in the audience marketplace regarding the institutionalizing of particular representations of the audience. When this mutual agreement breaks down—when the validity of the institutionalized audience begins to be called into question by a critical mass of stakeholders, as is happening now— then the conditions are likely right for an evolutionary change to take place.

A survey of advertising industry professionals conducted by the consulting firm Forrester Research found that virtually all respondents found traditional approaches to audience understanding to no longer be adequate. According to this study, nearly all respondents agreed "that they need audience metrics other than reach and frequency" (Kim 2006:6). Reflecting this finding, this study concluded that the traditional methodologies and metrics for understanding audiences were incapable of penetrating today's highly fragmented media environment (Kim 2006). Returning to the long tail terminology, as the tail comes to account for a greater proportion of overall audience attention, and as the audiences contained within this tail become increasingly fragmented, the proportion of the total amount of audience attention that can be effectively measured—and consequently monetized—via traditional approaches to the measurement of audience exposure decreases. The deleterious effects that the fragmentation of the media envronment is having on traditional exposure-based approaches to understanding—and trading in—media audiences are a fundamental driver of the growing willingness among media industry stakeholders to explore and embrace alternative approaches to understanding audiences.

AUDIENCE AUTONOMY

This drive toward alternative approaches to audience understanding is being fueled not only by increasing media and audience fragmentation, but also by increasing audience autonomy—that is, the extent to which media audiences increasingly have control over when, where, and how they consume media; and now increasingly have the power to affect the content they consume and to become content producers and distributors in their own right. Media and advertising industry pundits increasingly emphasize the "empowerment" that the new media environment bestows upon the consumer, and the flexibility in the dynamics of media consumption that these new technologies allow (e.g., Berman, Battino, and Feldman 2009; Donaton 2004).

Table 2.1 presents the various aspects of audience autonomy, illustrating the mechanisms that can today be employed to influence what, when, where, and how media are consumed. This table brings together many of the defining characteristics of the contemporary media environment, ranging from the greater control over the television viewing process afforded to those with DVRs, to the ability to consume media (whether it be video, music, or other

Web-based content) on the go via increasingly advanced cellular phones or technologies such as Slingbox,[29] to the ability to have one's particular interests better served by the ability either to customize Web pages, news feeds, channel guides, recommendation systems, or to program one's DVR to record content associated with particular genres or containing particular stars. Under this umbrella concept of audience autonomy we must also include the various means by which audiences can increasingly engage with and affect content, whether it be by voting or providing other forms of feedback that affect content decisions, as well as the ever-increasing ways in which audiences can themselves become content creators and distributors, whether via blogging, tweeting, creating and maintaining social networking pages, or via producing and uploading music, podcasts, and videos to Internet sites and services such as YouTube, iTunes, and Kazaa (see, e.g., Berry 2006; IAB 2008a; Prescott 2006; Stern 2010). Many of these activities can of course be placed under the heading of user-generated content, which has been defined according the following three criteria: (a) content made publicly available over the Internet; (b) content that reflects a certain amount of creative effort; and (c) content that is created outside of traditional professional routines and practices (Wunsch-Vincent and Vickery 2007).

From an academic standpoint, these developments have often been considered noteworthy for facilitating a more "active" notion of the media audience over the more traditional "passive" conceptualization that has characterized some strands of academic audience research that developed in conjunction with the traditional mass media, wherein the distinction between content provider and audience member was much clearer. (see, e.g., Clarke 2000; Croteau 2006; Springel 1999; Webster 1998).[30] Some observers have adopted the term "the former audience" to reflect this expansion of the audience's capabilities (e.g., Gillmor 2004:136). Nemirovsky, by contrast, contends that the audience terminology retains its value as long as the "new audience" is not conceptualized as a monolithic category, but rather as a "conglomerate of humans exploring the media space," with multiple social functions (2003:394).

As the previous section noted, it is important to recognize that the fragmentation of the media environment and the rise of user-generated content are not completely independent phenomena. The Internet in many ways represents the apex of media fragmentation, exceeding levels of intra-media fragmentation that have been achieved in previous media such as magazines

TABLE 2.1 Components of Audience Autonomy

What	When	Where	How
On-demand	on-demand	mobile	ad-skipping/blocking
Search	mobile	portable	community participation/ discussion
Informed recommendations	time-shifting	—	affect outcome
Personalization	—	—	user-generated content

and television. As the histories of these earlier media tell us, when the audience becomes increasingly fragmented, the economics of content production are forced to change. In the history of television, for example, as the audience fragmented, one of the only responses available to programmers was to rely increasingly on reality programming, given the lower production costs of such programming relative to traditional scripted entertainment content.

The rise of user-generated content on the Web essentially represents the next iteration of this phenomenon; indeed, it emerges from the same technological genealogy.[31] User-generated content is essentially the next logical step beyond reality television. In an environment that is even more fragmented (the Web), it is only natural—and inevitable—that the economics of content would evolve further, to the point that filling the available "channel capacity" could only be achieved economically if the consumers themselves became a key source of content production and distribution (not unlike the way average Americans have come to populate a television landscape increasingly dominated by reality programs) (see Terranova 2000). A key aspect of the transformation of media consumption that has been taking place has thus been one of fragmentation essentially compelling a shift in the economic burden of content creation and distribution from the traditional institutional communicator to the media consumer, whether it be your next-door neighbor showing up on *Survivor* or your work colleague blogging on the Web.

Again, the objective here is less to document the ways in which the dynamics of media consumption have changed than it is to explore what these changing dynamics mean for how media industries understand their audiences. At the most basic level, the fundamental parameters of what constitutes an audience are expanding. Terms such as "prosumers" and "produsage" have been coined to capture the ways in which the media audience is evolving, and the ways in which content production and distribution are consequently migrating beyond the traditional industrial paradigm (Banks 2002; Deuze 2003). As Benkler (2006) and others have demonstrated, the new media environment is one in which the tools of participation in public discourse and creative activity are much more widely distributed (Beer and Burrows 2007; Jenkins 2006; Mabillot 2007). Mass communication is now a much more egalitarian process, in which the masses can now communicate to the masses (Fonio et al. 2007; see also Deuze 2006). It is important to recognize that the one-to-many dynamic at the core of the meaning of mass communication (see Lang and Lang 2009) persists here. It is simply that there are many, many more instances of it.[32] It is this proliferation of the one-to-many capacity that represents the communication dynamic that was largely absent from previous incarnations of our media system, in which the capacity to mass communicate was technologically and economically constrained to a select few. As Beer and Burrows note, "Perhaps the key defining feature of Web 2.0 is that users are involved in processes of production and consumption as they generate and browse online content, as they tag and blog, post and share. This has seen the 'consumer' taking an increasingly active role in the "production" of commodities" (2007:8).[33]

One 2007 forecast estimated that by 2010, 70 percent of the content available online would be created by individuals (Slot and Frissen 2007).[34] Another study estimates that one-third of all new Web content is being produced via social media systems such as blogs, wikis, online forums, and social networking sites (Finin et al. 2008). Equally important are data indicating that such content is being consumed in substantial quantities. Research has projected that over 18 million U.S. households will be downloading podcasts on a weekly basis by 2010 (Berry 2006). More recent research estimates that the total amount of media consumption time devoted to user-generated content will reach 15 percent of television time and 25 percent of PC time by 2013 (IBM Global Business Services 2008).

This pattern highlights a very important aspect of the unique economics of media—the extent to which individuals will engage in the production and distribution of media content absent any real expectation of compensation. This has always been the case, ranging back to unpublished novels and short stories stashed in desk drawers and to garage bands toiling away without a recording contract (see, e.g., Knight 2007). What is different today, of course, is that these producers of content now have the access, thanks largely to the Internet, to potential audiences that was largely missing in previous generations. Indeed, one surprising characteristic of many user-generated content discussions is that the focus is often misguidedly on the revolutionary or disruptive aspects of user's ability to *produce* content.[35] Even the term, user-*generated* content, reflects this misplaced emphasis. This is not the aspect of contemporary developments that is new or of the greatest significance (Mabillot 2007). Users' capacity to generate content has been around for quite some time, due to the long-established availability of production technologies such as home video cameras, personal computers, typewriters, and home recording equipment. What is different today is the ability of users to *distribute* content, to utilize the Web to circulate their user-generated content (as well as, to media companies' dismay, traditional media content) to an unprecedented extent.[36]

What is also different today is that these uncompensated acts of content production can be monetized by media organizations (Deuze 2008; Reinhard 2008).[37] In this regard, the value of the media audience is increasingly extending beyond what they consume to what they produce as well. Again we find ourselves returning to Web 2.0 applications and the ways that they help the masses to mass communicate. Here, however, the concern is not just that such communication is taking place, but also that this communication itself often becomes a source of economic value for media organizations. The dynamic under consideration here is well expressed by Cohen:

> Web 2.0 has altered the terrain of the media business, notably by adjusting consumers' roles in the production process. Business models based on the notion of the consumer as producer have allowed Web 2.0 applications to capitalize on time spent participating in communicative activity and information sharing. In mass media models, the role of consumers has been just that, to consume, or to watch and read the product. Web 2.0 consumers, however, have become producers who fulfill a critical role.   (2008:7)

The advertising revenues that sites such as YouTube, Facebook, and MySpace generate are derived largely from audience attention captured by content produced by members of the user/audience community. Typically, these content contributors receive no compensation.[38] Aggregating or providing a common platform for user-generated content, and then selling advertising on these platforms, represents the core business model of most Web 2.0 applications. User-generated content such as comments, ratings, and reviews has also become an important source of added value for organizations involved in the production and/or distribution of more traditional institutionally produced content (Reinhard 2008). Examples along these lines include the user ratings/comments on sites such as Netflix and Amazon, and the increasing extent to which newspapers' Web sites are incorporating reader feedback and comments into their presentation of traditional journalism (Schultz 2000).

The development of this "new economy of free labor" (Johnson 2007) highlights the tremendous value that these "prosumers" place on obtaining access to an audience for their expression. This need helps to maintain a role for the institutional communicators who typically manage the Web 2.0 platforms that allow (via the aggregation of content and the investment in marketing resources) for greater audience reach than an individual communicator could likely achieve without such platforms. We could then argue that it is this enhanced ability to access an audience with one's creative expression that online media organizations are now providing in exchange for that creative expression—which they in turn monetize. This is obviously a very different content production–distribution–exhibition–consumption dynamic than has characterized traditional media.

Indeed, many of the de-institutionalized forms of mass communication that are now in existence do still involve traditional institutional communicators—only in more ancillary roles, as content aggregators, navigation services, or server space/platform providers (for instance, Google, YouTube, MySpace, and Facebook). These forms of integrated activity between the institutional communicator and the individual user are central to the emerging significance of the "work" of the audience (Napoli 2010).

The work of the contemporary media audience can be taken one step further. Increasingly, not only are audience members contributing content that can be monetized by content providers (typically via ad sales), but audiences in fact willingly engage in the work of the advertisers and marketers who traditionally support these content providers (Vogt and Knapman 2007). That is, audiences today engage in a wide range of activities that assist in the marketing of products, ranging from self-producing commercials to engaging in online word-of-mouth and endorsements (via blogs, tweets, etc.), to integrating brand messages into their own communication platforms (e.g., their MySpace or Facebook pages) (Cheong and Morrison 2008; Deuze 2007; Reinhard 2008; Spurgeon 2008).[39] Contemporary marketing and advertising strategies increasingly focus on taking the value of consumer "word of mouth" to entirely new levels and developing new methods for facilitating and encouraging consumers to do the work of marketers and advertisers in the dissemination of brand messages.[40] As one consultants' report declared, "Consumers are the new marketers" (Rasmussen, Ude, and Landry 2007).

The notion that media audiences work began well before the age of user-generated content, with economist Dallas Smythe (1977), who, in providing the initial influential formulation of the media audience as a "commodity" manufactured and sold by ad-supported media, argued that the act of consuming media represented a form of wageless labor that audiences engaged in on behalf of advertisers. According to Smythe, the key work that audiences engaged in on behalf of advertisers was to "learn to buy particular 'brands' of consumer goods, and to spend their income accordingly. In short, they work to create the demand for advertised goods which is the purpose of the monopoly capitalist advertisers" (1977:6). Smythe's observation was fundamental to his larger critique of what he saw as a failing by Marxist theorists to adequately account for the production of audiences in their analyses of the political economy of the media, which, according to Smythe, tended to focus overwhelmingly (and misguidedly) on the production of content.

Smythe's notion of the work of the audience was subsequently taken up and expanded by Jhally and Livant, who, focusing on television, argued that the advertising revenue that programmers earn that extends beyond the costs of the programming represents "surplus watching time" (1986:127). Jhally (1982) and Livant (1982), in earlier iterations of the ideas that would be central to their later collaborative piece, emphasized their departure from Smythe in their view that the audiences worked not for the advertisers but for the mass media (Jhally 1982:208; Livant 1982:213). The viewing audience, having already received their "wage" in the form of the free programming, was now, in their program viewing, working on behalf of the programmer. The programmer was then able to convert this surplus watching time into additional advertising revenue.

This perspective on the media audience was the subject of substantial debate and discussion at the time (see, e.g., Livant 1979; Murdock 1978;

Smythe 1978). In the years since, however, this perspective has received relatively little attention in communications scholarship (for exceptions, see Andrejevic 2002; Cohen 2008; Shimpach 2005).[41] However, it is clear that contemporary developments in the media environment have once again brought to the foreground this notion of the work of the audience.

AUDIENCE AUTONOMY
AND THE AUDIENCE MARKETPLACE

Audience autonomy not only blurs the boundary between audience and content producer (and affects the monetization of audiences accordingly)—it also undermines established audience information systems while simultaneously providing the foundation for alternative audience information systems. One industry analyst has described the contemporary media environment as one in which the consumer is "devastatingly in control" (Jaffe 2005:43). The use of the term "devastating" in this statement is particularly telling, as it suggests that audience autonomy, like fragmentation, is having damaging effects on the traditional dynamics of the audience marketplace.

And indeed this is the case. The damaging effects of increased audience control of the media consumption process have been felt particularly powerfully in terms of the audiences' increased ability to avoid advertisements (see, e.g., Berrios and Moyano 2005; Wilbur 2008). The commercial-skipping features of digital video recorders, online pop-up ad blocking software, and the growth of on-demand, ad-free, or ad-diminished content delivery platforms are just some of the mechanisms by which today's audiences can control their exposure to advertisements (IBM Global Business Services 2008). This increased control over ad exposure has dramatically undermined the viability of traditional exposure-based approaches to media audiences.

This development, like the transition to an increasingly fragmented media environment, also has undermined traditional institutionalized approaches to media audiences. As one analysis has noted, "Traditional measures that were designed for passive media fail to capture the important and differentiating dimensions of response to interactive communication" (Stewart and Pavlou 2002:382). In this regard, then, there is a growing recognition among the relevant stakeholders in the audience marketplace that traditional exposure-based systems of audience measurement are really only capturing the tip of the iceberg in terms of the dynamics of audience behavior. The wide-ranging dimensions of the autonomy and interactivity[42] that can now be found across the various platforms of our media system are forcing media industry stakeholders to confront the inherently limited and largely uni-dimensional conceptualization of the audience that has been embedded in traditional audience information systems.

We see this recognition of the inadequacy of the established approach to audiences well-reflected in the statement of an industry executive who recently noted that, in comparing an ad's performance online versus on television, "no matter what the click-through (rate) they get, it's infinitely larger than the click-through rate they get on TV. The click-through they get on TV is zero" (quoted in Nakashima 2008:1). It is important to recognize how greatly the advertising community is beginning to value the attributes of interactive media—which is a far cry from the prevailing attitudes ten years ago, when the documented low click-through rates of online ads were seen as hindering the Web's ability to draw ad dollars away from traditional media, in which such assessments of performance are virtually impossible (see Chandler-Pepelnjak 2008; Napoli 2003a). The time when ignorance was bliss has passed. If there is one term that recurs more than any other throughout the industry trade press, conferences, and conventions today, that term is "accountability" (see, e.g., Elms 2007; Magazine Marketing Coalition 2007; Magazine Publishers of America 2005). The key here, of course, is that once such perceptions of the inadequacies of established approaches to audiences reach a critical mass, the conditions are in place for the institutionalized audience to undergo change.

However, while the autonomy facilitated by the new media environment is undermining the traditional passive, exposure-focused conceptualization of audiences, it is also opening up new avenues of audience understanding. That is, the various interactive components of the new media environment are illuminating previously concealed dimensions of audiences; many of these are seem to have significant economic and strategic value and, perhaps most important, can facilitate the gathering of types of information that previously could not have been gathered (see Ross 2008).

This point is reflected in figure 2.3, which first illustrates, at the top, the traditional form of information that has flowed from the audience to the content provider (that being information on exposure to the content). Below the exposure arrow, however, are arrows representing some of the new audience information flows that are today reaching content providers. Search activities—whether via online search engines, interactive television program guides, or digital video recorder menu interfaces—represent an important source of information about audience wants and interests. Audience appreciation of the content they consume can today be expressed through a variety of means, such as the ratings and recommendations systems that audiences participate in via online content providers such as NetFlix and Amazon, or community review and ratings sites such as RottenTomatoes.com and IMDB.com, and via "thumbs up/thumbs down" functionalities such as those provided by TiVo (Garfield 2008; Thompson 2008). Audience participation today can take a variety of forms (see Nightingale and Dwyer 2006), ranging from voting online or via mobile phones in ways that affect the outcomes of programming such as *American Idol*, to emailing or instant-messaging radio hosts. Audience responses to content now take a number of forms, ranging from direct, immediate behavioral responses to online advertisements (in the form of a click-through or an actual purchase) to commentary or feedback that can be placed directly alongside individual online news stories or blog entries. The point here is that these new audience information flows bring with them the potential to broaden the institutionalized audience well beyond its traditional exposure-oriented model.

The key at this point is to recognize that today's media environment is one in which—thanks largely to its increasingly interactive nature—more of these dimensions of audience behavior can be monitored, and as a result can potentially be monetized by media industries and thereby become part of institutionalized approaches to audiences (see Harris and Chasin 2006; Sen et al. 1998). The Internet has been described by one marketer as making it "possible to record data about individual consumers at an unprecedented level of detail" (Mullarkey 2004:42). One industry analyst has even gone so far as to describe the Internet as "*too* measurable. . . . It is measurable in terms of audience delivery; it is measurable in terms of audience interaction; it is even measurable on the transactional/ROI front" (Jaffe 2005:113–114). Clearly, aspects of the audience other than exposure are now capturable via the measurement techniques facilitated by the new, highly interactive media environment, in which most of the ways in which audiences interact with media leave some sort of measurable data trail that can be aggregated and analyzed.

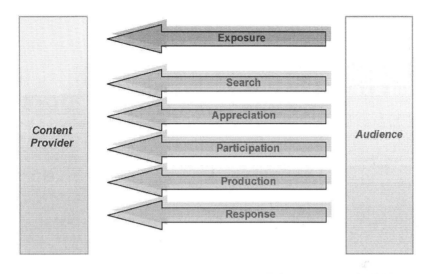

FIGURE 2.3 New Audience Information Flows

The audience marketplace thus finds itself in a situation where technological forces are simultaneously undermining established approaches to audience understanding and opening up new avenues for alternative approaches. These new avenues are the focus of chapter 3.

CHAPTER 3

THE TRANSFORMATION OF AUDIENCE INFORMATION SYSTEMS

The previous chapter illustrated the many ways in which the technological changes affecting the media environment are simultaneously undermining traditional analytical approaches to media audiences and creating opportunities for alternative analytical approaches. This chapter focuses on these alternatives by exploring exactly how the changing technological environment, and the associated changing dynamics of media consumption, are feeding into ongoing innovations in audience information systems. These innovations frequently (though not always) take advantage of the interactivity inherent in the new media environment to produce audience information systems that move beyond the traditional exposure metrics that have long held the dominant position in the audience marketplace.

These interactive infrastructures facilitate the flow of information not only from content providers to audience members, but also from audience members to content providers (typically referred to as "return path data").[1] Any platform on which audiences leave such a "digital footprint" (Madden et al. 2007) is also, to some extent, inherently capable of moving beyond exposure in terms of the dimensions of audience behavior that it can capture. Thus, as the media environment has grown more interactive, this has facilitated the gathering of new streams of data about audience members' media consumption habits, content preferences, degree of engagement, and levels of anticipation for, and appreciation of, the content they consume. Various dimensions of participation, appreciation, and feedback are now expressed in very public forms online that are accessible to, and are being accessed and analyzed, by industry researchers (Andrejevic 2008; Harris and Chasin 2006).[2] Internet audience measurement firm comScore has even begun assessing the performance of media companies in terms of the number of "data collection events" they engage in with audiences, under the presumption that such indicators provide useful insights into how well positioned individual media companies are to address the challenges, and capitalize on the opportunities, of today's media environment, in which interacting with audiences is becoming increasingly important to both understanding and monetizing them (Story 2008a, 2008b).[3] Today's new "smartphones" provide up to twenty pieces of information about individual audience members using their cell phones to visit a Web site or use an application (Clifford 2009b). As one advertising industry executive has stated, "Everyone's in an arms race to find out more about their users" (Clifford 2009b:2).

These developments raise the possibility of a fundamental transition in the marketplace—one in which the primacy of exposure is supplanted by a more multifaceted conceptualization of the media audience, and in which alternative dimensions of audience behavior play a much more significant role in the processes of buying, selling, and producing media audiences. The complex institutional dynamics surrounding any such transition will be discussed in chapter 4. The focus here is on the emerging alternative audience information systems, the dimension of audience behavior that they represent, and the ways they are beginning to be used in the audience marketplace.

EXPOSURE AND BEYOND:
DECONSTRUCTING AUDIENCE BEHAVIOR

In order to effectively address these emerging audience information systems, it is first important to thoroughly deconstruct the notion of audience behavior. That is, what are the various dimensions of audience behavior beyond basic exposure that can potentially be captured and aggregated by new audience information systems, and subsequently monetized by media organizations? Figure 3.1 breaks down audience behavior into a series of discrete units. Note that this model approaches audience behavior in a somewhat sequential manner, assuming a chronological progression from one unit to the next. Thus, in moving from left to right in the model, we begin with *awareness*. The decision to consume a particular piece of media content often begins with the audience member becoming aware of that content's availability in advance.[4] Should the information that the audience member receives about this content option resonate, then that awareness can translate into *interest*. Sufficient interest can then potentially lead to *exposure*, which, as has been noted, traditionally has served as the central metric of relevance in the audience marketplace.

Paralleling exposure to some extent are the phenomena of *loyalty* and *attentiveness*. These dimensions of audience behavior are situated in parallel with exposure because typically they are operationalized in terms of exposure data. Thus, for instance, audiences loyal to a particular television or radio program are typically defined in terms of the number of times they watch or listen to that program—the frequency of their exposure. Similarly, the loyalty of the audience to a particular Web site typically is defined in terms of the frequency of visits to the site.

Attentiveness can similarly be extrapolated from exposure data. Typically, attentiveness is defined in terms of the time spent per exposure. Thus, online, the notion of "stickiness" emerged to capture the amount of time that a visitor to a Web site spends with that site (Bermejo 2007; Napoli 2003a). The "stickiness" terminology has since migrated to other media, such as television (Friedman 2010). Today, a prominent metric in Internet audience measurement is "time spent," which is defined as the "amount of elapsed time from the initiation of a visit to the last audience activity associated with that visit" (IAB 2008c:8; see also Butche 2007). Along related lines, "time spent listening" is an important performance metric for radio stations (Arbitron 2006). Again, the key point here is that the notions of loyalty and attentiveness that arise frequently in the discourse of the audience marketplace are typically derived from audience exposure data.

That being said, exposure-based dimensions such as loyalty and attentiveness have also been utilized as some of the building blocks of the more complex—and persistently ambiguous—notion of *engagement*. The location of loyalty and attentiveness under the broader umbrella concept of engagement is reflected in figure 3.1. The emergence and ongoing evolution of this concept (see ARF 2006a, 2006b, 2007) will be discussed in greater detail below. For now, it is important to recognize that basically all of the post-exposure dimensions of audience behavior have been associated with one or more definitions and operationalizations of engagement.

Returning to figure 3.1, we move next to *appreciation* and *emotion(al response)*. These are related phenomena that reflect the immediate reactions that audiences have upon being exposed to a particular piece of content, in

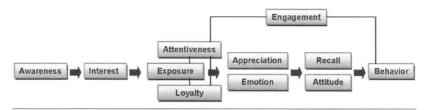

FIGURE 3.1 Audience Dimensions

terms of whether they liked it, and in terms of whether it affected them, positively or negatively, at an emotional level. *Recall* and *attitude* are placed next in the sequence to reflect the deeper and more lasting effects that can arise from exposure and that can logically be thought of as outgrowths of the level of appreciation or emotional response the audience member experienced from the content. Recall and attitude change can, in turn, can lead to *behavior(al responses)*—in the form of product purchasing, clicking on an advertisement, or engaging in some sort of online participation or content creation.

This model of audience behavior thus encapsulates a process that begins with an audience member first becoming aware of a particular content option and ends with whatever behavioral response this content may be able to generate. The key point of this chapter is that audience information systems are developing that are, in the aggregate, capturing virtually the full range of dimensions of audience behavior reflected in this model. This is in turn driving an evolution of the institutionalized media audience that extends beyond exposure (see chapter 5). The sections that follow examine these emerging analytical tools for a post-exposure audience marketplace.

PRECURSORS TO EXPOSURE: CAPTURING "BUZZ"

In the audience marketplace, media organizations and advertisers often want to acquire information about future audience behavior. That is, it is often desirable (even necessary) to have some idea of how audiences are going to consume a particular piece of media content before they have even had the opportunity to do so (McQuail 1969). This is an inevitable byproduct of the inherent perishability of media audiences. Within the realm of ad-supported media, audiences typically need to be purchased before they are even produced. And, in the realms of both advertising- and consumer-supported media, strategic decisions regarding content production, distribution, and marketing often are guided by assessments of the anticipated levels of consumption for individual pieces of content. As a result, predictions of audience consumption patterns are a fundamental element of the activities of both advertising- and consumer-supported media (Napoli 2003a). And so, efforts to predict audiences' media consumption behavior are well established, and can range from the movie industry's efforts to pre-test upcoming films to television programmers' pre-testing of new shows, to radio stations testing the appeal of individual songs (see chapter 1).

The key difference today is that the growth and rapid diffusion of the Internet has given media organizations, advertisers, and audience measurement firms a new laboratory for assessing the extent of audiences' awareness of—or interest in—upcoming content options. Online "chatter," as it is typically labeled, is increasingly being monitored and aggregated by firms who contend that such information is a valuable tool for predicting audiences' media consumption. From a methodological standpoint, audience information systems operating in this vein typically employ sophisticated Web-"scraping" software that can be programmed to scour the Web in search of specific key words, and then to capture and categorize the text surrounding these key words. These systems represent an effort to capture the elusive "word of mouth" that has always existed in off-line space, but that leaves much more tangible traces in online space. This extension is reflected in the occasional use of the term "word of mouse" in connection with approaches to analyzing buzz (see, e.g., Verhaegh et al. 2007). Such analytical approaches extend across a range of online platforms, including blogs, social networking sites, and discussion boards.

Perhaps the most visible service of this type is Nielsen Online's BuzzMetrics service. BuzzMetrics gathers information from over 100 million blogs, social networking sites, discussion groups, and other consumer-generated media platforms, using these data to provide analyses of various factors, including the levels of awareness, interest, and anticipation for upcoming events—including media products (see Nielsen Online 2009). Reflecting the relative newness of this platform for gathering this type of audience information, a number of competing services are currently available, from firms such as BrandIntel, E-Poll Market Research, Visible Technologies, TNS Media Intelligence, and Optomedia (see Pace and Moores 2008; Silver, n.d.;

Vasquez 2007, 2008a, 2008b). Such services typically provide information on both the quantity and the valence of online discussion, and of course also facilitate the analysis of trends over time. History tells us that we should expect substantial consolidation within this area, as there has been a pronounced tendency toward monopoly in all fields of audience measurement (see, e.g., Buzzard 2002, 2003b; Gluck and Sales 2008).

It is important to emphasize that efforts to gauge audience awareness of, and interest in, media content predate these new information systems, which are oriented around the inherent interactivity of the Web (see chapter 1). The motion picture industry, for instance, has for years engaged in systematic telephone survey research to track moviegoers' awareness of, and interest in seeing, forthcoming films (Hayes and Bing 2004).[5] The difference now, of course, is that the Web represents a way to more cheaply examine far more audience members in a far less obtrusive manner than do traditional survey research methods. The typical participants in an online chatroom or writers of blogs generally are not aware that their words represent the raw data from which analyses of the prospects for forthcoming media products are being derived. Participants in telephone survey research or focus groups, in contrast, are fully aware that they are being studied, and this awareness can affect responses. Online conversations represent behavioral demonstrations of awareness of, and interest in, forthcoming media products, unlike survey responses, which are self-reports of audiences' attitudes and cognitions.

The value of such audience information resides in the extent to which media organizations can utilize it in their strategic decision-making. Traditional motion picture tracking data, for instance, has for decades factored heavily into decisions related to release dates, theater bookings, and the allocation of marketing dollars (Hayes and Bing 2004). Online buzz data are similarly beginning to find their way into media organizations' decision-making about products ranging from motion pictures, to albums, to television programs. These assessments are factoring into various aspects of strategic decision-making, such as release strategies, the allocation of marketing dollars, and schedule placement. The logic here is that the more people are talking about upcoming films, albums, or television programs, the more likely it is that audiences will consume these content options once they become available.

The scheduling of television programs, for instance, is already being demonstrably affected by buzz data. Programs that have produced substantial advance buzz have in some instances been awarded better time slots as a result, so that they can better capitalize on the audience anticipation and interest that already exists (Ross 2008). Ross (2008) describes how ABC, convinced that high online buzz for its program *Ugly Betty* merited moving the program to a prime-time slot, placed it on Thursday night alongside its hit *Grey's Anatomy*, rather than airing it in the much more challenging Friday night timeslot for which it was originally slated. Online conversation data has also factored into the subsequent revamping of *Ugly Betty* as the producers have tested out various new looks for the main character via online polls and focus groups (Chozick 2009).

And so the Web today represents an evolving laboratory for analyses geared toward anticipating the consumption patterns of media audiences. The rise of user-generated content therefore has a significance that extends beyond the fact that audiences are now empowered to produce and distribute content, and to operate alongside traditional media organizations. These forms of expression serve as important new mechanisms by which media organizations can unobtrusively learn more about the tastes, preferences, and interests of their audiences.[6] Of course, the utility of such analyses of online discussions need not be confined to the analysis of awareness of, and interest in, *forthcoming* media products. Such information also can factor into assessments of *available* media products. As the next section illustrates, the new information systems are in fact playing a central role in ongoing efforts to develop analytical approaches to audiences that move beyond exposure.

THE EMERGENCE OF ENGAGEMENT

As was illustrated in figure 3.1, and discussed in some detail in chapter 1, exposure represents but one aspect of a much more complex and multifaceted notion of audience behavior. *How* media products are consumed, *why* they are consumed, and *what effects* their consumption may have all represent dimensions of audience behavior that extend well beyond the much more basic question of *if* a particular media product was consumed. Media industries have to some extent neglected these other aspects of audience behavior, which typically have been assigned the label of "qualitative" audience data (see Lloyd and Clancy 1991: Magazine Publishers of America 2006), for quite some time (see chapter 1). Today, however, thanks largely to the dramatic technological transformations that are taking place, we are seeing a resurgence of efforts to dig deeper into the nature of media consumption. And this time around many of these efforts are taking place under the rubric of understanding audience *engagement,* with the term "engagement" seeming to have emerged as the consensus umbrella concept, in lieu of related, perhaps even synonymous, terminologies such as *connectedness* and *involvement* (see, e.g., Lloyd and Clancy 1991; Lu and Lo 2007; Malthouse, Calder, and Eadie 2003; Russell and Puto 1999).[7]

The concept of engagement is not new, however. For years this notion has hovered at the margins of the media and advertising communities, taking its strongest hold within the context of the print media, as magazines and newspapers emphasized the engagement of their audiences in an effort to convince advertisers of the unique value of their readers. Today, however, the concept of engagement has moved from the periphery to the center of how media organizations and advertisers are thinking about audiences, thanks in part to technology's undermining of the exposure model documented in chapter 2, but also to its facilitation of new audience information systems. These new audience information systems are contributing to the growing prominence of engagement metrics across virtually all media (see, e.g., Neely 2008). The print, online, and television platforms have been the focus of particular activity in terms of efforts at defining, operationalizing, and of course seeking to monetize audience engagement (see, e.g., Atlas Institute 2008; Neely 2008). At the same time, there are a number of ongoing efforts to develop approaches to engagement that are transferable across media (see, e.g., Haven and Vittal 2008; Kilger 2008; Passikoff and Schultz 2007; Simmons Market Research Bureau 2007).

In 2005 the American Association of Advertising Agencies "declared . . . that 'engagement' would become the new metric for advertising accountability" (Sorce and Dewitz 2006:30). The embrace of engagement as a new metric for understanding audience behavior is widespread (see, e.g., Albiniak 2007),[8] as advertisers, content providers, and measurement firms have rather suddenly become willing to acknowledge the shortcomings in the criteria that long have dominated the audience marketplace and are beginning to embrace alternative—or at the very least, supplementary—analytical approaches (Albiniak 2007; Neely 2008).

However, the growing prominence of the concept of engagement has yet to result in any kind of clarity or consensus as to what "engagement" actually means. As one industry white paper has noted, "'Engagement' has very much become the dominant buzzword of the measurement industry, and there are a number of focused efforts attempting to define and measure engagement in meaningful and useful way"; however, the industry remains "quite far from achieving consensus on what the term means and how it should be measured" (Peterson and Berger 2008:10). As another report notes, "companies [have been] founded to measure it, and countless arguments spawned just seeking a reasonable working definition of the term to apply in a meaningful way" (Peterson and Carrabis 2008:2). According to one executive at an Internet audience measurement firm, "Engagement is like obscenity. None of us can define it, but we're all pretty sure when we see it."[9]

Reflecting this somewhat chaotic state, the Advertising Research Foundation (2006a) issued a white paper titled "Engagement: Definitions and Anatomy" that contained *twenty-five different definitions* of engagement as proposed by different industry stakeholders.[10] Table 3.1 contains a compilation of twenty fairly recent definitions of audience engagement, which have been obtained from a range of both industry and academic sources. This compilation is not intended to be comprehensive by any means, but rather simply to provide an illustration of the wide range of definitional approaches that have been applied to the concept of engagement in recent years.

The Advertising Research Foundation's (2006a) paper also contained a working definition of engagement that had been established by one of the ARF's subcommittees: "Engagement is turning on a prospect to a brand idea enhanced by the surrounding context" (ARF 2006a:9). This proposed definition certainly seems to lack the clarity necessary to resolve the persistent debates and discussions over what engagement should mean; and indeed, in the four years since this definition was introduced, the meaning of engagement remains very much contested territory. Obviously this proposed definition reflects the strong advertising focus of the ARF, highlighting the fact that approaches to engagement have tended to focus either on engagement with the advertisements and brands or on engagement with the content in which advertisements are embedded (see ARF 2006a).[11]

Such analytical distinctions are somewhat reduced in terms of importance, however, by the growing body of research suggesting significant relationships between engagement in content and engagement with embedded advertisements (see below).[12] In fact, this surging emphasis on engagement and its range of related subcomponents is in part the outcome of an

TABLE 3.1 Definitions of Audience Engagement

Definition	Source
A scale indicating the degree to which a consumer is likely to or has internalize(d) a communication	ARF 2006a
A measurement of involvement with a marketing communication	ARF 2006a
A prospective consumer's interaction with a marketing communication that can be proven to be predictive of sales effects	ARF 2006a
A brand idea/medium context experience selected and attended toby a category-involved consumer that leaves a positive brand impression	ARF 2006a
A measure of attention paid by a consumer to a piece of communication	ARF 2006a
The average time spent in a branded experience	ARF 2006a
A positive consumer attitude resulting from a communication	ARF 2006a
Emotional connection	ARF 2006a
A measure of concurrent response to advertising that can be proven to be predictive of sales effects	ARF 2006a
How a consumer relates to a medium and the advertising in it	ARF 2006a
A measure of the degree to which each brand or title provides a conducive environment for an ad to achieve its objective	ARF 2006a
The net effect of attentiveness to a program and an ad that brings about a measurable impact	ARF 2006a
Getting the right message in front of the right audience at the right time	ARF 2006a
Turning on a prospective consumer to a brand idea enhanced by the surrounding context	ARF 2006a
The amount of subconscious "feeling" going on when an advertisement is being processed	Heath 2007
Comprises the following dimensions: inspirational, trustworthy, life-enhancing, social involvement, personal timeout	Kilger and Romer 2007
Collective qualitative experiences with content	Malthouse and Calder 2007

(continued)

TABLE 3.1 Definitions of Audience Engagement (*continued*)

Definition	Source
A consumer's relationship with media content	Magazine Publishers of America 2006
The consequences of any marketing or communications effort(through any media touchpoint) that results in an increasedlevel of "brand equity" for a brand	Passikoff and Weisler 2006
A measure of the contextual relevance in which a brand's messages are framed and presented based on its surrounding context	Wang 2006

established but growing body of research indicating that the concept does indeed seem to resonate with advertisers in terms of criteria that matter to them the most, such as product attitudes, commercial recall, and purchasing behaviors.[13] That is, engagement with the media content does seem to be meaningfully related to engagement in the advertisements or product placements embedded within the content. Studies have found, for instance, that various measures of engagement are positively related to advertisement recall and persuasiveness (Moorman, Neijens, and Smit 2007; Wang 2006; Wood 2008), as well as to product assessments, purchase intentions, and behaviors (Eubank and Griffiths 2007b; Kilger and Romer 2007). Similar relationships have been found between certain subcomponents of engagement (such as appreciation) and advertising effectiveness (Kok and de Vos 2005; Lu and Lo 2007; Simmons Market Research Bureau 2007). Other studies have demonstrated that audience engagement varies across different media as well as across different demographic groups (Kilger and Romer 2007).[14]

Audience measurement organizations have devoted particular attention to the development of systems that examine audience engagement with the content that they consume, under the logic that "media should not be viewed as merely the passive vehicle through which consumers are exposed to advertisements. . . . The content of the media should itself be thought of as providing experiences for the viewer or reader. These experiences must be considered in evaluating an advertisement as a contact" (Calder and Malthouse 2005:357).

With audience engagement in both advertising and content, and the potential interactions between these two forms of engagement to be taken into consideration, it is perhaps not surprising that analytical approaches to engagement remain varied. In late 2006 the Advertising Research Foundation issued a second white paper on the topic, titled "Measures of Engagement," that sought to "summarize some of the leading efforts to measure engagement" (ARF 2006b:2). This paper contained summaries of more than twenty distinct analytical approaches to measuring engagement. Subsequently, the ARF released "Measures of Engagement, volume II," which summarized fifteen additional measurement approaches (ARF 2007).

Engagement can certainly mean somewhat different things depending upon the priorities and goals of different stakeholders.[15] It is also likely the case that as the "engagement" terminology gained traction in the audience marketplace, stakeholders began applying the label to a broad array of phenomena and analytical constructs—many of which in reality do not meet any kind of rigorous criteria in terms of what engagement should mean or how it should be operationalized. Because the term now resonates so strongly in the audience marketplace, it is likely being employed in a variety of contexts in which its applicability is questionable. It is also important to recognize that although the meaning and measures of engagement are at this point quite varied, the little research that has thus far sought to compare them has suggested that a number of the most common engagement metrics are highly related (Eubank and Griffiths 2007).

The point here is that in these early developmental stages of the concept, the stakeholders involved are not yet converging around any consensus definitional or operational approach. The concept of engagement has been described as being "in its infancy in terms of construct definition and implementation" (Sorce and Dewitz 2006). Engagement up to this point has been described as "lacking in clarity about how it works, what effect it has, and why we need yet another marketing construct" (Woodard 2006:353). And so "while content producers and advertisers generally agree that engagement is important, they are also unsure how to measure and use it" (Peer et al. 2007:15).

The concept of engagement remains at this point a complex one, to say the least; in its various incarnations it has encompassed virtually every postexposure dimension of audience behavior contained within figure 3.1.[16] This in many ways reflects the fact that theoretical approaches have broken the concept down into discrete components, including attention, memory, emotions, and social relations (Mast and Zaltman 2006).

However, it remains somewhat unclear at this point where exactly the concept of engagement ends and where the *effects* of engagement begin. This ambiguity leads to occasionally contradictory approaches to the definition and measurement of engagement, and its relationship to other aspects of audience behavior. For instance, some analytical approaches to engagement see audience recall as a defining element (see, e.g., Nielsen IAG 2009), whereas others see engagement as a precursor to—and cause of—recall (Eadie 2007). Clarification of these kinds of definitional conflicts can only be achieved when the specific parameters of engagement are clearly defined, and in a way that is embraced consensually in the audience marketplace. Should audiences' recall of a particular piece of content be seen as a result of their engagement (with engagement perhaps defined in terms of appreciation or emotional response) or as an indicator of engagement in and of itself? Such questions remain at this point far from resolved amid the various competing analytical approaches to engagement.

However, the goal here is not to assess and critique the various definitions of engagement, propose alternative definitions, or determine the concept's value or effectiveness, but rather to illustrate how engagement is being integrated into many new audience information systems that take advantage of the interactivity inherent in the new media environment. It is also important to recognize that each of the possible components of engagement discussed below also can potentially function as freestanding audience behavior metrics (independent of the overarching engagement umbrella). For organizational simplicity, however, all of these dimensions of audience behavior are discussed here within the broader context of engagement, given that all of them have been put forth by one or more stakeholders as components of the broader notion of engagement.

EXPOSURE-DERIVED APPROACHES TO ENGAGEMENT

Some analytical approaches to engagement have been based on the contention that engagement can be effectively quantified via the analysis of basic exposure data. That is, information about the patterns and duration of audience exposure to content can provide the analytical basis for determining how engaged audiences are in that content (see, e.g., Danaher and Lawrie

1998; Magazine Publishers of America 2006).[17] Within magazine publishing, for example, engagement has been defined in terms of: (a) readership frequency; (b) amount of time spent with each issue; and (c) the percentage of each issue that was actually read (Sorce and Dewitz 2006:31). All of these components are derivatives from basic exposure data.

New media technologies also are contributing to exposure-derived approaches to engagement. For instance, cable set-top boxes are being used to "go beyond simply counting the number of eyeballs and truly understand how the audience is interacting with content" (Dish Network/Rentrak Corporation 2009:5).[18] In 2006 DVR manufacturer TiVo created a division of audience research and measurement devoted specifically to providing advertisers, media buyers, and programmers with second-by-second DVR-viewing data—data that are being utilized to craft measures of engagement as part of what TiVo has labeled its Stop‖Watch ratings service (Klaassen 2006). In this case the much more nuanced and granular exposure data that can be obtained from an inherently interactive technology such as a DVR are being used to extrapolate a metric of engagement. With a TiVo or other DVR, information can be obtained not only about program viewing, but also about pausing, time-shifting, re-watching, and, perhaps most important, commercial fast-forwarding behaviors. TiVo has developed what it calls its "commercial viewership index," which is calculated by dividing the average commercial viewership within a program by the average viewership of the program itself. According to TiVo, "the higher the CVI, the more engaged viewers [are] with the commercials" (ARF 2007:30). Along similar lines, approaches to measuring online media consumption (e.g., online video consumption) have equated exposure duration with engagement (Peterson and Berger 2008). According to this approach, "thresholds can be used to measure the number of viewers who were engaged enough to surpass a certain viewing duration" (Peterson and Berger 2008:13).

The question that naturally arises from such analytical approaches is whether something as simple as the duration of media consumption represents a convincing and satisfying representation of engagement, which would seem to be inherently a bit more complex. It certainly seems reasonable that "time spent with a medium is a fundamental *component* of looking at engagement" (Wang 2006:357, emphasis added; see also Magazine Publishers of America 2006), but that the concept of engagement should imply something a bit more robust than simply how long an audience member spends with a particular content option. It seems quite plausible that there could be instances in which audiences appear to spend a long time with a particular content option specifically because they are *not* meaningfully engaged. One could imagine, for example, multitasking television viewers whose television is tuned to a particular channel while the bulk of their attention is devoted to the Web pages they're reading via the notebook computers on their lap. Such a media consumer may be spending a substantial amount of time with an individual television program or network, and therefore appear to be engaged, when in fact the length of time spent with the content would in this case be reflective of the extent to which the audience member is *not* engaged with the programming.

Moreover, as was noted in chapter 2, one of the key characteristics of the contemporary media environment is that generating accurate, reliable, and comprehensive exposure metrics is becoming more and more difficult, given the strains that fragmentation imposes on panel-based audience measurement systems. Under these circumstances, crafting an analytical approach to engagement that relies entirely on these increasingly unsatisfactory exposure metrics seems somewhat problematic—or, at best, an effort to pour old wine into new bottles. Going forward, therefore, it seems more likely that any institutionalized approaches to audience engagement directly tap at dimensions of audiences' media consumption that truly extend beyond exposure.

APPRECIATION AND EMOTIONAL RESPONSE

As was noted in figure 3.1, it seems reasonable to consider audience appreciation and emotional responses as fairly immediate byproducts of audience exposure. Here too we are not treading into completely unfamiliar territory in terms of efforts to assess these dimensions of audience behavior. Efforts to assess audience appreciation and emotional responses to media content have a long history, with academic audience researchers frequently advocating on behalf of a stronger integration of appreciation-based measurement approaches into commercial audience information systems (see, e.g., Danaher and Lawrie 1998; Gunter and Wober 1992; Lloyd and Clancy 1991).[19] However, for much of that history these efforts have resided at the margins of the audience marketplace. Today new technologies allow such analytical methods to play a more central role in institutionalized approaches to media audiences—enabling the analysis of audience appreciation and emotional response to serve as a counterweight to the diminishing viability of traditional exposure metrics, and making these criteria key building blocks for the broader notion of audience engagement.

As was discussed in chapter 1, the BBC has had a long history of looking beyond exposure and measuring the extent to which audiences appreciate the content they consume, and this trajectory continues into the present (see Smith and North 2006). The BBC has developed the concept of "audience value," which it defines as "appreciation multiplied by duration of consumption" (Holden and North 2008:3). Appreciation, in this case, is measured via the very simple question, "On a scale of 1–10, how do you rate this program?" (Holden and North 2008:4). Clearly this measure seeks to integrate an exposure-based indicator of attentiveness (duration of consumption) with an indicator of the perceived quality of the content (appreciation). Information is gathered from audience members via the Internet and onscreen program guides, as well as via more traditional telephone interviewing (Holden and North 2008; Smith and North 2006). And, perhaps most important, this information is gathered across the BBC's television, radio, and online platforms (Smith and North 2006), in reflection of the notion that engagement is an aspect of audience behavior that can be captured, analyzed, and even compared across different media platforms.

In the case of a public service content provider like the BBC, the assessment of appreciation is the reflection of an organizational mission that extends beyond simply trying to maximize audience size. However, audience appreciation is also emerging as a significant analytical construct in the context of ad-supported media. In Korea, for example, a metric called the "quality evaluation index" is being applied to the analysis of television audiences. This index assesses audiences' perceptions of programming across a variety of quality-related dimensions, with audience assessments being obtained primarily via online surveys (Lee, Ma, and Lee 2007). A number of European audience measurement services gather immediate audience appreciation information about individual television programs via People Meters (with participants entering their ratings for individual programs at the program's conclusion; see Beck 2009).

In the United States radio audience measurement firm Arbitron has begun developing an "affinity metric" in an effort to go beyond exposure in terms of providing radio stations and advertisers with information about radio audiences (PR Newswire 2009). In many ways this move by Arbitron is a throwback to some of the earliest days of radio audience measurement (see chapter 1), when the focus was much more on the extent to which audiences appreciated the program they had heard, rather than the extent to which they were simply exposed to programming. Clearly, after decades of reporting audience size and demographics, Arbitron has decided that the audience marketplace is changing in ways that require alternative approaches to audience understanding.

Audiences' emotional responses to content have also been posited as a central element of the broader concept of engagement.[20] The Advertising Research Foundation issued a report in 2007 that focused on the notion of emotional response and the various approaches to measuring audiences' emotional responses to content (particularly advertisements; see Micu, Plummer, and Cook 2007). Approaches for measuring audiences' emotional responses to content involve employing techniques such as facial recognition technologies (to detect smiles, frowns, etc.), heart rate monitoring, skin conductance analysis, and traditional surveys (see, e.g., Morrisson and Gomy 2008; Peacock, Purvis, and Hazlett 2007). Newer, even more technologically sophisticated approaches have involved the analysis of brainwaves to assess emotional response. Nielsen recently invested in a firm called NeuroFocus, which specializes in applying brainwave research to the analysis of advertising and content effectiveness ("Nielsen Makes Strategic Investment," 2008).[21]

Market research firm Marketing Evaluations, producers of the venerable "Q scores," which for years have been used to assess the recognizability and marketability of celebrities, has introduced a metric called "emotional bonding Q scores," which the firm applies to individual television programs as a comparative indicator of the level of emotional involvement that audiences have with programs (Friedman 2009c; Vasquez 2008b). The logic of the value of these scores is, according to an executive within the firm, that "emotionally committed viewers are more frequently exposed to and more receptive to advertising" (Friedman 2009c:1).[22]

As was noted previously, just as the analysis of certain types of user-generated content can be used to assess the level of awareness of, and interest in, forthcoming media content, so too can this analytical approach be employed to assess audiences' appreciation of, and responses to, media content that is already available. For instance, firms such as Nielsen Online and Networked Insights are offering large-scale analyses of online conversations and audience activity (including linking activities, sharing, and rating content) that can be employed as alternative, or at least supplementary, indicators of a piece of content's popularity and impact that extends beyond traditional exposure-based ratings. Such analytical approaches are being used to assess a variety of forms of media content, including songs, television programs, advertisements, and even videogames (see, e.g., O'Malley 2008; Plunkett 2008; Sullivan 2010). Thus, for instance, online conversations and blogs dealing with individual television programs, the extent to which people link to program-related Web sites, or the extent to which people post clips of individual programs can all potentially serve as sources of information about the programs' audiences. As Nielsen has noted within the context of its BuzzMetrics service, "Word of mouth, or CGM [consumer-generated media] is intertwined with engagement" (ARF 2006b:8). However—reflecting the unsettled definitional state of the concept—Nielsen simultaneously states that consumer-generated media can be viewed as "an indicator or proxy of engagement; a form of engagement; or a result of engagement" (ARF 2006b:8).

Reflecting the perceived value of user-generated content in reaching a deeper understanding of audiences, the Nielsen Company went so far as to set up its own social networking Web site in 2007 called Hey! Nielsen (www.heynielsen.com), which was intended to "give lovers of pop culture an opportunity to sound off online and to make their voice heard by decisionmakers" ("Nielsen Unveils Hey! Nielsen," 2007:1). Participants on the site were able to offer their opinions and ratings on movies, television programs, and music. These opinions and ratings were then aggregated and integrated with other Nielsen data sources to create detailed reports for individual media properties and brands. The site attracted over 175,000 members before being shut down in late 2008 for a planned revamp and relaunch (Mandese 2008b).[23]

Networked Insights measures the engagement of television programs via an analysis of seventeen thousand consumer-generated media sites. Networked Insights' approach involves measuring various possible forms of "interactions," including the posting of video clips or photos about a show, discussion board comments, and inviting friends to join online fan groups (Abels 2008). Each of these types of activities is presumed to be an indicator of an audience member's level of engagement with individual television programs. The obvious irony in such a measurement approach to engagement is that the concept is being operationalized in part by means of some

activities (such as posting clips) that many content providers have historically sought to discourage due to copyright concerns.[24]

Of course, analytical approaches that rely on the analysis of various forms
of online conversation and activity are hampered to some extent by the fact
that online participation remains limited to certain sectors of the population; findings therefore lack the generalizability to the population as a whole
that is typically demanded of audience information systems. Audience information systems that scrape the Web for online conversation, or that solicit,
and then analyze, forms of feedback or participation from the audience do
still run aground to some extent against the fact that participation in such
activities remains far from representatively distributed across the population
as a whole. According to some estimates, 90 percent of the people online are
best categorized as "lurkers"; 9 percent engage in some online participation/
content creation; and it is only the remaining 1 percent who are actively
engaged in online participation and content creation.[25] Other estimates have
classified 15 percent of the online audience as active participants and the
remaining 85 percent as the "silent majority" (Networked Insights 2008),
though other studies suggest a significantly greater distribution of online
participation and content generation (Nielsen Online 2008).[26] These somewhat divergent results seem to reflect the different definitions of online
participation and content creation being employed. An accurate answer is
key to determining the generalizability—and therefore the decision-making
value—of such data.

Some research already suggests that media organizations are allowing the
data gathered from online discussions to exert too strong an influence over
strategic decision-making. Ross (2008), for instance, describes a case in
which television network programming executives butted heads with program producers over the extent to which online message board comments
should influence the creative direction of an individual program. The producers expressed concerns that such online commentary "was not necessarily representative of the average viewer" (Ross 2008:148), and therefore
should not play too strong a role in affecting decision-making about the
creative direction of the program.

In addition to the asymmetries in participation among the online audience, online audience information sources are themselves not equally
accessible. For instance, some social networking sites have resisted allowing third-party measurement firms to access their user data (Kanaracus

2008). Here again, if large portions of the online conversations that are taking place are inaccessible for analysis, then the results of such analyses will be skewed and the generalizability of any results can be called into question. This situation online is no different from what we have seen for years in traditional audience measurement contexts, where, for example, large retailers such as Wal-Mart have refused to provide their book and music sales data to measurement firms, which of course undermines the accuracy of book and record popularity charts (see, e.g., Andrews and Napoli 2006).

Finally, if we step back even further, we need to recognize that any methods of gathering audience information via newer interactive technologies such as the Web will run up against persistent "digital divide" issues. Communication and information technologies are quite widely diffused in some sectors of the population, but far less prevalent in other sectors (see, e.g., Norris 2001; van Dijk and Hacker 2003). This divide in access to digital platforms is widely acknowledged as a social problem of increasing significance, given the growing importance of these technologies for effective political participation and for taking full advantage of available economic opportunities (Norris 2001). It is still the case that only about 70 percent of the U.S. population, for example, has regular Internet access (Hindman 2009). And perhaps more important, we see significant variations in levels of Internet access across different demographic groups, with low income, rural, and minority households still lagging significantly (see, e.g., Fox and Livingston 2007; Marriott 2006).

Reflecting these persistent asymmetries in Internet access, Rochet has argued that efforts to gather generalizable audience information via the participation and discussions that take place on the Web run aground against the likelihood that "what could be exceptionally valuable data is [sic] fundamentally biased and skewed, an outcome owing to the disproportionately low amount of minority user-generated media on the Web. Therefore, as reliance upon this inaccurate information proliferates, commercial entities and politicians neglect a significant portion of potential consumers and constituents" (2006/2007:40). Researchers have identified a "participation gap" (Jenkins et al. 2006), in which online content production and distribution is heavily skewed toward individuals of higher socioeconomic status (Hargittai and Walejko 2008). From this standpoint, then, audience information systems that rely upon the Web to gather information must confront the fact that the online world still does not provide an accurate representation of the offline world.

RECALL AND ATTITUDES

Audiences' recall of content and advertisements also has been treated as an element of engagement, and in some instances recall has even been treated synonymously with engagement. Nielsen, for example, provides a service called IAG, which measures audience engagement for individual television programs.[27] Each day, more than five thousand panelists answer questions via online surveys about the details of the programs they watched the previous day.[28] The higher the average number of questions answered correctly by the panelists, the higher the "program engagement score" for that program (Nielsen IAG 2009). The presumption here is that the better audiences are able to recall the details of the programs they are watching, the greater the likelihood that they were attentive to the advertisements contained within the program. More important, perhaps, is that these recall scores are labeled "engagement scores" by IAG, suggesting that recall may in and of itself represent a viable representation of the concept of engagement. The IAG data have already begun to be utilized as currency in transactions between television programmers and advertisers (Neff 2007), suggesting that a recall-based approach to audience engagement may have the potential to take hold and become institutionalized in the audience marketplace.

Recall can potentially be accompanied by attitude change (toward either the content or products advertised or integrated within the content). Some audience measurement firms have also sought to incorporate measures of attitude change into their broader efforts at assessing audience engagement. For example, audience research firm Roy Morgan International measures whether consumers' attitudes toward advertised products change as a result of exposure to advertisements (ARF 2007). Obviously such analyses require that measurement take place both before and after exposure to the relevant content/advertisements.

BEHAVIORAL RESPONSES

As should be clear from the preceding discussion, audience information systems clearly have the ability to measure not only what media options are consumed by audiences, but also, to some extent, the effects that such exposure has upon them. Thus far this discussion has focused on effects related to attitudes, cognitions, and emotional responses. The next stage in the process would naturally be to determine whether such effects result in tangible behavioral responses. Some approaches to engagement have extended the definition of the term to incorporate such behavioral responses (ARF 2006a).[29] Audience information systems that focus on behavior also represent the potential for the audience marketplace to operate without relying upon the demographic variables that traditionally have served as proxies for audience behavior. As one audience research executive has stated, "We need better proxies for behavior [and] the best proxy for behavior is behavior."[30]

Typically within the realm of ad-supported media, the behavioral response of particular concern involves audiences' product-purchasing behaviors. Thus for decades a wide range of efforts have been undertaken to produce what is typically referred to as "single-source" audience measurement (for a history of such efforts, see Wood and Gloeckler 2007). The term "single source" refers to the fact that such a service would gather media consumption and product-purchasing behavior data from the same panel of participants, thereby allowing both direct analysis of the impact of commercial messages and, perhaps even more important, the targeting of media audiences not by the traditional age-income-gender demographic breakdowns that have historically dominated the audience marketplace, but rather by the actual product-purchasing behaviors for which these demographic categories long have served as fairly weak proxies (McClellan 2008c; Napoli 2003a).[31] For these reasons, single-source measurement systems that gather information about audiences' media consumption and product-purchasing behaviors simultaneously have frequently been described as the "Holy Grail" of the advertising industry (Gertner 2005; Harvey 2009; Wood and Spaeth 2008). As one recent industry research report noted, "the natural evolution of audience measurement services is the aggregation of knowledge throughout the entire consumer purchase process, starting at the basic gauge of exposure and ending at the actual product purchase" (Duarte and Beauchamp 2007:2).

Although a variety of efforts have been launched over the years to produce such data, they have virtually always foundered under the challenges of maintaining data of sufficient quality and reliability to be appealing to clients; such data must also be produced at a manageable cost that is not prohibitive to the necessary critical mass of subscribers (Gertner 2005; Wood and Gloeckler 2007). The most recent example of this pattern can be seen in the short lifespan of Project Apollo, a collaboration between audience measurement firms Nielsen and Arbitron that was launched in 2005. Project Apollo combined media consumption data obtained via Arbitron's Portable People Meter (see chapter 2) with product-purchasing behavior data obtained via Nielsen's Homescan service (McClellan 2008a; Wood and Gloeckler 2007).[32] Approximately five thousand U.S. households participated in Project Apollo (Kennedy et al. 2008). Research that emerged from Project Apollo provided indications of how advertising exposure affected product loyalty (e.g., Kennedy, et al. 2008), as well as evidence of significant inefficiencies and inaccuracies in the usage of demographic categorizations in the targeting of advertisements (Wood and Gloeckler 2007).

Despite Project Apollo's apparent potential to move audience measurement into what we can think of as the final stage of audience behavior (behavioral response), Nielsen and Arbitron terminated the initiative in early 2008, because the service had not attracted enough clients to remain viable (McClellan 2008a). No sooner did Project Apollo fold, however, than a new firm (TRA Inc.) emerged to pursue the same goal—to simultaneously measure media consumption and product-purchasing behaviors (see Collins 2009). In this case media consumption and product-purchasing behavior data are being aggregated from multiple sources, including cable set-top boxes, TiVo boxes, and frequent shopper cards (TRA 2008).[33] Even Nielsen has re-entered this field with a joint venture with Catalina Marketing, a firm that gathers shopping data (Friedman 2009).

Of course, in a highly interactive media environment, such as online or, increasingly, television, it is possible to obtain audience data that link media consumption directly with behavioral responses, including not only product-purchasing behaviors, but also activities such as clicking on an advertisement or submitting a request for additional information about a product. Ironically, this direct linking of media consumption data with behavioral response data—a natural outgrowth of an inherently interactive medium such as the Web—was, in the Web's early years, something of an impediment to its growth as an advertising medium, as low "click-through" rates for online advertisements were perceived primarily as evidence of the medium's ineffectiveness, thereby handicapping the medium relative to other, more established media where no such direct indicators of effectiveness were even available (Campbell and Carlson 2002; Napoli 2003a).[34] For a time it seemed that ignorance was bliss in the audience marketplace: stakeholders preferred to have no information about a message's effectiveness rather than information indicating low levels of effectiveness.

The developments outlined in chapter 2 have contributed to a change in perspective, however, and today the ability to capture content consumption and behavioral response data simultaneously within any medium is highly valued. Such information can be used both to better assess advertising effectiveness, and to develop strategies for delivering messages that more directly address individual audience members' particular interests. Today there is growing enthusiasm—and controversy (see chapter 4)—surrounding development of "online behavioral advertising" (see Federal Trade Commission 2009). Online behavioral advertising involves the delivery of targeted advertising to different members of the audience based on their demonstrated patterns of media consumption or behavioral responses such as information requests and other possible advertisement responses, such as click-throughs or product purchases. This information is gathered via tools such as cookies placed on an individual's Web browser, and, more recently, techniques such as "deep-packet inspection," which involves monitoring online behavior via hardware devices attached to ISPs' networks (Clifford 2008).[35] With behavioral targeting different audience members receive different (and presumably more appealing/interesting) advertising messages based upon their behavioral profiles (Federal Trade Commission 2009).[36]

Such behavioral targeting possibilities are not confined to the Web. For instance, as television grows increasingly interactive via more advanced set-top boxes (see, e.g., Bachman 2009b; Spangler 2009b), information can be gathered about television audiences that includes not only their viewing patterns but also their responses to any advertisements they've seen, such as requesting additional information or even making an immediate purchase via their television. All of these categories of information can then be utilized to deliver more targeted advertisements to different audience members (Clifford 2009a; Spangler, Gal-Or, and May 2003).[37] Such developments could potentially reverse to some extent the trend toward commercial avoidance facilitated by the diffusion of the DVR, as the advertisements that individual audience members would receive would more likely speak to their particular interests.

The cable industry launched an initiative called Project Canoe (now titled Canoe Ventures) that is focused on gathering the necessary information via set-top boxes to deliver such targeted advertisements (Arango 2008; Spangler 2009b). The underlying logic of this initiative is that it is essential for cable television to at least approximate the interactive data gathering and behavioral targeting capabilities inherent in the Web, particularly given the extent to which advertisers have embraced search-based advertising (in which ad placements are based on the terms entered into search engines).[38] The development of such functionality in the television space is seen as essential for that industry to combat the defection of advertising dollars to the online space. It also enhances the likelihood of attracting advertising dollars from other media that lack the interactivity to engage in such behavioral targeting (Arango 2008).[39] Included in this venture are plans for an enormous database, called TV Warehouse, capable of storing a full year of data gathered from digital set-top boxes in more than 16 million homes (Spangler 2009a).

INTEGRATED APPROACHES TO AUDIENCE BEHAVIOR

Although this overview of new audience information systems has sought to organize them according to the particular dimension of audience behavior that each tries to capture, it is also important recognize that many emerging audience information systems seek to integrate *multiple* dimensions of audience behavior into their assessments of audiences. Typically these approaches work to combine traditional exposure-based metrics with other, more "qualitative" measures, such as audience engagement. Media-buying firm Optimedia, for instance, recently launched what it calls its "content power ratings," which rank "the relative reach and power of the top 100 television programs, based on the number and quality of viewers across important digital and traditional media" (PR Newswire 2007:1; see also Vasquez 2008a). These ratings involve the integration of various forms of audience exposure and engagement data, including traditional Nielsen television ratings, comScore online audience estimates, and online "buzz" data from E-Poll (PR Newswire 2007), to form a measure of engagement that Optimedia refers to as "our staple currency" (Young 2008:2). Online audience research firm Web Analytics Demystified has developed a multifaceted engagement metric comprising seven different dimensions, including number of page views, time spent on a site, propensity to supply feedback, and level of interaction with the site (Peterson and Carrabis 2008).[40]

We also see this notion of the integration of engagement with traditional exposure metrics in the efforts of some media buying agencies to create and utilize what they term "eGRPs." The term "GRP" refers to "gross ratings points," a metric used in assessing the reach of any advertising campaign, particularly within the context of television, where each rating point represents 1 percent of the television-viewing population. Advertising campaigns, as they are developed, often include a targeted number of rating points. The use of eGRPs would essentially involve weighting traditional GRPs according to the results of an engagement index that would be applied to each piece of content (in this case, each television program) in which an advertisement was placed (Eubank and Griffiths 2007).[41] Obviously such an approach requires that each program's audience engagement be assessed alongside its audience size, and that these two performance metrics then be combined.[42]

AUDIENCE INFORMATION SYSTEMS AND AUDIENCE EVOLUTION

As should be clear at this point, recent years have seen a tremendous amount of activity in terms of efforts to define, redefine, and empirically capture those aspects of the media audience that should matter most to participants in the audience marketplace. The result is a state of disruption, disorder, and even, to some extent, confusion about the predominant performance criteria that should guide the operation of the audience marketplace going forward. The extent to which changing technologies are facilitating new analytical approaches to media audiences has built upon the damage that these same technologies have inflicted upon traditional analytical approaches to media audiences.

These alternative analytical approaches are beginning to make inroads into the operation of the audience marketplace—particularly in the television industry.[43] For instance, cable network Logos, which targets gay and lesbian viewers, and has only 30 million subscribers nationally, is one of the many cable networks that does not attract a sufficiently large audience to qualify for detailed ratings reports by Nielsen. Logos is also one of the growing number of cable networks that are consequently turning to engagement metrics in their efforts to attract advertising dollars, either as an alternative to traditional exposure metrics or as a supplement intended to bring a premium for more engaged audiences (Carter 2009; Crupi 2008a). NBC, which of course doesn't suffer from the same audience verification problem as cable networks such as Logos, nonetheless has begun offering guaranteed levels of audience engagement to advertisers in the same way that the network has traditionally guaranteed certain levels of ratings points (Neff 2007). These examples would seem to support the contention that "in some respects the fragmenting media environment means less emphasis on numbers and more concern with establishing and maintaining a bond with audiences" (Davies and Sternberg 2007). In 2008 ABC introduced its "advertising value index," which allows advertisers to choose from more than fifteen criteria, including traditional demographic factors such as age, income, and employment status, as well as length of tune-in to commercials and level of program engagement. This system, with its effort to be flexible in terms of the criteria associated with audience value, is certainly reflective of the transitional process that is affecting the audience marketplace (Kang and Vranica 2008).[44]

In the online space the pattern at this point has the exposure-based pricing model of display advertising continuing to be supplanted by cost-per-click pricing models (Shields 2008a), which in turn are in some quarters being supplanted by cost-per-action models, which are based on even more robust behavioral indicators than simple click-throughs (Spencer 2007).[45] In the social media space, the largest brands are primarily buying the audience on such behavioral "key performance indicators," rather than on the more traditional basis of "impressions."[46] Impression based pricing continues to lose ground to performance based pricing in the world of online advertising, such that, according to one estimate "there are more than 3 trillion impressions each year that go unsold" (Koretz 2009: 2).

Behavioral responses can of course be seen as a particularly robust indicator of audience engagement. However, the challenges for content providers that arise from monetizing only those audiences that exhibit some form of behavioral response have compelled efforts within the online space to develop audience metrics that capture the extent to which ads may be affecting even those members of the audience who do not exhibit a specific behavioral response (Shields 2008a). Some stakeholders have even called for the adoption of a "cost-per-engagement" pricing model online (Morrissey 2009b). The likely end result, once again, is a scenario in which multiple success criteria exist side by side. This likely represents the future of the audience marketplace, in which multiple approaches to conceptualizing, valuing, and purchasing media audiences operate simultaneously.

It is important to recognize how unusual it is that so many different audience information systems, that address so many different dimensions of the media audience, are currently in various stages of development and deployment. The typical state of the audience marketplace is one of much greater stability in terms of how media audiences are defined and measured (Gluck and Sales 2008). Today, however, the same new interactive communications technology platforms that are undermining traditional exposure-based analytical approaches to audiences (see chapter 2) also are giving birth to new analytical opportunities—opportunities not only to measure aspects of audience behavior that previously were unmeasurable, but also to more easily and more rigorously analyze aspects of audience behavior that long have been measurable but have tended to reside at the margins of institutionalized approaches to audience understanding, perhaps only because other aspects of audience behavior were both easier to measure and considered acceptable currencies in the audience marketplace.

The fact that the institutionalized media audience is in such a state of flux is a key indicator of the ongoing process of audience evolution. Old models are breaking down and new ones are emerging to supplement, if not replace, them. But underlying this somewhat chaotic situation is a consistent progression toward a greater rationalization of audience understanding (see Andrejevic 2007a, 2007b; Gandy 2000). Efforts to go beyond audiences' media consumption and to analyze their various responses, as well as their content production activities, can be seen as natural extensions of fundamental components of the process of rationalization, including the refinement of the techniques of calculation and the increased reliance on specialized knowledge (see chapter 1).[47] The processes described here—breaking down certain elements of audience behavior into more granular units of analysis, and extending the reach of quantitative analyses into previously neglected aspects of audience behavior—represent the latest steps in the long and continuing process of the rationalization of audience understanding. For the process of audience evolution to continue forward, however, this period of flux will need to eventually conclude in the emergence of consolidated, unified, and institutionalized set of analytical approaches to the media audience.

Any shift in the dominant institutionalized conceptualization of the media audience can happen only after a process of resistance and negotiation has taken place among the various stakeholders that either participate in or oversee the audience marketplace. It is important to keep in mind that some level of consensus among all stakeholders in the audience marketplace regarding the validity and value of particular performance metrics has always been fundamental to the efficient functioning of the marketplace (Napoli 2003a), and remains an imperative even in this period of disruption (see Wurtzel 2009). Nonetheless, the media audience has been, and always will be, contested territory among the various stakeholders involved in the audience marketplace, who seek to have their own best interests fully reflected in whatever consensus emerges. It is these processes of stakeholder resistance and negotiation that are the focus of the next chapter.

CHAPTER 4

CONTESTING AUDIENCES

The previous two chapters have emphasized the technological forces that are in so many ways compelling media organizations to reconceptualize their audiences. This chapter shifts the emphasis to the broader institutional contexts in which these technological changes are occurring. Research on the social shaping of communications technologies has emphasized the importance of considering a wide range of social actors with the potential to influence the ways that technologies are used, the form that these technologies take, and the impact that they ultimately have (see, e.g., Boczkowski 2004b; Lenert 2004).[1] Interpretive battles are inevitably fought among these various actors (industry players, policymakers, users, etc.) over the path that any new communications technology travels. The repercussions of these battles can be wide-ranging. As Carlson states, "Institutional entities exercise control over the shape of new technology, which in turn impacts users of that technology as well as the society into which it becomes embedded" (2006:99).

This analytical framework applies directly to the process of audience evolution being discussed here. The audience marketplace is a complex and contentious institutional environment, with many divergent, competing stakeholder interests that are frequently brought to bear in an effort to influence technologies in terms of both how audiences consume media and how these consumption behaviors are represented—sometimes in an effort to prevent, or at least impede, certain technological transitions from taking place. It is often the case that particular reconceptualizations of audiences are beneficial to certain stakeholder interests while harmful to others. The power dynamics surrounding the key institutional actors therefore play a central role in the determination of any reconceptualization of audiences.

Thus, this chapter emphasizes that the notion of the media audience is very much a contested space, with a diverse array of institutional interests at stake. By focusing on the role and impact of institutional pressures and interests in this evolutionary process, this chapter will demonstrate that dominant conceptualizations of audiences are, in fact, often negotiated outcomes between key stakeholders, including media firms, advertisers, technology companies, audience measurement firms, and even policymakers and public interest organizations.

The chapter begins this assessment by providing a grounding in the current state of knowledge about how organizations respond to technological change. It then examines the specific institutional dynamics surrounding the contemporary media audience, in which processes of resistance and negotiation have arisen in response to some of the key technological transformations discussed in chapters 2 and 3. Particular attention is given to the fact that media organizations have resisted the technological changes that place media audiences on a closer to equal footing with traditional content providers; also a factor here is multi-stakeholder resistance to new audience information systems that may represent unacceptable levels of intrusion into the privacy of media audiences. The chapter then examines recent stakeholder battles surrounding the introduction of new television, radio, and Internet audience measurement systems and the thorny economic, legal, and public policy issues around which such battles revolve.

ORGANIZATIONAL RESPONSES
TO ENVIRONMENTAL CHANGE

As the previous chapters have illustrated, the process of audience evolution is being driven by two interrelated factors: (a) technological changes that are altering the dynamics of media consumption; and (b) technological changes that are facilitating the gathering of new forms of information about the media audience. Thus at one level it is the mechanisms by which audiences *use* media that are changing; at the second level, it is the mechanisms by which *representations* of this media usage are constructed that are changing. It is important to maintain this distinction between the transformation of audience behavior and the transformation of the *representation* of audience behavior, not only because they clearly represent fundamentally different— though certainly interrelated—phenomena, but also because, as we will see, the stakeholder conflicts and negotiations that are taking place tend to focus on one level or the other. Moreover, when we consider the processes of stakeholder resistance and negotiation that have emerged around new media technologies, the institutionalized conceptualization of the audience has been identified as a focal point for "the playing out of competing conceptions of the threat/potential of the new medium" (Uricchio and Pearson 1994:44), suggesting an intertwining of these two factors.

There are important differences between these two levels of transformation, particularly in terms of how they can be approached theoretically. When we speak, for instance, of the contemporary technological changes that are affecting the dynamics of media consumption, and how various institutional actors respond to them, we find ourselves within the thoroughly researched territory surrounding how organizations respond to competitive threats that emerge from the environment in which they operate (see, e.g., Daneels 2004; Herbig and Kramer 1994; Tushman and Anderson 1986). As Tushman and Anderson note, "Technology is . . . an important source of environmental variation" (1986:440).

The study of organizational responses to innovation—both within and outside the specific context of media industries—typically focuses on the introduction of a new product or process and its impact on the providers of the precursor(s) to this new product or process. Thus, for instance, within the media industry there is a fairly extensive body of literature examining how different sectors of the industry responded to—and were affected by—the advent of television (see, e.g., Baughman 1997; White 1990). Similarly, studies of the television industry have examined how it has responded to innovations such as digital broadcasting and cable (Auletta 1992; Litman 1983; Galperin 2004). More recently we have seen detailed explorations of how various industry sectors, including the newspaper industry, have responded to the technological opportunities and threats posed by the Internet (e.g., Boczkowski 2004b).

One of the most common responses identified by researchers who have studied organizational responses to technological change has been a concerted effort to reinforce the status quo (e.g., Fligstein 1996; Hannan and Freeman 1984). This is likely a reflection of the documented tendency within organizations to perceive technological innovations primarily as threats to existing business models or organizational practices (Cooper and Schendel 1976; Cooper and Smith 1992). Jackson and Dutton (1988) identify a tendency among organizational decision-makers toward a "threat bias": managers are more sensitive to characteristics associated with threats than those associated with opportunities. Thus, it is more likely that new technologies will be perceived in terms of the potential harms they may cause than in terms of the potential benefits they may provide. Consequently, organizations often react to technological innovations with strategic responses designed to eliminate, minimize, or simply defer the perceived technological threat (Cooper and Schendel 1976; Cooper and Smith 1992).

Many of these behavioral patterns have surfaced in research that has focused specifically on responses to environmental/technological changes within media industries. In earlier research (Napoli 2003b), for instance, I found a tendency within the broadcast television industry to respond very slowly to environmental change—a finding that to a certain degree echoed themes in journalist Ken Auletta's (1992) popular account of the behavior of the Big 3 broadcast networks in the late 1980s and early 1990s. Auletta attributed the decline of the Big 3 broadcast networks to their failure to effectively recognize and respond to the environmental changes wrought by the diffusion of cable television and VCRs. Research by Boczkowski (2004b) examined how the newspaper industry had responded to the innovations of online publishing, uncovering a strong tendency to integrate established structures and practices (whether appropriate or not) into the new media enterprise, which suggests the common organizational propensity for maintaining the status quo amid dramatic environmental or technological change (see also Singer 2004). Studies of how the Hollywood studios responded to the VCR have illustrated what has essentially become a signature instance of a media technology that ultimately proved enormously beneficial being initially treated as a threat, so much so that the studios went all the way to the Supreme Court in their failed effort to have the new technology banned—a clear case of "threat bias" (Greenberg 2008; Lardner 1987; Picker 2004).

Much of the work in this vein has contributed to the more macro-level literature on media evolution (see Lehman-Wilzig and Cohen-Avigdor 2004; Napoli 1998a) that was discussed in chapter 1. And it is within this context of how media organizations are responding to these technological forces that compel a reconceptualization of the audience that this work on media evolution becomes particularly relevant. Specifically, this chapter will identify the historical pattern of resistance to technological developments that alter the dynamics of the media system which is a central element of the process of media evolution that in turn feeds into the ongoing process of audience evolution.

Of course, these organizational responses to the changing dynamics of media consumption also feed into institutional responses to the associated emergence of new audience information systems. It is important to recognize that audience measurement represents a fundamentally different type of innovation from the standpoint of the traditional approaches to the study of organizational responses to innovation—one that has received significantly less research attention. A new (or simply altered) audience information system does not represent a new product market or a new competing technology confronting the organization; nor does it represent an innovation to the internal production or distribution process to which the organization must adapt. Rather, a new audience measurement system represents a new representation of the audience marketplace; a new "market information regime." Anand and Peterson define a market information regime as "regularly updated information about market activity provided by an independent supplier, presented in a predictable format with consistent frequency, and available to all interested parties" (2000:271). Such socially constructed information regimes become the means by which marketplace participants form their cognitions of their own performance, the performance of their competitors, and the activities of their consumers (Anand and Peterson 2000).

New audience information systems represent the introduction of a new mechanism by which industry stakeholders can "make sense of their actions and those of consumers, rivals, and suppliers that make up the field" (Anand and Peterson 2000:271). Of particular importance is the fact that these new measurement systems, through their revised depictions of the market, have the potential to disrupt existing competitive arrangements, organizational strategies, and content production decisions (Adams 1994; Barnes and Thomson 1988, 1994). New audience information systems can produce a radically different portrait of the type of content that audiences are consuming, or the type of audiences that are consuming it. They can introduce new types of information into the decision-making process; or they can impact the rate at which information is available to decision-makers, and the overall quantity of information available (Barnes and Thomson 1994; Peterson 1994). In these ways, "the methodology used for framing market information is vital to the social construction of a market" (Anand and Peterson 2000:272). Research has shown that organizations will respond to new performance metrics that present their organization in a less favorable light by engaging in activities such as emphasizing alternative performance criteria and calling into question the validity of the measurement system (Elsbach and Kramer 1996).

Because market participants provide the economic foundation for any market information regime (through their financial support of the service), the dynamics surrounding innovation in audience measurement are particularly complex. Different stakeholder groups may have varying perspectives on the costs and benefits of the new measurement system; different sectors of the market may therefore vary substantially in terms of their willingness to support a change. A new measurement system represents the possibility of a dramatic reconfiguration (possibly positive, possibly negative) of all stakeholders' perceptions of their market and their organization's place within it. Consequently, just as stakeholder resistance and negotiation can focus around the changing dynamics of media consumption (see above), so too can they focus around the dynamics of audience measurement.

The main focus of this chapter will be these processes of resistance and negotiation, which can affect the ability of technological innovations to produce changes in the dynamics of the media system (Winston 1999), or, at the very least, affect the rate at which these changes take place. These behavioral patterns will then be considered in relation to how they may influence the ongoing process of audience evolution.

ORGANIZATIONAL RESPONSES TO THE CHANGING DYNAMICS OF MEDIA CONSUMPTION

The process of audience evolution is being driven in large part by technological changes that are fundamentally reconfiguring the dynamic between media audiences and content providers. Because these developments alter the traditional balance of power between the media and their audiences, they are wreaking havoc with many long-established business models. It is therefore not surprising that the past decade has seen a wide range of efforts by a variety of media industry stakeholders to preserve the status quo.

These efforts are seldom completely successful; they can, as Yochai Benkler has argued, raise "the costs of becoming a user—rather than a consumer—of information and undermine the possibility of becoming a producer/user of information" (2000:562–563). Benkler maintains that efforts at reproducing the traditional media consumer-producer relationship have been directed at all three "layers" of the new media environment: (a) the "content layer" (which involves issues such as copyright and fair use); (b) the "logical layer" (which involves encryption) and (c) the "infrastructure layer" (which involves the structure and operation of communications networks). The examples discussed below all fit neatly into one of these layers.

It is important to emphasize that the goal here is not to examine the full range of issues that have emerged as the new media environment has brought media organizations and audiences into conflict, or to determine what the appropriate resolutions to these issues should be. Detailed examinations of this type can be found in the work of Benkler (2006) and Lessig (2004, 2008), among others. The goal here is simply to illustrate the key ways in which these conflicts relate to—and can potentially affect—the ongoing process of audience evolution.

COMBATING FRAGMENTATION AND AUDIENCE AUTONOMY

According to Shimpach, "The ideal audience to emerge from the culture industry's construction is largely passive, observing the products of the culture industry, waiting around to be counted, measured, and receive intervention" (2005:350). As was noted in the introduction, this tendency toward passive constructions of the media audience was fueled in large part by the development of commercial mass media (particularly broadcasting) in the early part of the twentieth century. Today technological developments are undermining this established construction in ways that directly challenge, and in some cases obliterate, established business models, which have historically proven quite lucrative. These business models have relied on the more uni-directional relationship with audiences that was an outgrowth of the centralized (i.e., de-fragmented) distribution models and high-entry barriers that emerged as defining characteristics of the traditional media.

Given the record of success of the old models, and the economic uncertainty surrounding the technological transformations that are taking place, it is not surprising that various industry stakeholders have initiated a wide range of efforts aimed at preserving the more traditional construction of the media audience, using strategies and tactics that target the technologies that facilitate enhanced audience autonomy and greater media and audience fragmentation (see, e.g., Bhattacharjee et al. 2006; Dekom and Sealey 2003;

Lassica 2005; Lessig 2004; Waterman, Ji, and Rochet 2007).[2] These efforts can take a variety of forms, ranging from legal challenges to new technologies and how they are used, to the creation (or alteration) of technological interfaces that prevent or limit certain behaviors, to network designs and operations with intentionally restrictive capacities.

It is important to emphasize that the nature of these resistance efforts is much more complex than media organizations versus audiences, though the desired end result is often to limit certain audience behaviors. These conflicts often represent battles across various industry sectors among any number of stakeholders, including content producers, distributors, consumer electronics manufacturers, and software and application developers. Reflecting this point, one recent industry analysis concluded that the changing role of the media audience will likely emerge as a key source of tension in the relationship between media content producers and distributors, with producers seeking to capitalize on the growing array of increasingly open distribution channels, thereby neglecting—or at least denying privileged access to—traditional distributors; and distributors seeking to erect and maintain walled communities that increasingly rely on user-generated content, to the detriment of traditional media content (Berman et al. 2007). This scenario suggests stakeholder conflict, as "the actions each party takes, in some way, injure the others' business over time" (Berman et al. 2007:17).

And very often these conflicts are resolved in ways that to some extent curtail the dramatic changes that technological developments initially appear capable of imposing on the media system. This "suppression of radical potential" (Winston 1999) can be achieved not only by threatened stakeholders challenging new technologies or services, but also by subsequent efforts by these same stakeholders to diversify into the market for these new technologies or services and influence the direction of their development from within.

The introduction of the DVR is illustrative of the kinds of conflict and resolution processes that can arise when a new technology empowers audiences in ways that challenge established business models. When the DVR was first introduced by firms such as TiVo and ReplayTV in the 1990s, the fact that these devices included the capacity to skip commercials in their entirety, as well as the capacity (in the case of ReplayTV) for subscribers to share recorded programs among themselves, prompted aggressive responses from program producers and distributors, who argued that both the capacity to share programming and the capacity to avoid advertisements represented copyright violations. Then-chairman and CEO of Turner Broadcasting, Jamie Kellner, famously declared that DVR users who used the device to skip commercials were stealing programming (Kramer 2002). Legal challenges to both the commercial skipping and program-sharing functionalities were initiated by the major motion picture and television studios (*Paramount Pictures Corp. v. ReplayTV* 2004).

In the case of the DVR, although the legal actions taken against it played an influential role in its development—particularly in terms of the disabling of the program-sharing feature—perhaps more important is that traditional programmers (such as NBC, in the case of TiVo) elected to become major investors in, and providers of (in the case of most major cable system operators), DVR technology and services. In so doing, these content providers were able to ensure that the DVR lacked not only the capacity for program-sharing across users (Carlson 2006; Picker 2004), but also its initial feature allowing users to skip commercials in their entirety, instead forcing users to fast-forward through them (Cohen 2005; Donaton 2004; Notkin 2006; Piccalo 2004). The full extent of this technology's ability to transform the media audience has thus been somewhat curtailed. One TiVo executive noted, "There's great resistance. . . . No matter what the technology is, you're dealing with the entrenched dynamics of an industry that don't move simply because someone builds a better mousetrap. The economics of the business models make such that change comes about slowly, begrudgingly" (Donaton 2004:79).

The emergence of user-generated and user-distributed content represents perhaps the most direct challenge to the centralized, uni-directional production and distribution models of the past, and has therefore been a particular point of focus for ongoing resistance efforts. As was noted in chapter 2, one of the key transformative aspects of the contemporary media audience is that audiences' increasing abilities to produce and distribute content are placing them on a closer to equal footing with traditional content providers. Obvious threats that this pattern poses to traditional media are its facilitation of a further fragmentation of the media audience (with audience attention shifting somewhat from traditional media content to user-generated content; see chapter 2), and a possible reduction in traditional media consumption, as time once spent consuming traditional content is now being spent producing content. In either case, the end result is a diminished amount of audience attention devoted to traditional media content.

A threat that has received much more attention from media industry stakeholders is that much of what we might broadly categorize as user-generated content relies to some degree on content produced by traditional media. This usage can range from direct posting of traditional media content, whether these be clips—or the entirety—of television programs or movies, or newspaper or magazine stories (or excerpts) on blogs (categories of usage that are fairly easily identified as "copied" content; see Hilderbrand 2007), to less direct uses, such as the creation of "mash-ups" or the posting of "fan fiction" that utilizes already-created characters for new stories generated by fans of the original content (what can be categorized as "appropriated" content; see Hilderbrand 2007; see also Jenkins 2006). In instances such as these, not only is the diversion of audience attention discussed above taking place, but the original content creators may potentially be deprived of revenues that their content is generating via other distribution channels. And, of course, audiences may be accessing this content via channels that allow them to consume it without having to pay for it at all (nor does any intermediary, for that matter).

The exact amount of unauthorized use of copyrighted material taking place within the various emerging venues for the production and distribution of user-generated content remains a significant point of contention. One study, for instance, estimated that roughly 10 percent of videos posted on YouTube were posted in violation of copyright law (Vidmeter.com 2007),[3] an estimate that many industry stakeholders saw as too low. Critics of the study noted, for instance, that the estimate was based only on those videos that were *removed* in response to copyright violation claims, and therefore neglected those videos for which copyright holders remained unaware of the unauthorized posting (Li 2007). In its highly publicized lawsuit against YouTube, Viacom noted that identifying material on YouTube that is potentially in violation of copyright law is impeded by a number of aspects of YouTube's functionality, including, for instance, the fact that YouTube's search engine identifies a maximum of one thousand videos for any given search, though there may be well more than one thousand postings of copyrighted material related to any one media property (*Viacom v. You Tube* 2007).

However, we are beginning to see the institutional resistance to video file-sharing services such as YouTube subside, with many companies opting instead to enter into revenue-sharing arrangements with YouTube that include more intensive commitments on the part of YouTube to police piracy (see, e.g., Stelter 2009b). Former Viacom subsidiary CBS entered into such an agreement even as Viacom's billion-dollar lawsuit against YouTube continued (Stelter 2008a). One approach allows copyright owners to insert ads into unauthorized video clips that have been posted online but subsequently identified via digital fingerprinting of the content (Sandoval 2008). As these developments progress, it seems a fairly safe bet that we may see the YouTube interface altered so that users are prevented from fast-forwarding through advertisements, as many online video providers already do. Developments such as these suggest that the death of the thirty-second spot, which it has been argued may soon come to pass on traditional television, may be accompanied by its rebirth in the online space.

This would be a prime example of a new media technology failing to induce changes to the dynamics of the media landscape that are as dramatic as it initially seemed capable of producing (Winston 1999). Traditional media content providers (such as CBS, Showtime, and Universal) have even established "channels" on YouTube, in further homage to the "old" medium of television (Shields 2009). One recent report claims that YouTube is in the process of redesigning its site specifically to make it more suitable for "media company content" (Stelter 2009b:2), in an effort to better appeal to advertisers, who at this point assign little value to most user-generated content.[4] Another recent report has gone so far as to claim that while YouTube has a tremendous amount of content, "from the perspective of advertisers, much of it is utterly worthless" (Lyons 2009:1). Hulu, the newer video-streaming site launched by traditional media content providers such as NBC and FOX, has already emerged as a more profitable enterprise than YouTube, hinting at the entrenched preferences among both advertisers and media audiences for more traditional media content (Lyons 2009).

As these developments suggest, innovations such as online video-streaming services can easily become extensions of—rather than fatal threats to—established media enterprises.[5] Hilderbrand notes, "As has been historically apparent with entertainment technologies, initial novelty often gives way to familiar content. Convergence usually means content redundancy across platforms, and YouTube perhaps relies more on mainstream media for source material than it threatens to displace it" (2007:50).

Along related lines, the newspaper industry has been aggressively pursuing bloggers who excerpt news stories within their blogs (Stelter 2009a).[6] Research has shown that traditional media content provided by newspapers continues to play a very prominent role in blogs (Reese et al. 2007), something that the newspaper industry sees as increasingly harmful, especially as its own revenue streams dwindle in the face of increased competition for advertising dollars and audience attention. The Associated Press (A.P.) recently announced that Web sites that post articles or portions of articles produced by A.P. members must obtain permission from, and share revenue with, the A.P. (Pérez-Peña 2009). In some ways these actions by the newspaper industry recall what occurred in the early days of radio, when the newspaper industry took legal action against the radio industry for what was deemed "news piracy," which involved radio news reports that consisted primarily of the daily newspaper being read over the air (Chester 1949; Jackaway 1995).

Search engines such as Google also have been a target of resistance, from both traditional media actors and policymakers. Media executives such as Rupert Murdoch have called for search engines to pay royalties for the ability to link to online newspaper articles (Smillie 2009). In Germany such a model is already being implemented, with the German government pledging to institute a system in which online content aggregators such as Google must pay royalties when they link to online news stories.[7] In the midst of these controversies, Google has instituted changes that limit the extent to which Google can be used to access paid content (Saas 2009b).

It is important to recognize that these resistance efforts are directed not only at the increased audience autonomy facilitated by the contemporary media environment,[8] but also at increased media and audience fragmentation. That is, activities such as the posting of clips on YouTube, the uploading of songs on Kazaa, and the posting of news articles on blogs all represent mechanisms for the further disaggregation of media content into smaller, more discrete units, which is a fundamental aspect of the ongoing process of media fragmentation (see chapter 2). These practices run counter to the long-established strategy of monetizing media content in "bundles," whether it be the bundling of multiple cable networks into a subscription package, multiple songs into an album, multiple stories (and sections) into a newspaper, or even multiple segments into a television program (Owen and Wildman 1992). Here again we see that audience autonomy and fragmentation are not entirely distinct technological processes. The implications of both factor into the resistance that has been leveled against many media technologies and services.

As these disputes often illustrate, the line between piracy and user-generated content continues to be a point of contention. Nonetheless some paths of resistance to the empowering capabilities of newer media technologies are clearly more broadly targeted, in that they are directed against *all forms* of user-generated content, not just those forms of audience expression that draw to some extent upon copyrighted material. For instance, the persistence of asymmetrical bandwidth—the speeds at which ISP subscribers are able to download content are much faster (as much as ten–fifteen times faster [see Jesdanun 2006]) than the speeds at which they are able to upload content (see Winseck 2002)—can be interpreted as a further effort by media industry stakeholders to preserve the content provider–audience distinction that was much more clearly defined within the traditional media. This practice has been criticized as an effort to "turn users into simple appendages of the network" (Winseck 2002:807). One industry analyst has described this situation as "a hangover of the old mass media days" (Jesdanun 2006:1).

Similar issues are playing out in the news industry, where questions about the future of the news business often revolve around if, or to what extent, user-generated content should be embraced by traditional news outlets in an effort to craft what has been labeled "participatory journalism" (see, e.g., Paulussen et al. 2007; Paulussen and Ugille 2008), which encompasses "the variety of initiatives undertaken by mainstream media to enhance the integration of all kinds of user contributions in the making of news" (Paulussen and Ugille 2008:25). The question here involves whether the platforms operated by traditional news outlets should also serve as an access point for journalism produced outside of the confines of traditional journalistic institutions, creating "hybrid configurations" of user-generated and traditional media content (see Banks and Humphreys 2008:406). Research to date suggests that while many online news sources are embracing the notion of participatory journalism (see, e.g., Thurman 2008), they are doing so with some reluctance, and certainly not to the full extent that technology at this point would allow (Boczkowski 2004a, 2004b; Chung 2007; Ornebrink 2008). According to Boczkowki (2004a), this is because newspapers have tended to view their readers primarily as consumers of content and have thus constructed online platforms that reflect this perception and provide little opportunity for readers to speak alongside reporters and editors.[9] This tendency also may be reflective of Lowrey's contention, made in reference to blogging: "News organizations may be more interested in containing and directing the blogging phenomenon than in fostering democratic participation" (2006:493). The end result again may be a reconfiguration of the audience–content provider relationship that is not as dramatic as technological developments could allow.

IMPLICATIONS FOR AUDIENCE EVOLUTION

The patterns of stakeholder resistance and negotiation discussed here affect both the actual dynamics of audience behavior and the representations of the audience that can be achieved through certain emerging audience information systems. In terms of actual behavior, the discussion above suggests a continuing struggle by many industry stakeholders to maintain a more traditional relationship dynamic between media organizations and audiences, one in which senders and receivers of content remain more easily distinguishable. This is not meant as a broad generalization characterizing the entirety of the media system. As this section has also illustrated, there are a number of instances in which the integration of a new, more egalitarian dynamic between media and audiences is being embraced, and monetized, by media organizations. Rather, the point here is that the persistence of the response patterns involved in institutional efforts to resist or modify the influence of new technologies on the content provider–audience relationship will have lasting effects on the ways this dynamic is ultimately reconfigured.

From the standpoint of new audience information systems, how much the various forms of audience activity are curtailed bears directly on the functionality of the emerging audience information systems discussed in chapter 3. That is, where emerging audience information systems are, for instance, seeking to quantify engagement via online activities such as the posting and sharing of video or audio clips, methods of preventing or discouraging such activities (such as content providers seeking to prevent the sharing or use of copyrighted material) affect the representations of the audience provided by such analytical approaches, and likely undermine their reliability as an indicator of any dimension of audience behavior. Similarly, some online content providers, such as news organizations, limit audiences' ability to participate in, and provide feedback on, the news organizations' activities, by providing only limited online discussion forums and few opportunities for audiences to comment on or rate stories. Whether such decisions are strategic in nature or simply a function of resource-allocation decisions, the end result is still that the development of another analytical path of audience understanding is cut off. In these ways, the process of stakeholder resistance and negotiation surrounding the changing dynamics of media consumption feeds directly into the conceptualizations of the audience employed by media industry stakeholders.

ORGANIZATIONAL RESPONSES TO NEW AUDIENCE INFORMATION SYSTEMS

The processes of stakeholder resistance and negotiation have also, in some instances, been targeted directly at new audience information systems that play a key role in the process of audience evolution. As was noted above, new audience measurement systems inevitably enter a highly charged environment, in which the potential benefits of a new system (more, faster, or better data) are weighed by stakeholders against a wide range of potential costs (see Buzzard 1990). These potential costs extend well beyond the costs of subscribing to the measurement service. They also include potential costs in terms of lost market share (as reflected in the new audience measurement system), an increased commitment to analytical resources, or becoming reoriented to the altered consumption dynamics of the media environment in question (see Beville 1988; Buzzard 1990). In light of these many potential costs, the tremendous institutional resistance to new measurement systems is not surprising (see Beville 1988; Napoli 2003b). In many cases, however, systems are adopted despite such resistance, and media industry sectors are subsequently transformed as a result of the infusion of the new data, which often provide a significantly different portrait of the media audience (Adams 1994; Barnes and Thomson 1988, 1994).

Audience information systems ranging from the Soundscan system of measuring music sales (Anand and Peterson 2000; McCourt and Rothenbuhler 1997),[10] to the Bookscan system of measuring book sales (Andrews and Napoli 2006),[11] to the Nielsen People Meter system of measuring television audiences (Napoli 2005; see below), to the Arbitron Portable People Meter system of measuring radio audiences (Napoli 2009; see below) have all had to overcome the significant stakeholder resistance that arose in response to their introduction, which emanated from a variety of sources. Content providers may resist a new system because of the costs it imposes (see, e.g., Andrews and Napoli 2006), and because the new system indicates lower levels of performance than were characteristic of the previous system (Napoli 2005). Policymakers have resisted new audience information systems on the basis of their impact on social policy objectives such as media diversity and individual privacy. Even audience measurement firms themselves have been accused of being a key source of resistance to the migration to new audience information systems. As one media executive has stated in reference to the Nielsen Company, "They're very good at stifling innovation and managing the environment. They slow the pace of change down" (Gertner 2005:6).[12] In many instances, these various sets of stakeholders and interests can become simultaneously intertwined in the context of a single new audience information system. This is often the case in many of the examples discussed in this section.

THE INTRODUCTION OF THE LOCAL PEOPLE METER

The introduction of the Local People Meter (LPM) system of measuring local television audiences has encountered resistance (and outright hostility) unprecedented in the history of audience measurement (see Napoli 2005). The Local People Meter initiative is an effort by Nielsen to convert the 210 local television markets that it measures in the United States from paper diaries to electronic set-top meters that are essentially identical to those used since the late 1980s to measure national television audiences (Nielsen Media Research 2006a, 2006b). As was noted in chapter 3, set-top meters, with their ability to gather and report minute-by-minute television viewing data, have the capacity to feed into many of the developing analytical approaches to audience engagement that are derived, at least in part, from very granular exposure data, in ways that the diaries—with their much more basic, and less granular, exposure data—cannot.

Resistance to the Local People Meters began immediately upon the introduction of the first test system in Boston in the late 1990s. This resistance emanated primarily from local broadcast television stations (as opposed to other major stakeholders such as advertisers or cable companies). The focal points of resistance at this early stage in the LPM's introduction were: (a) the sudden dramatic shift in methodology that was taking place (and the disruption it would cause to established practices); (b) the costs associated with this shift (since subscribers would have to bear the increased costs associated with the more expensive measurement system); (c) local station research directors' and media buyers' inability to cope with the enormous information flow provided by the LPM service (see Lotoski 2000); and (d) Nielsen was instituting the shift before receiving full accreditation from the Media Rating Council (although accreditation ultimately came six months after the launch) ("For Nielsen, Fear and Loathing in LA," 2004).

The Media Rating Council (MRC) is a nonprofit organization created by the media and advertising industries to oversee and accredit audience measurement services. It originated (as the Broadcast Rating Council) in the aftermath of a series of hearings held by Congress in the 1960s in response to the well-known quiz show scandals investigating television ratings and audience research (see Goldberg 1989). The MRC engages in detailed assessments of the methodological rigor and soundness of new audience measurement systems, accrediting those that attain minimum standards of rigor, accuracy, and reliability. Services meeting these qualifications receive a formal accreditation from the MRC. However, the MRC does not have any binding regulatory authority over the firms that produce audience data. Measurement firms are not required to subject their methodology to the MRC accreditation process; and, more importantly, if a measurement service is denied accreditation by the MRC, it is in no way required to postpone the launching of the service until accreditation is received.[13]

Resistance to the LPM system emanated almost exclusively from the local broadcasters, which is important to note given that broadcast stations experienced significant ratings declines under the LPM system, while many cable channels experienced significant increases ("For Nielsen, Fear and Loathing in LA," 2004; see also Napoli 2005). Broadcasters were resistant to a measurement system that was likely going to alter the competitive dynamics of their market in a manner that would enhance local cable's ability to compete with local broadcasting for advertising dollars. Resistance to the LPM mirrored what took place at the national level in the 1980s, when the switch to the People Meter also resulted in sudden ratings increases for cable at the expense of broadcast ratings (Adams 1994; Barnes and Thomson 1994).

The most widely accepted explanation for this alteration in ratings patterns is that the participant recall component of the diary system creates a bias in favor of broadcast programs. For a variety of reasons, participants are more likely to recall viewing—or even exaggerate viewing—broadcast than cable programs; that is, diary keepers are more likely to recall and record broadcast television viewing than they are to recall and record cable television viewing. Unhappy with the results of the new system, as well as the increased costs associated with subscribing to it, many broadcasters went for months without subscribing to Nielsen data (Bachman 2002a, 2002b).

As the LPM rollout continued, however, the expressed rationales for broadcaster resistance to the new system changed dramatically, with the resistance focusing on the possibility that the LPM system was under-representing minority television viewers in relation to non-minority viewers (see Hernandez and Elliott 2004a). This claim quickly attracted attention in political and policymaking circles (see Bachman 2004; Hernandez and Elliott 2004b), leading to the formation of an advocacy organization called the Don't Count Us Out Coalition (2004), which comprised a collection of minority advocacy groups and which received its primary financing from News Corp, owner of the FOX broadcast station group (Hoheb 2004; NewsCorp 2004).

Broadcaster resistance to the LPM went further still, resulting in a failed lawsuit seeking an injunction against the rollout of the Los Angeles LPM system (*Univision Communications Inc. v. Nielsen Media Research* 2004), as well as congressional hearings (U.S. Senate 2004), requests by members of Congress for a Federal Trade Commission investigation (Burns 2004), and proposed congressional legislation seeking to establish more direct government oversight over media audience measurement (Fairness and Accuracy in Ratings Act 2005). This legislation was introduced not only in response to specific concerns about the accurate measurement of minority audiences but also because of more general concerns about the dangers of monopoly situations in audience measurement that emerged in the wake of the LPM controversy (ARF 2005).[14]

No legislation was passed, nor was any FTC oversight imposed, and the Nielsen LPM system, though delayed somewhat from its original timetable, has continued its roll-out across the nation's major television markets, with most broadcasters essentially begrudgingly subscribing to the new service. Nielsen did, however, make some concessions, adopting a number of methodological alterations, and doing more to engage with minority communities (see Napoli 2005). The revised audience "currency" that has emerged from this new audience information system was thus affected by the process of stakeholder resistance and negotiation. In addition, these controversies seem to have opened the door to competing local television audience measurement systems (see, e.g., Mandese 2009).

THE INTRODUCTION OF THE ARBITRON
PORTABLE PEOPLE METER

This pattern demonstrated by the Local People Meter case, in which the economic concerns among industry stakeholders and the social policy concerns of policymakers became tightly intertwined, recently repeated itself, with Arbitron's introduction of its Portable People Meter (PPM) radio audience measurement service. The PPM is a portable electronic device intended to gradually replace Arbitron's much-maligned paper listening diaries. The PPM carrier need only carry the device all day (attached to a belt or a purse, etc.), then dock it at night in an Arbitron-provided docking station. All of the relevant listening data are uploaded, aggregated, and linked with the subject's demographic data, so that detailed radio listening reports can be produced—much more quickly, and presumably much more accurately, than can be accomplished via paper diaries, which need to be filled out by each participant and mailed back to Arbitron for tabulation at the end of each week (Arbitron 2007a). Like the LPM, the PPM, with its minute-by-minute data on radio audiences' listening behaviors, has the capacity to contribute to analytical approaches to audience behavior that extend well beyond the very basic exposure metrics that are possible with the much more rudimentary paper diaries.

Arbitron began rolling out its new system via trials in test markets such as Wilmington, Delaware, and Philadelphia, Pennsylvania (McBride 2007). The PPM went "live" in Philadelphia in March 2007 and in Houston in June of the same year (Arbitron 2008). This meant that as of those dates, the PPM data officially replaced the diary data as the "currency" to be used in setting the rates for the buying and selling of radio audiences. PPM data have since become the currency in more than thirty of the largest radio markets in the United States (as of February 2010; see Arbitron 2010).

However, the introduction of the PPM was quickly met with resistance by many within the radio industry and within the public interest and advocacy communities.[15] Industry associations such as the National Association of Black-Owned Broadcasters, the Spanish Radio Association (2008), and the Association of Hispanic Advertising Agencies (2008) asked that Arbitron delay the roll-out of the PPM service (McBride 2007). Public interest and advocacy organizations such as the NAACP (Jealous 2008) and the Minority Media and Telecommunications Council (Miller 2008) soon began expressing concerns about the PPM roll-out as well. Spanish-language broadcaster Univision refused to encode its broadcasts with the PPM signal in a number of markets in which Hispanic audiences comprised a significant portion of the overall radio audiences (Bachman 2009a). Once again, the key criticism being leveled at the new audience measurement system was that the new ratings estimates showed substantially lower listening levels for programmers targeting minority audiences (see Napoli 2009).[16]

The PPM indicates an overall average decline in the average quarter-hour ratings of radio stations of between 15 and 30 percent, with more established and more popular formats experiencing larger ratings declines than new formats.[17] These patterns suggest that the more popular programming, which tends to be consumed in a more habitual manner, was likely being over-represented by diary keepers, while the less habitual listening to less popular stations was being under-reported.[18] Thus, as was the case with the LPM, there appears to be a complex intertwining of self-interest and the public interest in the concerns that have arisen in regards to the PPM.

The Media Rating Council has also been critical of the PPM system. When Arbitron launched its PPM service in Houston, that service did receive accreditation from the MRC prior to "going live" (Arbitron 2007b). However, Arbitron subsequently went live with the PPM in nine other markets without the services in each of those markets receiving MRC accreditation (Downey 2008). Arbitron has continued to go live with the PPM service in dozens of individual radio markets, despite the fact that only the Houston and Riverside, California, PPM systems were operating with MRC accreditation.[19] Critics of Arbitron's willingness to roll out the PPM service without MRC accreditation pointed to the fact that Arbitron executives' performance bonuses were tied to the commercialization of the PPM service (Radio Business Report 2008). Within this context, it should be noted that the PPM service generally carries a subscription price tag that is 60 to 65 percent higher than a subscription to diary data.[20]

As was the case with Nielsen's Local People Meter, concerns about the accuracy of these unaccredited iterations of the PPM service, and their potential impact on minority-targeted radio, have spilled into the governmental arena. At the local level, in September 2008 the New York City Council issued a resolution calling upon the Federal Communications Commission to open an investigation into the PPM service. At the state level, the attorneys general of New York, New Jersey, Florida, and Maryland filed lawsuits against Arbitron, asserting both fraud and civil rights violations,[21] and seeking damages and the cessation of the unaccredited PPM services. Arbitron tried to preempt the action by the New York attorney general by filing its own lawsuit in federal court (*Arbitron v. Andrew Cuomo* 2008a). And at the federal level, in September 2008 the Federal Communications Commission (2008) opened an inquiry into the PPM service aimed at the question of whether a formal FCC investigation into the PPM was appropriate; and in June 2009, the Oversight and Government Reform Committee of the U.S. House of Representatives initiated an investigation into Arbitron's use of the PPM ("Towns opens investigation," 2009; "Towns subpoenas Media Ratings Council," 2009; see also Towns 2009).

The question of whether a formal FCC investigation into the PPM will take place remains unanswered at the time of this writing. The lawsuits filed by the states of New York, New Jersey, and Maryland have all been settled, with Arbitron agreeing to make a number of methodological alterations to its PPM service, most of which focus on the process of sampling individuals to participate in the measurement process—so once again the representation of the audience provided by the new audience information system has been affected.[22] The settlements also include agreements by Arbitron to include more pronounced disclaimers about the limitations of the PPM data in its ratings reports and to provide a small amount of monetary relief to the states and minority broadcaster associations (see, e.g., *Anne Milgram v. Arbitron* 2009; *New York v. Arbitron* 2009).

QUESTIONING THE SPEECH STATUS OF AUDIENCE DATA

What was particularly interesting about these lawsuits was the fundamental questions they raised about the appropriate regulatory treatment of audience measurement services, particularly whether ratings data should be afforded free speech protection under the First Amendment, and therefore be free from any potential government intrusions. The answer to this question has a direct impact on whether policymakers and the courts have the right to influence the operation of audience information systems; this in turn determines the magnitude of any potential role that these stakeholders can play in the process of audience evolution. In some ways it is surprising that the speech status of audience data remains unclear at this point in time. This suggests that this issue will continue to be debated in any future instances in which policymakers or the courts seek to influence or regulate the behavior of audience measurement firms. For this reason, it is important to examine here the specifics of the dispute over the speech status of radio audience ratings that took place between Arbitron and the New York Attorney General (of the three states that have concluded lawsuits against Arbitron, it was the New York lawsuit that proceeded the furthest before being settled).

Looking first at Arbitron's arguments, the firm contended that the states' ability to enjoin the company from issuing PPM-based ratings ran aground against the ratings' status as noncommercial speech. According to Arbitron, any efforts to enjoin distribution of the PPM data represented a prior restraint on protected, noncommercial speech, and were thus a violation of the company's First Amendment rights (*Arbitron v. Andrew Cuomo* 2008a). Noncommercial speech generally receives stronger First Amendment protection than commercial speech (see, e.g., *Central Hudson v. Public Service Commission of New York* 1980). False or deceptive commercial speech is wholly unprotected by the First Amendment. Noncommercial speech, on the other hand, is immune to the forms of prior restraint that were being sought by the attorneys general in their efforts to prevent Arbitron from switching over from the diary to the PPM ratings reports. From this standpoint, any effort to prevent Arbitron from moving forward with its PPM roll-out would represent an unlawful infringement on the company's First Amendment rights. Arbitron went so far as to argue that because the concerns of the attorneys general were directed at the representations of African-American and Hispanic audiences within Arbitron's ratings data, their efforts to prevent the dissemination of the LPM data "constitute a content-based regulation of speech" (*Arbitron v. Andrew Cuomo* 2008b:16).

Unfortunately, the Supreme Court has never offered a clear and definitive set of criteria as to what constitutes commercial speech (see, e.g., Boedecker, Morgan, and Wright 1995; Earnheardt 2004). The court has articulated different criteria in different decisions (Boedecker, Morgan, and Wright 1995).

At the general level, the Court has defined commercial speech as speech that does no more than propose a commercial transaction (*Virginia State Board of Pharmacy v. Virginia Citizen's Consumer Council* 1976). In some decisions, however, additional characteristics have been identified, including (a) whether the communication is an advertisement; (b) whether the communication refers to a specific product or service; (c) whether the speaker has an economic motivation for the speech (see, e.g., *Goran v. Atkins* 2006/2008); (d) whether the speech involves a matter of public rather than private concern; and (e) whether the speech conveys information of interest to audiences beyond potential customers.[23] Some commercial speech decisions also have suggested that expressions of opinion are less able to meet the threshold of classification as commercial speech than are expressions of fact (*Kasky v. Nike* 2002).[24]

The fact that the application of these different criteria has varied across different commercial speech cases helps explain the multifaceted arguments put forth by Arbitron and by the state attorneys general on this issue. In support of its argument that its audience ratings are noncommercial speech, Arbitron emphasized that its ratings "do not propose any offer of sale or other commercial transaction by Arbitron to its subscribers" (2008b:20). Arbitron also referenced the earlier lawsuit (see above) in which Nielsen Media Research was sued by Spanish-language broadcaster Univision over representations of the Spanish-language audience provided by Nielsen's Local People Meter. In this case the court denied Univision's motion to have the LPM service suspended because in the court's view, Univision had failed to demonstrate that the LPM service was flawed, and therefore the motion *had* be denied on this basis (*Univision Communications, Inc. v. Nielsen Media Research* 2004). However, the court also touched on the First Amendment issue, noting that the motion "*should* be denied" on the basis that "the ratings system may qualify as non-commercial speech because, though [the] defendant is a commercial speaker, the intended audience is not necessarily likely to be actual buyers of [the] defendant's services" (*Univision Communications, Inc. v. Nielsen Media Research* 2004:3)." The use of the terms "must" and "should" suggests that the court was less willing to make a definitive statement about the speech status of audience ratings, an interpretation that is further supported by its later statement that "even if the speech is considered commercial, plaintiffs have failed to show that the speech is false" (*Univision Communications, Inc. v. Nielsen Media Research* 2004:3). Here again the court conveys a somewhat tentative perspective on the speech status of audience ratings, which perhaps explains why the attorneys general chose to pursue this line of argument in the PPM case despite this court's decision in regards to the LPM.

Arbitron also contended that its ratings do not qualify as commercial speech because the ratings are "a matter of public interest and concern" (*Arbitron v. Andrew Cuomo* 2008a:5). In support of this point Arbitron noted that its radio ratings are published in a wide variety of mainstream media outlets and trade publications.[25] From this standpoint, Arbitron's construction of the radio audience has a public relevance that extends well beyond those who subscribe to its ratings service, and this broader public relevance is indicative of speech with implications that extend beyond narrow commercial transactions.[26]

Arbitron also contended that its ratings represent "its *opinions* as to the size of radio audiences and station rankings" (*Arbitron v. Andrew Cuomo* 2008a:61; emphasis added). According to Arbitron, "Simply because the final audience measurement estimates are arrived at through statistical analysis and the results are expressed in numerical form does not make them objective facts, nor does it make them unworthy of First Amendment protection" (*Arbitron v. Andrew Cuomo* 2008c:60). Characterizing audience ratings as opinions makes it more difficult to categorize Arbitron's PPM ratings as fraudulent commercial speech, unprotected by the First Amendment, than if the ratings are considered facts. A false opinion is generally seen as an oxymoron in First Amendment jurisprudence, whereas the expression of a false fact can much more easily be characterized as fraudulent and has less First Amendment protection (see *Gertz v. Welch* 1974).[27]

The New York attorney general contended that Arbitron's ratings data are a "statistical service" sold commercially, and thus regulatable "pursuant to state consumer protection and civil rights laws without running afoul of the First Amendment" (*Arbitron v. Andrew Cuomo* 2008d:10). The attorney general argued that the extent to which Arbitron emphasizes the "objectivity" of the PPM service contradicts the company's efforts to characterize its ratings as "opinions," and thus they are more appropriately classified as facts (*Arbitron v. Andrew Cuomo* 2008d:9). The New York attorney general countered Arbitron's characterization of its ratings data as information of "public interest and concern" by noting that Arbitron's full data do not circulate very widely, as they are fully available only to "subscribers who purchase the data for a fee" (*Arbitron v. Andrew Cuomo* 2008d:9). Finally, the New York attorney general also contended that the Supreme Court has established that commercial speech is not limited to advertisements and that commercial speech need not reference a particular product or service (*Arbitron v. Andrew Cuomo* 2008d:10).

Because these lawsuits were ultimately settled out of court, these fundamental questions about the appropriate speech classification for audience ratings, and thus the permissible regulatory approaches to the institutionalized media audience, remain unresolved. As much as the institutionalized media audience has been described in various analyses as a "discursive construct," the specific *kind* of discourse that the institutionalized media audience represents has yet been clearly defined in the legal and policymaking arenas. To the extent to which the construction (and reconstruction) of the institutionalized media audience is increasingly spilling over into the legal and policymaking arenas, this is an issue that requires much more discussion and analysis, so that a workable resolution to this fundamental question regarding the legal status of the institutionalized media audience can be reached.

THE EMERGENCE OF COMPETITION

Finally, within these institutional dynamics surrounding the introduction of the Portable People Meter, it is important to note that the controversy surrounding the PPM's introduction spurred Nielsen to enter the radio audience measurement market as a competitor to Arbitron (Saas 2009a). Nielsen has launched a competing audience measurement service in fifty medium-sized radio markets. Ironically, Nielsen is employing a modified version of the paper diaries that Arbitron is seeking to move away from, though in conjunction with Internet-based "EDiaries," in an effort to make participation more appealing to younger listeners, who tend to resist participating in the diary method (Zornow 2008).

This action suggests that Nielsen may perceive the stakeholder resistance to the PPM to be substantial enough to provide an opening for Nielsen to gain a foothold in the United States radio audience measurement business, which has essentially been a monopoly for decades. And the fact that a less sophisticated methodology is being employed as the mechanism for making inroads into this market is a reminder that technological developments alone do not necessarily drive the construction of the institutionalized media audience.

THE DVR AND THE TRANSITION TO C3 RATINGS

The introduction and diffusion of the DVR is particularly interesting, not only in that it has begun to fundamentally alter the dynamics of television consumption, but because it has done so in such a way as to be directly responsible for the institution of a new currency in the market for television audiences. It was the diffusion of the DVR that ultimately compelled the institution of the C3 rating system, which changed the standard from one based on the size of the audience of a program to one based on the size of the commercial audiences within that program. C3 ratings are the average rating for a commercial contained within a program (Steinberg 2007a). The "3" refers to the fact that the commercial ratings are calculated on the basis of all viewing that takes place within three days of the initial airing, in order to account for the increasing amount of time-shifted viewing facilitated by the growing DVR penetration. Via the C3 ratings, it is now possible to consider the ratings performance of individual programs independently of the ratings performance of commercials, and vice versa. This "unbundling" of information about advertising exposure from information about program exposure is achievable only with the granularity of the minute-by-minute data obtained via People Meters (Picker 2004; see also Kent 2002). Absent audience data gathering and reporting systems capable of distinguishing between content viewership and advertisement viewership (e.g., paper diaries), the unbundling facilitated by the DVR that illuminates how audiences consume television would not be reflected in the representations of audience behavior that serve as the currency in the audience marketplace.

Obviously, the migration to C3 ratings represents a fundamental shift in the dynamics of how television audience exposure is bought and sold (see Atkinson 2008). Advertisers and media buyers in the United States had long been clamoring for some form of commercial ratings that would allow them to pay only for those audiences who were actually exposed to their advertisements. This was a demand that predated the DVR, with origins dating as far back as the widespread diffusion of the remote control device. However, the resistance of program producers and distributors to such a transition was intense, given their interest in preserving an economic model in which all audience members could be monetized, not just those who were exposed to advertisements (see Myers 2007).

The introduction and diffusion of the DVR, with its profound effects not only on commercial exposure but on the timing of program consumption, created a set of circumstances in which some sort of negotiated change to the established currency was unavoidable—particularly in the light of the increasing attractiveness of the Internet as a substitute for television for many advertisers. The result of this process of stakeholder negotiation was the introduction of the C3 ratings system. One key point of dispute in this negotiation process involved the issue of how many days after an initial broadcast should be included in the "currency" rating. Three days was ultimately settled upon as the standard, which means that those viewers who watch a program/commercial beyond the first three days do not count toward the reported size of the commercial audience.

The other key point of dispute involved exactly how a commercial rating would be calculated. In theory each commercial aired could have its own distinct rating calculated—based upon the specific time interval in which it aired. Or, individual commercial "pods" could be rated separately. The final outcome, however, was one in which Nielsen reported an "average commercial minute" for each program, derived from the average ratings level for all commercials within a program (see, e.g., Lafayette 2006; Steinberg 2006). This outcome reflected the interplay of interests of not only programmers, advertisers, and media buyers, but also Nielsen, which faced substantial increases in its own data-processing costs under the more granular options for reporting time-lagged commercial audiences.[28] And it should be noted that as was the case with the LPM and the PPM, the C3 ratings system was instituted without Nielsen first obtaining accreditation from the Media Rating Council (Goetzl 2008).

The processes of stakeholder resistance and negotiation that emerged around the C3 transition and the LPM transition resulted in a near revolt by Nielsen subscribers. In 2009 fourteen of Nielsen's largest clients formed a consortium called the Coalition for Innovative Media Measurement (Hampp 2009a). The purpose of the coalition is to both pressure Nielsen to improve its measurement systems and to assess and consider alternative data providers. The coalition is particularly interested in exploring set-top box measurement systems, as well as systems capable of measuring television audiences across multiple platforms (Atkinson 2009). This action is the latest in a long history of efforts by industry stakeholders to pressure incumbent audience data providers via the threat of supporting emerging competitors. And as has typically been the case in the past, the end result will likely be continued market dominance by Nielsen, but with alterations to Nielsen's technologies, methodologies, and pricing structures.

INTERACTIVITY, AUDIENCE INFORMATION SYSTEMS, AND PRIVACY

Another significant focal point around which stakeholder resistance to new audience information systems has revolved of late has been the issue of appropriate privacy protections for data regarding audiences' media consumption and related behaviors such as search and product purchasing activities. As was noted in chapters 2 and 3, a fundamental element of interactive media is that their users leave a variety of traces that can then be gathered, aggregated, analyzed, and potentially monetized in the audience marketplace. These opportunities to gather information about media audiences—often without their awareness and consent—collide with some interpretations of the level of privacy protection that should be afforded to citizens.

For instance, some privacy scholars have argued that individuals possess a fundamental "right to read anonymously" (Cohen 1996). Modern media platforms increasingly impel audiences to leave behind "digital footprints" of their media consumption, undermining the expectation of privacy established with traditional media—the consumption of which often takes place without audiences leaving behind tangible traces of their activities. Cohen ties this right to read anonymously to broader First Amendment rights, from the standpoint that "the activities of speaking and of receiving information are symbiotic; one cannot exist without the other, and any definition of 'speech' in the constitutional sense properly encompasses both" (1996:1014). Certainly the contemporary media environment, in which the boundary separating speaker from audience is increasingly blurred (see chapter 2), would seem to be one in which the logic of this perspective becomes more compelling. Thus, resistance among many stakeholders—particularly policymakers and privacy advocacy organizations—to ongoing developments in the gathering of audience information via interactive media technologies has remained strong, and this despite the fact that research suggests that individual citizens are becoming less concerned about the privacy issues raised by new communications technologies (see, e.g., Madden et al. 2007).

Perhaps the most high-profile context in which this resistance to new audience information systems has taken place has been the monitoring of online audience behavior. From very early in the history of the Web, media organizations have sought to take advantage of the medium's interactivity in order to engage in detailed monitoring of audience behavior, and to utilize the data gathered from such monitoring for a number of purposes, ranging from the delivery of targeted advertising, to the delivery of more appealing media content, to the delivery of more granular audience data to advertisers. These activities have inspired a tremendous (and growing) body of work in the academic arena dealing with the issue of online privacy (see, e.g., Andrejevic 2007b; Campbell and Carlson 2002; Gandy 1996, 2000; Montgomery 2007; Solove 2004). And more important to this analysis, these activities have motivated substantial resistance from the public interest and advocacy communities (see, e.g., Cooper, Grant, and Murray 2008; Harris 2008) as well as from various government bodies (see, e.g., Federal Trade Commission 2009; Ruane 2009).

The key piece of legislation relevant to these issues is the Electronic Communications Privacy Act (1986), which prohibits the interception of electronic communications, with certain exceptions. The most relevant to the issue of online audience measurement is the exception that allows for the interception of communications with the consent of one of the parties. If, for instance, in the interaction between a Web site and an audience member, the Web site chooses to allow the "interception" of the communication to take place by an audience measurement firm, or by behavioral advertising firms such as DoubleClick or NebuAd, then it would appear that no violation of the Electronic Communications Privacy Act has taken place (see Ruane 2009). However, agreements between Internet service providers and audience measurement or online advertising firms to gather information about audiences' visits to individual Web sites do not necessarily involve the consent of either of the parties to the communication (the audience member or the Web site). Such arrangements are therefore much more likely to represent violations of the Electronic Communications Privacy Act (Ruane 2009).[29]

The Federal Trade Commission (2009) has been investigating the state of online behavioral advertising in an effort to encourage industry self-regulation according to a set of agreed-upon guiding principles.[30] The Federal Trade

Commission (2009), in consultation with industry representatives, the public, and various privacy-focused public interest and advocacy organizations, has proposed a set of self-regulatory principles based on four governing concepts: (a) transparency and control (addressing whether audiences know that their online behavior is being monitored and have some choice about whether to allow the practice); (b) security and limited data retention (addressing whether the data that are gathered are secure and not retained longer than necessary); (c) material changes to privacy policies (addressing whether companies inform audiences of any changes in data collection practices/policies); and (d) affirmative express consent regarding sensitive data (addressing whether companies obtain information related to topics such as children, health, or finances for use in behavioral advertising). Congress has also become deeply enmeshed in the issue of the privacy of online media consumption, holding a number of hearings on the privacy implications of online advertising (see, e.g., U.S. House of Representatives 2008; U.S. Senate 2008a, 2008b) in response to calls from many within the public interest and advocacy communities for more intensive government oversight of these activities (Cooper, Grant, and Murray 2008; Harris 2008).

Many firms operating online have begun to incorporate the FTC's suggested principles into their behaviors (Federal Trade Commission 2009), and the extent to which this continues will ultimately demonstrate how much the evolution of these types of audience information systems is affected by resistance put forth by governmental stakeholders. Along related lines, in the light of Congress' scrutiny of the practice of deep-packet inspection (and the associated threat of direct government regulation of online audience data-gathering), a number of Internet service providers have abandoned its use, at least for the time being (Clifford 2008), indicating a more prolonged time frame for the emergence of this particular audience information system; if it should it ever reemerge, it will likely do so in a modified form that is less intrusive from a privacy standpoint.

On a related front, privacy concerns have also motivated resistance to online platforms that support and aggregate some forms of user-generated content. This resistance has limited the extent to which the data derived from such platforms can feed into the audience information systems that are being developed around them. Social networking sites such as Facebook have been a particular point of focus, in the light of the variety of ways such sites have sought to utilize the incredible volume of data related to individual users (see, e.g., Grimmelmann 2009; Mayle 2008). A complete Facebook profile can contain as many as forty pieces of recognizably personal information, ranging from name, gender, and birthday, to contact information, favorite books and movies, educational and employment history, and product-purchasing behaviors (Grimmelmann 2009). Efforts by Facebook to expand the analytical utility and economic value of such data—by, for instance, changing its terms of service to allow the company *permanent* rights to users' personal information (even after account deletion)—have been met with resistance not only from individual users but also from public interest and advocacy organizations such as the Center for Digital Democracy (Mayle 2008) and the Electronic Privacy Information Center (EPIC) (2009), the latter of which threatened to file a complaint with the Federal Trade Commission. Facebook abandoned its plan to alter its terms of service hours before EPIC filed its complaint with the FTC (Electronic Privacy Information Center 2009).[31] Thus, once again, we see a case of the threat of government intervention resulting in an alteration of the available mechanisms for gathering and analyzing data about media audiences.[32]

IMPLICATIONS FOR AUDIENCE EVOLUTION

As these examples make clear, the introduction of a new audience information system is often a long and contentious process, one in which the audience information system that ultimately emerges can be significantly different from what was originally intended, or from what is technologically feasible, and may in fact face a much longer process from introduction to the widespread adoption that allows it to impose any transformational effects on the audience marketplace. These examples highlight the importance of considering the process of audience evolution as not just a technological phenomenon, but an economic phenomenon, a legal phenomenon, and a political phenomenon as well.

From the standpoint of the evolution of audience information systems currently underway, the ongoing processes of stakeholder resistance and negotiation are directed at a variety of points of transition. These include the greater granularity in exposure data that feeds into some emerging engagement metrics, as well as the ability to exploit as much as is technologically possible the ways in which interactive media are able to provide tangible traces of audience exposure, content creation, and product-purchasing behaviors. The end results of these processes of resistance and negotiation are conceptualizations of the media audience that do not necessarily reflect technology's full potential to capture audience information, and that reflect, to some extent, the specific interests of individual stakeholder groups. In this way, the evolution of media audiences is a reflection not only of new media and new audience measurement technologies, but also of the organizational dynamics of the environment into which these new technologies have been introduced.

CHAPTER 5

THE IMPLICATIONS OF AUDIENCE EVOLUTION

In an interview with the trade publication *Advertising Age,* Alan Wurtzel, president of research and media development at NBC Universal, characterized the current state of audience measurement as a "primordial soup" (quoted in Steinberg 2008b:1). Wurtzel's description of the tools that media organizations use to understand their audiences is certainly in keeping with the evolution analogy around which this book is structured. As this book has attempted to illustrate, the ongoing technological transformations in media consumption and in audience information systems are combining to produce an evolution in the nature of the institutionalized media audience in which the emphasis on exposure, which has predominated since the earliest stages in the rationalization of audience understanding (see chapter 1), is giving way to alternative analytical approaches.

We are now beginning to see the outcomes of this process, as the audience marketplace begins to adjust to the decline in its established conceptualization of the media audience and the rise of alternative approaches to audience understanding. The level of stakeholder consensus around individual performance metrics essential to the traditional functioning of the audience marketplace has yet to emerge (Wurtzel 2009)—but when it does, we are more likely to see the institutionalization of what one audience measurement executive has described as "a basket of currencies."[1] This statement reflects the likelihood that we are in the early stages of the migration to a *post-exposure audience marketplace.* This transition, and its causes, are represented in figure 5.1, where the exposure dimension has becomes a diminished component of a much broader, more multidimensional conceptualization of the audience, and in which the pressures provided by both the transformations in the dynamics of media consumption and the development of new audience information systems simultaneously serve to both reduce the prominence of exposure-based approaches and facilitate the institutionalization of alternative analytical approaches. According to one estimate, more than 20 percent of advertising revenue will shift from impression-based to impact-based formats by 2011 (Berman et al. 2009).

One point that needs to be emphasized about this transition is that the pressures undermining the traditional exposure model are *combining* with the additional audience information obtainable in the new media environment and *together* propelling the current process of audience evolution. The relationship at work is one of mutual causality, in which declines in the viability of the traditional exposure model are compelling alternative analytical approaches, and in which the development of these alternative analytical approaches is a key factor undermining the established exposure model.

Thus a key contention here is that both conditions have to be in place for this evolutionary process to take place. Not only must the dynamics of media consumption be changing in ways that undermine established approaches to audiences, but new audience information systems must be capable of capturing alternative approaches to audiences. Neither element alone can compel an evolution in the institutionalized audience. This is well illustrated by the fact that mechanisms for capturing aspects of audience behavior beyond exposure have existed for many decades, yet they have never been meaningfully embraced by media industries (see chapter 1). The methods of tapping into dimensions of audience behavior that extend beyond exposure existed prior to the advent of the Web and other newer interactive media technologies such as DVRs, mobile phones, and interactive television services (Danaher and Lawrie 1998). As Gunter and Wober note, "Although measurement of audience reactions pre-dated that of audience size measurement, it was the latter which attained prominence" (1992:1).

These alternative audience information systems were never fully institutionalized. They have remained secondary, at best, to exposure-focused information systems. Certainly, interactive media technologies have expanded the boundaries of what can be done in terms of gathering various alternative forms of audience information, but the fact that less technologically sophisticated approaches to gathering this information have long been available is fundamental to one of the central premises of the notion of audience evolution being developed here—that the dominant institutionalized

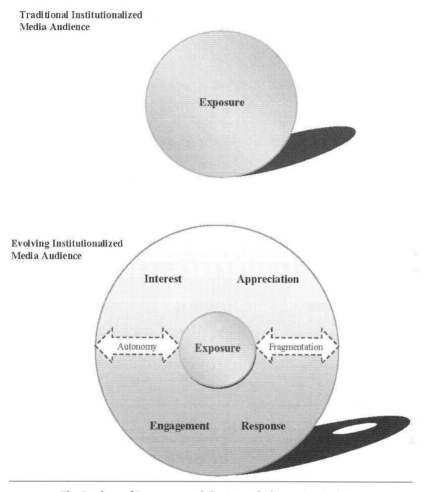

FIGURE 5.1 The Decline of Exposure and the Rise of Alternative Audience
Conceptualizations

conceptualization of the media audience will not change unless the ability to
gather alternative audience information is accompanied by a substantial
breakdown in established audience information systems. Such is the strength
of the institutional forces in favor of the status quo.

As long as the dynamics of media consumption were stable enough to
facilitate the persistence of the exposure model, no evolution in the institutionalized audience was likely to take place. Similarly, without audience

information systems capable of capturing any reconfigured dynamics of audience behavior, then the marketplace would continue to operate under the established approaches to audiences, *even* if the dynamics of media consumption were changing. Research illustrates that media industries responded to the changing dynamics of media consumption only after the emergence of audience information systems capable of reliably documenting these changes. Barnes and Thomson (1988, 1994), for instance, demonstrate that advances in the processing and analysis of audience data spurred advertisers and content providers to begin targeting audiences at the individual, rather than the household, level, in reflection of the fragmenting of the media audience that was already taking place. Absent audience currencies that accounted for this fragmentation, the audience marketplace would have continued to operate under the established conceptualization of the media audience.

When we consider these developments within the context of the overarching process of the rationalization of audience understanding discussed in chapter 1, it may be that the concept of audience evolution that has been developed for this analysis is generalizable to other periods in media history in which substantial alterations in the institutionalized conceptualization of the media audience have taken place. It may thus be worthwhile to explore the applicability of the various components of this concept to important transitional points, such as when individuals, rather than households, become the primary unit of analysis employed by advertisers and content providers (see above), or, for that matter, the point in time coinciding with the rise of our traditional mass media, when audiences first began to be conceptualized primarily as largely passive aggregations (see introduction). These are possible avenues of inquiry for future research.

In any case, this process of audience evolution exemplifies the contention of organizational scholars who have emphasized that the organization of a field is not permanent, but rather is contingent upon institutionalized definitions of what is being transacted (Leblebici et al. 1991:333). Certainly, in terms of the audience marketplace, "the audience changes as we change our perspective" (Freidson 1953:316). However, as this analysis has suggested, the process of audience evolution to some extent follows a path of least resistance, in terms of encapsulating those dimensions of the audience that are most amenable to aggregation and monetization at particular points in time (see, e.g., Gandy 2000; Sorce and Dewitz 2006).

TOWARD A POLITICAL ECONOMY
OF AUDIENCE EVOLUTION

As should certainly be clear at this point, the institutionalized media audience is a highly contested and malleable terrain, susceptible to technological change as well as political and economic pressures. From this standpoint, this analysis has articulated the basic contours of a political economy of audience evolution, one which must account for the interaction of political and economic interests directed at *both* the dynamics of media usage and the dynamics of audience information systems. Each of these contexts demonstrates a complex interplay of political and economic interests capable of influencing the path which the process of audience evolution will follow.

The stakeholder dynamics surrounding many of the new audience information systems discussed in this book illustrate one of the most important aspects of the political economy of audience evolution—it is often questionable at best whether improved accuracy and reliability in audience information systems is something that is legitimately sought by the majority of stakeholders in the market. Frequently, flaws in established systems may in fact serve to tilt the competitive balance in the marketplace in a direction that benefits certain stakeholders to the detriment of others. It is unlikely then that these stakeholders that benefit from the status quo will embrace a new system that adjusts this imbalance.

Research on the measurement of product attributes and its influence on the organization of markets has shown that sellers are motivated to suppress or distort potentially harmful information about their products (Barzel 1982). However, stakeholder resistance that is in all likelihood grounded primarily in economic self-interest can become entangled in broader political concerns (e.g., privacy, diversity), bringing complex, interacting political and economic forces to bear on the process of audience evolution that are certainly capable of influencing the direction the process takes. In his book *The Politics of Numbers*, Paul Starr (1987) introduces the concept of the "statistical system," which he contends consists of both a social and a cognitive structure. The social structure incorporates the social and economic relations of the individuals and organizations involved "in producing flows of data from original sources to points of analysis" (p. 8). The cognitive structure is the structuring of the information itself, "including the boundaries of inquiry, presuppositions about social reality, systems of classification, methods of measurement, and official rules for interpreting and presenting data" (p. 8). A key point that arises from the present analysis is that these two structures are tightly intertwined, with the political and economic dynamics surrounding the social structure feeding into the parameters of the cognitive structure, and the characteristics of the cognitive structure (or any actual or proposed changes to it) having the potential to lead to a wide range of activities and institutional changes at the level of the social structure.

AUDIENCE EVOLUTION AND CONTENT PRODUCTION

A story in the *New York Times Magazine* about the business of audience measurement noted that when you change "the way you measure America's cultural consumption . . . you change America's culture business. And maybe even the culture itself" (Gertner 2005:2). This statement highlights the importance of considering the implications of this process of audience evolution for the production of cultural products.

Sociologists who have studied the production of culture have emphasized the importance of understanding the organizational forms through which cultural products are produced (see, e.g., Pratt 2004). According to Peterson and Anand, "The production of culture perspective focuses on how the symbolic elements of culture are shaped by the systems within which they are created, distributed evaluated, taught, and preserved" (2004:311). The process of audience evolution certainly touches on virtually all of these systems. On the one hand, this analysis has to some extent highlighted a fundamental process of *de-institutionalization* taking place in the realms of content production and distribution, in which audiences are taking a much more active and prominent role than has been the case at least since the dawn of the traditional mass media. From this standpoint, the very definition of creative industries may require reconceptualization (Uricchio 2004); as a result, the processes and systems of cultural production (expanded as they are becoming) may well merit renewed inquiry.

At the same time, the audience autonomy–enhancing technological developments that are facilitating the rise of user-generated content also may encourage the appearance of alternative forms of traditional, institutionally produced media content, as the ways by which audiences can engage with the content—and with each other about the content—continue to expand. Thus one recent analysis has contended that the process of television viewing today—with its increased capacity for re-viewing of episodes, and the ways in which online platforms facilitate not only program promotion, but also extensions of program narratives and interactions amongst audience members—is one that encourages greater narrative complexity and innovation (Ross 2008). Today content producers can feel increasingly comfortable that audiences will engage in a range of activities that extend well beyond the passive watching of a single episode, and that these activities will contribute to audiences' understanding of—and appreciation for—the program (Andrejevic 2008; Costello and Moore 2007). According to Ross (2008), the narratively complex television program *Lost* is very much a product of today's media environment of enhanced audience autonomy and interactivity, since fans can easily re-watch and decipher episodes, as well as engage in online debate, discussion, and information-sharing about the program. Such activities are practically necessary for an audience member to effectively appreciate a program such as *Lost*.

Motion pictures are evolving along a similar path, as the Web continues to develop as a mechanism for engaging movie audiences and extending the moviegoing experience, both before and after the movie is watched. A certain amount of narrative ambiguity is built into films such as the recent monster movie *Cloverfield*, under the expectation that audiences will go online to "connect the narrative dots" (Kung 2008:1). These developments suggest a future not only of greater narrative complexity and ambiguity in our cultural products, but also where the narrative experience associated with any media product extends beyond the primary medium for which it was produced.

In addition, we need to consider the ways in which any evolution in the analytical orientation that media industries apply to their audiences may impact both the process of cultural production and the nature of the cultural products that are produced. We should certainly expect media organizations to respond directly to any change in the criteria by which success is judged. As organizational scholars have noted, organizations will work to conform more closely to the criteria used to construct the measures that assess their performance (Espeland and Sauder 2007). In this regard, the ongoing transition to alternative market information regimes, in which alternative success criteria are likely to operate alongside of (and possibly instead of) traditional exposure-focused success criteria, raises the question of how these changing criteria may affect the nature of the media content that is produced and distributed. This is perhaps one of the most intriguing—if as yet difficult to answer—questions raised by this ongoing process of audience evolution.

We have seen indications that when it comes to certain measures of online audience engagement with advertisements, for instance, social media sites perform significantly better than other types of sites (Morrissey 2009). Data also indicate that, across a number of emerging engagement indicators, reality television programs perform significantly better than scripted programs (Friedman 2009d). Such findings point to possible ways in which new performance metrics may ultimately alter the competitive playing field in the audience marketplace and encourage the production of certain content types over others.

Related to such findings, we have also seen indications that media content that performs well according to traditional exposure-based performance metrics does not necessarily perform well according to alternative metrics, such as engagement, recall, or appreciation, and vice versa (see, e.g., "Optimedia U.S. Launches Content Power Ratings," 2008). For instance, songs and television programs that do not rate very high according to traditional exposure-based measures (such as sales charts and Nielsen ratings) often prove to be among the most popular when they are assessed by alternative measurement criteria, such as how much songs and television programs are featured in the online conversations found in social networking and social media sites (O'Malley 2008; Lafayette 2008b), or in terms of the "stickiness" of (i.e., time spent with) the content (Friedman 2010).

These patterns suggest that should the criteria for success truly become somewhat more diverse, we would see a greater diversity of types of content produced. Alternative success criteria may ultimately support—and encourage—the production of content that would not have been viable under traditional metrics of success. The breaking down of the absolute primacy of attracting large numbers of the right kind of audience members (i.e., audience size and demos)—and with the right kind of audience members defined in such a way as to be at best tenuously linked to the reality of who is and who is not the right kind of audience member (see Napoli 2003a)—has the potential to be monumentally liberating to the processes of cultural production. A media environment in which audiences' engagement in, and appreciation of, the content they consume is as valuable (or perhaps even more so) as the size and demographic composition of the audience is one that has the potential to support content forms that resonate powerfully with segments of the media audience that would otherwise be too small to encourage the production of content serving their particular needs and interests.

However, while we may have reason to be optimistic about the diversifying effects of the rise of alternative success criteria, these possibilities must be weighed against the possible negative effects of the even further rationalization of audience understanding that is reflected in the development and institutionalization of alternative audience information systems. As was noted in chapter 1, critics of the rationalization of audience understanding have frequently emphasized its potentially stultifying effects on the creative process. The primary critique often revolves around how appropriate it is for the creative process to be guided by extant information about audiences' tastes and preferences.

These concerns can be elevated to an entirely new level today, as new audience information systems provide new opportunities to gauge audience tastes and preferences—and to utilize this information in content production decision-making—to a perhaps unprecedented extent. Journalism, for instance, is being confronted with a variety of new opportunities for audience information to guide journalistic decision-making. The term "calibrated journalism" is now being applied to the ways in which online news sources utilize the wealth of audience data obtained through the Web to make determinations about which kinds of stories to cover, as well as which columnists to hire and fire (Anderson 2009; MacGregor 2007; Wasserman 2008). While it is certainly the case that the news business has become increasingly sensitive to audience tastes and preferences over the years (McManus 1994), these new tools bring a level of granularity to the analytical process that is only possible in today's media environment of enhanced interactivity and the disaggregation of content into smaller, more discrete analytical units (e.g., individual stories, individual columnists, etc.). Some research has suggested that these new information sources are undermining traditional journalistic "instincts" and established "news values" in ways that suggest a fundamental evolution in news professionalism (Anderson 2009; MacGregor 2007).

The influence of the increasingly interactive media environment on journalism is perhaps most dramatically reflected in the emergence of "community-funded journalism" sites such as Spot.us, which proposes a set of possible topics for its investigative journalism and then investigates those that receive the largest financial contributions via online payments from the site's visitors. Exactly how the journalistic product changes in a media environment in which information about consumer demand can be even more extensively gathered and analyzed should be a focal point for journalism research going forward.

Some research suggests that innovation in content production is inhibited when audience information plays a prominent role in decision-making (see, e.g., Ahlkvist and Fisher 2000; Born 2002). Is this a pattern that will persist in this next stage in the rationalization of audience understanding? Or will the nature of the new audience information that is being gathered affect content production differently? Answering these questions will involve examining the similarities and differences in the representations of audiences' tastes and preferences provided by new versus traditional audience information systems, as well as identifying any possible alterations in how, and to what extent, new audience information is influencing decision-making relative to the role of traditional audience information. Future research also needs to investigate if, and to what extent, content producers' perceptions of the analytical utility of new audience information systems, and the extent to which they rely upon them, differ from their views of more traditional audience information systems.

Nevertheless, today much of the work of strategic thinkers and management consultants who serve the media and communications industries consistently emphasizes the need for decision-making processes to be even further guided by the systematic analysis of audience data. As one consulting report recently noted:

> Media companies need to build a foundation of data, information and customer relationship management. . . . Content owners, often new to this game, will have to learn fast about data mining, profile building and predictive analytics. Historically, they have been one or two steps removed from actual transactions with consumers. To get access to the information they need, content owners will have to invest in more direct consumer interaction or structure distribution deal terms to include information-sharing components.   (Berman et al. 2007:19)

At the same time, however, there are substantial concerns within the media and advertising industries that the scope and granularity of today's audience information represents a potential information overload[2] scenario, given that the analytical resources that many organizations are devoting to audience information are by many accounts not keeping pace with the increasing volume of available data.[3] Some industry observers have identified what they see as a "talent gap," in which individuals with the necessary analytical expertise are not yet filling media industry positions that increasingly require more advanced analytical skills.[4] The literature on the role of information in organizations tells us that in such situations decision-makers typically carve out a subset of the available information to be relied upon in their analyses and decision-making (Edmunds and Morris 2000). This is a common technique for coping with information overload. The danger, of course, is that the subset of information that is relied upon will, when analyzed, lead to very different (and possibly incorrect) conclusions than would have been reached had a larger subset, or perhaps even the entirety, of available information been analyzed.

The irony here is that while the sphere of institutionalized cultural production continues to become ever more rationalized in its approach to understanding audiences, this sphere of cultural production is now increasingly competing with an array of cultural products originating from well outside of traditional institutional production contexts (e.g., user-generated content) that, for the most part, arise from no such highly rationalized approaches to audience understanding. Of course, these differing approaches to audience understanding represent only one of a number of important points of distinction between the processes surrounding the production of traditional media content and user-generated content. Further exploration of the differing production and consumption dynamics of—and possible tensions between—traditional and user-generated media content should be a focal point for future scholarship.

AUDIENCE EVOLUTION AND MEDIA POLICY

From a media policy standpoint, the issues addressed in this book touch upon two spheres of media policymaking. The first, more specific sphere, involves policymaking surrounding the operation—and possible regulation—of audience measurement firms. The second, more general sphere, involves media policy more broadly, and the ways in which the evolution of media audiences may affect the analytical frameworks and normative goals that guide regulation and policymaking related to media and communications industries.

THE REGULATION OF THE AUDIENCE MEASUREMENT INDUSTRY

At a very specific level, this analysis has touched upon an issue that has received an increasing amount of attention in recent years (particularly in the U.S.)—that of the appropriate regulatory treatment of organizations involved in the business of audience measurement. As was noted in chapter 4, the controversy surrounding Nielsen's introduction of the Local People Meter spurred the introduction in Congress of the Fairness and Accuracy in Ratings Act, which proposed more direct regulatory oversight of audience measurement firms. And more recently, a similar controversy surrounding Arbitron's introduction of the Portable People Meter, and the potentially privacy-invading activities of Web sites such as Facebook and online audience measurement firms such as DoubleClick and NebuAd, have spurred further governmental inquiries and actions. Finally, and perhaps most important, many of the clients of these audience measurement firms are among the most vocal advocates for some form of governmental regulation (see, e.g., Chagrin 2005) or, at the very least, some more intensive form of industry self-regulation.[5]

It is striking that current debates about the pros, cons, and even the legality (as was illustrated in chapter 4) of government intervention in the audience measurement industry do not yet seem to be grounded in any concrete consensus as to the speech status of audience data, and consequently the permissibility of government regulation in this context. The stakeholder debates over the speech status of audience ratings discussed in chapter 4, however, neglected some potentially relevant analytical perspectives, which are briefly touched on here.

Audience Data as "Social Facts"

The question of whether audience data are best characterized as fact or opinion remains largely unresolved in the rather sparse jurisprudence surrounding audience measurement. The Supreme Court has been reasonably precise in articulating its definition of a fact. Facts, according to the Court, are not original; they are discovered rather than created.[6] Historical accounts of the meaning of a fact have emphasized the centrality of numbers. Poovey, for instance, notes that "numbers have come to epitomize the modern fact, because they have come to be seen as preinterpretive or even somehow noninterpretive at the same time that they have become the bedrock of systematic knowledge" (1998:xii). This perspective strengthens a possible association between facts and audience data. An opinion, by contrast, is something that cannot be proven right or wrong. Key defining elements of an opinion that courts have used to distinguish opinion from fact include: (a) whether a statement has a precise core of meaning for which a consensus of understanding exists; (b) the verifiability of the statement; (c) the broader context or setting in which a statement appears (see Shapo 1997).

There is no doubt a certain amount of cognitive dissonance that emerges from the contention that audience data on the one hand represent the *opinions* of measurement firms, but on the other hand serve as what these firms describe as *accurate* and *objective* currency in the audience marketplace (see *Arbitron v. Andrew M. Cuomo* 2008b). The term "accurate" suggests some sort of relationship to factuality. Representations of the audience produced by measurement firms, however, are the outgrowth of a number of subjective decisions and opinions about how best to go about constructing the audience. Decisions about technology design, sample generation and recruitment, and data processing all affect the construction of the audience that ultimately serves as the currency in the audience marketplace (Webster, Phalen, and Lichty 2006). Changes in the process can lead to very different audiences. It is hard to accept a construct that is this malleable as a fact (see, e.g., Ang 1991; Buzzard 1990; Meehan 1984).

However, in making this fact versus opinion determination, perhaps it is also appropriate to consider how audience data are used by subscribers. Even if audience data do not clearly meet the threshold associated with the traditional definition of facts, they nonetheless seem to operate as facts in the functioning of the marketplace for media audiences. Media sociologist Todd Gitlin, for instance, noted that "in the tumult of everyday figuring and judging, network executives, even research specialists, often commit the standard occupational error of unwarranted precision. . . . Once managers agree to accept a measure, they act as if it is precise. They 'know' there are standard errors—but what a nuisance it would be to act on that knowledge. And so the number system has an impetus of its own" (1983/2000:53).[7]

Clearly then, audience data seem frustratingly resistant to categorization as either fact or opinion. There may be a tenable intermediate position, however, that can be ascribed to constructions of the audience produced by audience measurement firms. Specifically, some legal scholars have asserted the need for the courts to acknowledge a category of "'created facts,' . . . in which the expressive work brings the very facts themselves into existence" (Hughes 2007:45; see also Gordon 1992). John Searle offers a potentially valuable middle ground that acknowledges that "there are portions of the real world, objective facts in the world, that are only facts by human agreement" (1995:1). Such instances have been termed "social facts." According to Searle (1995), a social fact arises when: (a) someone declares or states that something is the case; and (b) when it becomes widely accepted that something is the case. This notion of facts by human agreement seems particularly applicable to the nature of audience constructions that serve as currency in the audience marketplace. Such audience currencies involve the unanimous acceptance and utilization of a particular set of social constructions as facts. Searle even uses currency as a prime example of a social fact (1995:55).

Drilling deeper into this notion of social facts, we find subcategories that seem particularly attributable to audience data. Specifically, legal scholar Justin Hughes identifies what he terms "evaluative facts," which involve quantitative or qualitative evaluations made by private parties that "can become so widely accepted and so relied upon for substantial non-expressive activities that they become social facts" (2007:68). Hughes' examples of evaluative facts include a publisher's estimates of the resale value for used automobiles, price estimates for collectible coins, and settlement prices established by a commodities exchange committee. All of these examples involve the setting of values for products, not unlike the way audience measurement firms' assessments of media audiences set values for advertisers.

Such efforts to develop an intermediate construct between fact and opinion/expression have been focused primarily on the copyright implications of such a shift. Hughes (2007), for instance, has advocated on behalf of the notion of "created facts," but has done so while also advocating for maintaining copyright protection for such facts when judged appropriate. This is relevant here because it is important to recognize that a legal path could potentially be traveled in which audience data are classified as facts of a sort for the purposes of fraud assessments and commercial versus noncommercial speech determinations (see below), but such a classification would not necessarily deny measurement firms the copyright protection needed to sufficiently incentivize them to produce their product (given that facts typically are not copyrightable).

Audience Data as Non-Speech

Just as the strict fact/opinion dichotomy may be an inadequate basis for legal and public policy decisions regarding audience data, so too may be the strict commercial/noncommercial speech dichotomy on which legal debates about audience measurement have focused. The difficulties (discussed in chapter 4) associated with assigning audience data to either the commercial or the noncommercial speech category suggest that perhaps we should dare ask the question: Are audience data speech at all? Many scholars of media industries and media audiences have often critically described the media audience as represented in ratings as a "discursive construct," suggesting that audience ratings should very much be considered a form of speech. How, however, do we reconcile the fact that something can be simultaneously described as a *discursive construct,* the *currency* used in economic exchange, and an *opinion,* yet marketed and purchased on the basis of its claimed *objectivity* and *accuracy*? Perhaps with audience data we are not really talking about something that fits within the parameters of speech established in First Amendment jurisprudence.

A number of legal scholars have emphasized the wide range of forms of communication that take place in the commercial sector that have very little, if any, First Amendment protection (see Weinstein 2002). Frederick Schauer, for instance, notes that there is "a universe of communication relating only to business activity, having no explicit political, artistic or ideological content, and yet differing substantially from the kind of widespread hawking of wares" traditionally associated with commercial speech (1988:1183). Examples range from

> communications to offerees, stockholders, and investors now regulated by various state and federal securities laws, including the Securities Act of 1933 and the Securities Exchange Act of 1934; numerous communications among business executives about prices and business practices now regulated by the Sherman Antitrust Act; communications about working conditions and the like now regulated by the National Labor Relations Act; representations about products and services now regulated by the Federal Trade Commission and the Food and Drug Administration; representations about products now regulated by various consumer protections, by the Uniform Commercial Code, and by the common law of

warranty and contract; statements about willingness to enter into a contract now regulated by the common law of contract; and so on and on. (Schauer 1988:1183–1184)

From this perspective, "Commercial speech doctrine is thus not merely about the boundary that separates commercial speech from public discourse, but also about the boundary that separates the category of 'commercial speech' from the surrounding sea of commercial communications that do not benefit from the protections of the doctrine" (Post 2000:21). The point here, then, is that there are essentially some forms of communication that take place in the commercial sector that do not even trigger the need for a First Amendment analysis.

This perspective of course raises the question of what then does trigger a First Amendment analysis. As Post (2000) illustrates, the answer comes largely from *Spence v. Washington* (1974), in which the Supreme Court acknowledged that not all forms of conduct can be labeled as speech, even if the individual engaging in the conduct intends to express an idea. Instead the Court determined that First Amendment scrutiny would be triggered only when "an intent to convey a particularized message was present, and in the surrounding circumstances the likelihood was great that the message would be understood by those who viewed it" (pp. 410–411). This *Spence* test has been used by lower courts to guide their decisions about whether to apply First Amendment protection (Post 2000).

Post (1995) however, contends that the *Spence* test provides an inaccurate set of criteria regarding when the First Amendment has been brought to bear, arguing that the determination as to whether a First Amendment analysis is appropriate has also considered the social context. He illustrates this point with the example of flight navigation charts, which, while certainly a medium of communication for particular messages, have, when accused of being inaccurate, been treated in the courts as products under product liability law rather than as speech receiving First Amendment protection. This is the case because, "First Amendment analysis is relevant only when the values served by the First Amendment are implicated. These values do not attach to abstract acts of communication as such, but rather to the social contexts that envelop and give constitutional significance to acts of communication" (Post 1995:1255).

The question then is: Does the production and dissemination of data such as those produced by audience measurement firms necessarily meet these criteria for consideration as the type of expressive activity that falls within the purview of the First Amendment? A number of analyses that have focused on the appropriate analytical lens to apply to commercial databases have concluded that the answer may be no, that the information contained within commercial databases does not meet the criteria necessary to trigger a First Amendment analytical framework (see, e.g., Richards 2004). One could certainly see that the same logic would be equally applicable to a subject such as audience data. Essentially, audience data may be closer to a navigation chart or medicine label than they are to a book or a newspaper, and thus may perhaps best be considered within the large collection of forms of commercial communication that long have resided largely outside of the parameters of First Amendment protection.

MEDIA POLICY IN AN ERA OF AUDIENCE EVOLUTION

One of the key developments that has been chronicled in this book has been the breaking down of the traditional distinctions between media audiences and content providers—a process that essentially heralds the de-institutionalization of our media system, in that the privileged position of our traditional media institutions is declining, as the high barriers to entry and access and capacity limitations of existing distribution systems that historically have maintained this separation diminish. The policy implications arising from these reconfigured dynamics are only just beginning to be thoroughly assessed (see, e.g., Benkler 2006; Pascu et al. 2007; Zittrain 2008). One thing, however, is clear: policy or First Amendment models that overwhelmingly focus on, or inherently privilege, the traditional institutional communicator no longer make any sense.

For decades public interest advocates and legal scholars advocated an approach to media policy that emphasized citizens' right of "access to the media" (see, e.g., Barron 1967). The essence of this argument was that in a media environment characterized by scarcity of media outlets (given the limited range of broadcast frequencies, or the high financial barriers to entry associated with other mass media such as newspapers, magazines, cable systems, or cable networks), media policy needed to carve out a small amount of space within these media for access that extended their use beyond the select few owners of these outlets. Thus we saw policies such as the Fairness Doctrine in broadcast television and public access channels in cable television that sought to grant some access to the media for speakers other than the institutional communicators who owned those media outlets.

With the diffusion of the Internet to the point where it is a communications platform that is arguably as pervasive, if not more pervasive, than any of our traditional mass media platforms, and its relative ease of access (i.e., very low barriers to entry), individual Internet users stand on closer to equal footing with the traditional institutional communicators in terms of their access to the media. Consequently, one could argue that the access to the media problem is now much less of a problem than it once was (Barron 2007).[8] We are therefore much closer today to being able to achieve the inherent First Amendment objective of a "democratic culture," which is a culture where "individuals have a fair opportunity to participate in the forms of meaning making that constitute them as individuals" (Balkin 2004:3). A democratic culture is one in which "ordinary people [participate] freely in the spread of ideas and in the creation of meanings that constitute them and the communities and subcommunities to which they belong" (Balkin 2004:4).

In an environment in which most audience members have an opportunity to be speakers, the performance criteria for our media policies need to be recalibrated to reflect the performance potential for our media system. And, in a media environment in which our major media institutions are increasingly serving functions focused on content aggregation, recommendation, and location (i.e., search), policymakers' focus needs to shift as well, to ensure that these functions are being performed in a way that maximizes the communicative potential of our dramatically reconfigured media system.[9]

For this kind of widespread distribution of the ability to freely participate in both the *creation* and the *spread* of ideas to be fully realized, policymakers need to focus their attention on the issues that arise after access to the media has been achieved. This next stage in the access process involves access to audiences (see, e.g., Napoli and Sybblis 2007). The difference between access to the media and access to audiences is that the notion of access to the media essentially stops with access to the means of producing and distributing a message. Access to audiences picks up where access to the media leaves off by encompassing the *extent* of the speaker's capacity to distribute a message, and how the capacities to do so are distributed across speakers. Thus, access to audiences goes beyond speakers' rights to express themselves; it also encompasses, to a greater extent than the right of access to the media, their right to have an opportunity be heard—their right to participate in the spread of ideas that is a fundamental element of a truly democratic culture.

Two speakers with access to the media can vary tremendously in their level of access to audiences. A broadcast licensee in New York City traditionally has had much greater access to audiences than a licensee in Omaha. A cable network available in 80 million homes traditionally has had much greater access to audiences than a cable network available in 10 million homes. A musician signed with a major record label traditionally has had much greater access to audiences than a musician signed to an independent label. A Web site that is among the top five sites returned on a search query has greater access to an audience than a Web site ranked 1,012 in that same search query. Differing levels of access to audiences are widespread and to some extent unavoidable, and certainly do not necessarily represent policy problems requiring attention. But these examples do illustrate that the notion of access to audiences can provide a somewhat more rigorous and more nuanced set of analytical criteria than does the notion of access to the media.

Perhaps the most important difference is that the right of access to audiences has a more established foundation in First Amendment theory than the right of access to the media. From a First Amendment standpoint, the right of access to audience is grounded in the traditionally privileged First Amendment rights of the speaker, whereas the right of access to the media emerged from, and has been justified by, the less traditional notion that the audience has a First Amendment right of access to a diverse array of sources of information (see Napoli and Sybblis 2007). This means that policy arguments grounded in a right of access to audiences are on stronger First Amendment footing than policy arguments grounded in a right of access to the media. This also means that media policymaking that promotes and is reflective of the full array of traditional First Amendment values must also focus on protecting and promoting speakers' First Amendment rights of access to audiences. And in pursuit of a truly democratic culture, policymakers should work toward equality in the distribution of this First Amendment right.

As the examples above show, there have always been different levels of access to audiences, even among those with access to the media. These differing levels are commonplace and to some extent unavoidable. These variations have generally seldom been thought of as violations of anyone's free speech rights or as policy problems requiring attention, and more often than not they are not. Most imbalances in speakers' access to audiences could be thought of as unavoidable byproducts of the technological and economic characteristics of our media system. Differentiated levels of access to audiences do represent a potential policy problem requiring attention, however, when the processes of aggregation, recommendation, and search that are the focus of activity for many contemporary media organizations involve discriminatory criteria or practices. According to one recent analysis of this issue, "if selection intermediaries block or discriminate against a speaker on grounds that listeners would not have selected" (Chandler 2007:1095), then a denial of a speaker's right of access to audiences has taken place.

For instance, the net neutrality issue can be approached as an access to audiences issue. The discriminatory mechanisms that broadband service providers can employ to selectively block, disrupt, or slow the flow of Web traffic are essentially mechanisms for creating differentiated levels of access to audiences among speakers (Chandler 2007). And most important, broadband service providers are engaging in these activities from a position more akin to that of a common carrier than of a publisher or programmer. In this regard, from a First Amendment standpoint the net neutrality issue is about online speakers' rights to reach audiences and how those rights stack up against the First Amendment claims of broadband service providers, who would seem to bear a much more tenuous resemblance to traditional speakers than do the operators of the Web sites who communicate across the Internet, but who nonetheless are in a position to act as gatekeeper for the content that travels over their networks.

The protocols in the operation of Web search engines also raise significant access to audience issues, as the placement order of Web sites in search engine listings is a key factor in determining the level of access to audiences enjoyed by different sites (see Chandler 2007; Napoli 2008). Some analysts have suggested that regulatory oversight of the operation of search engines is necessary, appropriate, and fully defensible on First Amendment grounds, given the importance of search engines to online communication and the wide range of mechanisms via which search engine operators can distort and block the results of search queries (see, e.g., Bracha and Pasquale 2008; Helft 2008). Yet these arguments have tended to focus on the First Amendment rights of search engine operators (and the limits of these rights), to the neglect of the First Amendment rights of the Web sites seeking access to audiences via search engines. Here the incorporation of an access to audiences analytical framework could potentially strengthen arguments surrounding the need for regulatory oversight of search engines, as a relevant First Amendment concern would be brought to the table that has to this point been largely neglected.

As should be clear, in a media environment in which the processes of production and distribution are becoming increasingly de-institutionalized because of the elimination of many of the technological barriers that traditionally have separated media organizations from audiences, policy objectives need to become de-institutionalized as well. That is, policymakers need to shift their orientation away from the traditional functions of traditional media organizations and instead focus on preserving and promoting a media system in which individual audience members and media organizations are on equal footing in terms of their ability to access audiences. Doing so involves focusing on those remaining chokepoints in the dissemination and reception of information that enable institutional actors to operate in ways that undermine the potential for a truly democratic culture that is inherent in how the new media environment is changing the nature of the media audience. As audiences evolve, media policy needs to evolve along a similar trajectory as well.

AUDIENCE EVOLUTION AND MEDIA SCHOLARSHIP

Finally, it is important to consider what the process of audience evolution means for the study of media industries and audiences. That is, what does the ongoing reconceptualization of the institutionalized media audience that is taking place mean for media scholarship? Media scholars have long taken a diverse range of approaches to the study of media audiences, some of which have tracked fairly closely with industry approaches (e.g., ratings analysis), and some of which have taken widely divergent—even oppositional—approaches.

Let us first consider what the process of audience evolution means for academic approaches that are more closely aligned with those of the media and advertising industries. As Mosco and Kaye (2000) have noted, the convenience of using commercially produced audience data has likely played an influential role in academic conceptualizations of the audience. This is particularly the case for the sector of academic audience research typically referred to as ratings analysis (Webster, Phalen, and Lichty 2006), which historically has relied upon the syndicated audience data sources used by media organizations and advertisers to engage in a wide range of analyses of media audiences. Some of these analyses address questions and problems reflective of those of interest to media industries; some utilize commercial audience data sources to explore questions and problems that extend well beyond those of concern to industry stakeholders (see Webster, Phalen, and Lichty 2006). However, regardless of the specific questions being asked, the answers are explored via data that reflect the established conceptualization of the audience within the media industries and the audience measurement firms that serve them.

The ongoing process of audience evolution raises interesting questions about how the field of ratings analysis should be defined. Is the focal point of the definition the aspect of media consumption that is being analyzed? That is, is ratings analysis to be defined in terms of the measurement and analysis of *audience exposure* via syndicated data sources? This is the focus of the definition of ratings analysis provided by Webster, Phalen, and Lichty (2006) in their well-known ratings analysis text. According to the authors, ratings analysis involves the analysis of "a body of data on people's exposure to electronic media" (p. 11). However, if ratings analysis continues to be defined so narrowly, then its academic utility may diminish, given the declines in the comprehensiveness and analytical utility of exposure data that were described in chapter 3.

For the academic audience researcher, ratings data are becoming an inadequate representation of audiences' media exposure—particularly if that researcher is interested in the distribution of audience attention across the full range of available content options, as opposed to just the most popular ones (which are still measured comparatively well by traditional measurement approaches), or across a broad range of demographic groupings. It may be the case that many of the questions central to the operation of the audience marketplace can still be answered by audience information systems capable of rigorously capturing data on only a portion of available television networks, radio stations, or Web sites. However, it seems an increasingly tenuous proposition that a thorough understanding of the full scope of audience behavior, with the level of rigor that should characterize academic social science, can be achieved by data sources that are becoming less and less comprehensive in terms of their ability to capture the distribution of media audiences. In this regard, the range of questions that can be effectively answered via traditional ratings analysis is narrowing. These developments suggest that a definition of academic ratings analysis that is oriented around the analysis of audience exposure is one that spells an inevitable decline for this field of inquiry.

More appropriate would be an alternative approach in which ratings analysis is defined in terms of the source and purpose of the data being analyzed. That is, ratings analysis may be more usefully defined as the analysis of the data (whatever their orientation) used by media industry stakeholders to assess performance and success in the audience marketplace. Such a definitional approach imbues the field with the flexibility necessary to adapt to various stages of audience evolution. If this definitional stance is adopted, then we see that we are simply at the beginning of an evolutionary stage in academic ratings analysis, as alternative criteria for monetizing media audiences—such as recall, engagement, and appreciation—emerge alongside exposure and are accompanied by the same kind of large-scale syndicated commercial databases that have long been associated with ratings analysis. From this standpoint, the nature of "ratings" is changing—or more accurately, expanding; and the nature of the questions that can be investigated by ratings analysis can expand accordingly. From this perspective, this is a very exciting time to be engaged in ratings analysis, as this research tradition is essentially in a period of reinvention.

Those academic approaches to audience research that have traditionally deviated significantly from media industry approaches tend to focus on issues such as how audiences interpret, interact with, and respond to media content (see Nightingale 1996). These approaches have often taken particular issue with the oversimplifications of audiencehood inherent in the conceptualizations of media audiences employed in the media industries (see, e.g., Ang 1991; Bielby and Harrington 1994; Mosco and Kaye 2000). Much of the work in this vein has also taken a strongly oppositional stance to approaches to audience understanding that employ quantitative rather than qualitative research methods. From a methodological standpoint, then, the gulf between academic audience research in this vein and the audience information systems utilized by media industries is likely to remain substantial, because the approaches emerging to examine aspects of audiencehood such as appreciation, engagement, and response continue to rely upon highly quantitative methodological approaches, as industry stakeholders as a whole continue to remain resistant to more qualitative approaches to audience understanding. According to Davies and Sternberg (2007), qualitative approaches to audience understanding remain "undervalued by the industry. At best, alternative forms of research such as focus groups appear an interesting supplement to the ratings. At worst . . . a challenge to the ratings authority" (Davies and Sternberg 2007:38).

However, from a conceptual standpoint, a tighter alignment between media industry approaches to audiences and those of the academic audience researchers who have traditionally been critical—if not hostile—to industry approaches seems possible. One cannot help but wonder whether it might be possible to bridge the substantial disconnect between these academic audience researchers and their industry counterparts that developed soon after the days in which Paul Lazarsfeld worked closely with the motion picture and radio industries (Livingstone 1998). Might, for instance, the ongoing transition in the nature of the institutionalized media audience represent a window of opportunity for scholars who have already been examining these aspects of audience behavior—which have traditionally resided at the margins of media industry concerns—to offer input into how the industry's ongoing reconceptualization of media audiences should take shape?

From a purely academic standpoint, these developments would also seem to represent an opportunity for a bridging of the gulf that has developed between those audience researchers who engage in ratings analysis and those who engage in more qualitative approaches to audience behavior, given the greater congruence (at least superficially) that appears to be developing in the aspects of audience behavior under examination in these historically divergent research traditions. If the nature of this gulf is purely methodological (i.e., quantitative versus qualitative), then the developments taking place will likely have no effect in terms of unifying the audience research field, as the "new" audience information systems will still cater to the media and advertising industries' established (and likely unchangeable) desire for quantitative data and performance metrics. Similarly, if the nature of the gulf is primarily ideological (i.e., focused around opposition to, versus cooperation with, the interests of commercial media organizations), then there is once again relatively little likelihood of seeing a coming together of these research traditions, as the data utilized in ratings analysis still will reflect the commercial imperatives of media industries.

However, if the nature of this division is more theoretical (i.e., involving the appropriate conceptualizations of audiences' media consumption), then it would seem that the move within the media industries and audience measurement organizations to look beyond exposure has the potential to narrow, at least somewhat, the divide between these research traditions. This prediction presumes that scholars currently engaged in ratings analysis will be flexible and adaptable in response to changes taking place in the realm of audience measurement, and will embrace the new audience metrics emerging in place of the declining exposure metrics. Since such researchers tend often to approach their subject from a standpoint grounded in the economics of media industries or the behavior of media institutions, this would seem to be a safe presumption. Scholars with such an analytical orientation are often less concerned with understanding the audience per se than with understanding media industries and institutions via their engagement with audiences—whatever analytical form these audiences take.

It is obviously this perspective on the relationship between media and audiences that has been the focus of this book. This book has made clear that the process by which the meaning of the audience is determined by our media institutions is as important to our understanding of them as the particular meaning that is reached.

NOTES

INTRODUCTION

1. For exceptions, see Roscoe 1999 and Siapera 2004.
2. Oswell goes so far as to argue that "audiences are invented" (2002:2). Bratich describes audiences as "discursive constructs" (2005:243). Similarly, Allor contends that the "audience exists nowhere; it inhabits no real space, only positions within analytic discourses" (1988:228). For alternative perspectives on Allor's (1988) assertion, see Hartley 1988 and Lull 1988.
3. Napoli (2003a) discusses the "double jeopardy effect" that often has been found in audience research, in which content with small audiences suffers from the compounded problem that these small audiences also tend not to be very loyal (see, e.g., Barwise and Ehrenberg 1988). Napoli notes that the fact that the audience data for content that attracts small audiences is typically less accurate and less reliable than the data for content that attracts larger audiences represents an additional challenge for niche content providers, leading to a "triple jeopardy effect" (2003a:90).
4. Anand and Peterson (2000) use the term *market information regimes* in reference to the various environmental surveillance tools—including audience data sources—used by industries to make sense of their competitive environment. Thus anything ranging from the *Billboard* music charts (McCourt and Rothenbuhler 1997), to television and radio ratings (Webster, Phalen, and Lichty 2006), to publishing industry best-seller lists (Andrews and Napoli 2006; Korda 2001), to monthly reports on the top 100 Web sites (Bermejo 2007), all represent fundamental market information regimes used by industry decision-makers to assess their environment and formulate appropriate responses to environmental changes.
5. Razlogova, for instance, documents how, by the 1940s, the commercial radio industry in the U.S. had embraced a "closed formal process" (1995:3) in terms of program production that largely ignored audience responses and feedback except in the more limited form associated with syndicated program ratings.

Billings (1986) similarly chronicles a "silencing of [the audience's] voice" that took place in both the live theater and motion picture industries in the U.S. and the U.K.

6. From this standpoint, the traditional passive-active dichotomy that often has been used to characterize audiences across different media, or across different points of time, can be seen as something of a "historical fallacy" (van Dijck 2009:43; see also Andrejevic 2008; Griffen-Foley 2004), or at least should be thought of primarily as a reflection of institutionalized manifestations of the audience, rather than direct representations of actual audience behavior.

7. It is important to emphasize, however, that a number of accounts of the history of media audiences contest the accepted notion that the relationship between media and audiences has been one of increasing passivity on the part of audiences (Black 2005; Peters 1996; Shimpach 2005). These accounts propose "an alternative, but equally viable, construction of the audience . . . that renders the audience active, social, and imbued with rights and subjectivities by emphasizing the work, the labor that is involved in participating in and as a cultural audience. This is proposed as an alternative to the inert object of knowledge and intervention that currently constitutes the predominant constructions of the audience" (Shimpach 2005:349).

8. See Razlogova, for instance, for a discussion of "recurring cycles of audience participation" in the history of broadcasting (1995:262). Cover suggests that "it is possible to review—or at least provide a particular view of—the history of media and communication as a struggle for interactive participation with the text and co-creation of a textual narrative" (2004:180).

9. For an overview of this literature, see Peterson and Anand 2004.

1. CONTEXTUALIZING AUDIENCE EVOLUTION

1. For further discussion of early research illustrating disconnects between fan mail and other forms of audience data, see Socolow 2004.

2. In his description of the evolution of advertising and media buying in response to the advent of radio, Leo Bogart notes that "the creation of advertising and the management of media selection became more complex, more technical, and more specialized, and the structure of agencies changed accordingly." As a result, "agencies developed specialized departments for research, for sales promotion, for merchandising, for public relations" (1988/89:50).

3. This section addresses only a few key developments in the methods employed by media organizations to understand their audiences. A wide range of much more detailed discussions of the methodologies of audience measurement across different media and national contexts, and how they have evolved over time, is available. See, for instance, Balnaves and O'Regan 2002; Banks 1981; Bermejo 2007; Beville 1988; Buck 1987; Buzzard 1990; Chappell and Hooper

1944; Eaman 1994; Handel 1950; Hurwitz 1983; Kent 1994; Klopfenstein 1990; Meehan 1993; Starkey 2004; and Webster, Phalen, and Lichty 2006.

4. Today paper diaries are being replaced by Portable People Meters in many of the largest radio markets in the United States. The majority of the radio markets in the U.S., however, continue to be measured via the paper diary (Arbitron 2008). Similar portable meters are replacing paper diaries in other nations as well (Mytton 2007).

5. As broadcast researcher Hugh M. Beville noted in 1940, "audience size [is] certainly the most important consideration in a mass medium such as radio" (p. 204). It is also important to note, however, that at various points in time the exact criteria for what constitutes exposure have been the subject of debate (see, e.g., Allen 1965; Bermejo 2007; Clancey 1993).

6. As Bakker notes, early motion picture audience research "was closely connected to methods developed for the radio industry. P. F. Lazarsfeld, who ran the Bureau of Applied Social Research at Columbia University, primarily researched radio audiences, for example, but at times diverted to motion pictures" (2003:108).

7. For a detailed account of the evolution of Internet audience measurement, see Bermejo 2007.

8. Downing examines the somewhat similar context of alternative media (which often are noncommercial in their orientation) and finds a comparable pattern, in which resistance to audience research is a function of such factors as a desire to resist "the ethos of commercial user research," as well as fundamental resource inadequacies that discourage media outlets from engaging in systematic research about their audiences (2003:627).

9. A similar critique during this time period argued that there was a "fundamental weakness of today's audience research: failure to study the listener except in terms of his numbers. It has long been realized in psychological research that in social situations measurement in and of itself rarely produces knowledge, either useful or theoretical. It is in the combination of statistical and motivational research that most meaningful socio-psychological knowledge is made" (Robinson 1947:50).

10. For other examples of early radio research that focused on audience appreciation of radio programming, see Coutant 1939 and Longstaff 1939. Lazarsfeld's influence can be seen in later work produced by Columbia University's Bureau of Applied Social Research, which looked at early television audiences (see Steiner 1963).

11. Ross and Nightingale provide a detailed overview of the major critiques that have been leveled against the prioritization of exposure within commercial media industries and their associated audience measurement firms (see 2003:55–57).

12. For discussions of the areas of intersection between citizen- and consumer-oriented approaches to audiences, and their relationship to early audience research, see Glickman 2006 and Schudson 2006.

13. For a detailed overview of both academic and commercial research initiatives related to audience appreciation of media content, across a variety of national contexts, see Gunter and Wober 1992.

14. For a discussion of similar concerns in relation to the publication of best-seller lists in the book publishing industry, see Korda 2001.

15. For a contemporary critique of ARI's methods, see Borneman 1947.

16. From the earliest days of the rationalization of audience understanding, some critics have seen efforts to empirically gauge and predict audience tastes and preferences as an exercise in futility by audience and market researchers who fail to realize that most "of their research practices were not adaptable to the cultural field. . . . Obviously, the premise of a stable audience with reasonably permanent and objectively verifiable needs does not hold in the cultural field. Transplanted from economics to culture, this premise became an obvious interference with the free play of human intelligence" (Borneman 1947:33; see also Seldes 1950).

17. A critical perspective on the relationship between data and control within the realm of audience behavior can be found in Susan Ohmer's study of public opinion pollster George Gallup and his role in the development of motion picture audience research, in which she argues that "numbers connote *a sense of control* and *foster the illusion* that the multiplicity of experience can be contained" (2006:7; emphasis added).

18. According to Bogart the result of this tendency is that resources are not likely to be appropriately allocated, as the emphasis on audience size over message impact creates "a disproportionate demand for the media at the top of the list and a disproportionate handicap for those that rate low" (1976:109).

2. THE TRANSFORMATION OF MEDIA CONSUMPTION

1. According to a presentation by a media industry researcher at the 2009 Advances in Audience and Consumer Measurement conference in Miami, Florida (attended by the author as part of the participant-observation data-gathering for this study), the average length of a video viewed online is 2.5 minutes, which this researcher characterized as "snacks" rather than "meals."

2. This relationship has been established in the "circulation spiral" literature, which has demonstrated that declines in ad pages lead to declines in readership, which in turn cause further declines in ad pages, creating a continued downward spiral in both circulation and ad pages (see, e.g., Furhof 1973; Rosse 1980).

3. This statement comes from field notes taken during participant-observation research conducted at the IAB's 2008 Audience Measurement Leadership Forum in New York.

4. Anderson's "long tail" scenario has inspired a substantial amount of academic research over a relatively short time. See, for example Aigrain 2006; Brynjolfsson, Hu, and Smith 2006; and Hillesund 2007.

5. For critiques of Anderson's (2006) conclusions, see Elberse 2008, Gomes 2006.

6. For evidence that information technologies that lower search costs can contribute to less concentration in the distribution of product purchases, see Brynjolfsson, Yu, and Simester 2007. Importantly, this study holds the products available for purchase constant across traditional and online sales platforms. Of course, the implications of these findings for the transition to a media environment in which not only do search costs decrease, but product choices increase, are at best unclear.

7. For instance, research on home video sales indicates that from 2000 to 2005 the number of titles in the top 10 percent of weekly sales dropped by more than 50 percent (Elberse 2008).

8. This statement comes from field notes taken during participant-observation research conducted at the IAB's MIXX 2008 conference in New York.

9. This statistic was presented during a presentation by an audience measurement executive at the ARF's 2008 Audience Measurement 3.0 conference, attended by the author during the participant-observation component of this study.

10. This quotation comes from field notes taken during participant-observation research conducted at a cable company's informational/recruiting session held in 2005 at the Graduate School of Business at Fordham University in New York.

11. It is for this reason that the concerns expressed by authors such as Cass Sunstein (2007) about the fragmentation of the media environment contributing to a loss of shared culture seem a bit extreme. So much of the activity of today's media system revolves around repeating or recycling content from other "channels," or around reporting on the activities or content of other media channels, that the end result is a very powerful echo chamber in which it is often the case that individuals are inevitably exposed to much of the same content because there are so many routes by which that content can reach someone.

12. This despite the fact that on a typical night viewing of basic cable networks accounts for almost 60 percent of household viewing, compared with only 35 percent for the Big Four broadcast networks (Fitzgerald 2009b).

13. For additional research examining the tendency of audience attention online to cluster around relatively few sources, see Dahlberg 2004, 2005; Webster and Lin 2002; and Yim 2003.

14. As one audience measurement firm executive has stated in the context of television, "Once you begin to drill into the un-rated networks and local TV markets, the effect of the 'long tail' of content offerings and distribution outlets that TV now represents cannot adequately be portrayed by a relatively 'tiny' sample of panel data" (Oscar 2008:2).

15. Nielsen intends to have a national television household sample of thirty-six thousand homes by 2011 (Learmonth 2007).

16. This estimate of 25 percent comes from cable system operator Charter Communications' analysis of set-top box data in the Los Angeles market (McClellan 2008b). According to an executive with the Nielsen Company who was interviewed for this study, the national average in terms of unreported viewing is closer to 8 percent of total television viewing. A cable industry executive leading the effort to measure television audiences via set-top boxes has stated that "Nielsen can only measure the top 102 programs," leaving all other programs bereft of systematic audience data (Kaplan 2008:1).

17. This statistic came from a presentation by Scott McDonald of Conde Nast Publications at the ARF's Audience Measurement 2.0 conference, held in New York in June 2007.

18. These methodological details come from a presentation by a Scarborough executive delivered at the Advances in Audience and Consumer Measurement conference, held at the University of Miami in March 2009 and attended by the author as part of the participant-observation data-gathering conducted for this study.

19. This estimate of fifteen thousand comes from a comScore Media Metrix 2.0 promotional flyer titled "Realize the Power of Panel-Based Online Audience Measurement," obtained during participant-observation research conducted at the IAB's MIXX 2008 conference. Nielsen NetView estimates that their panel service can provide detailed audience estimates for approximately twenty-eight thousand online brands/channels.

20. This statement was made during a presentation at the ARF's 2008 Audience Measurement 3.0 conference, attended by the author as part of the participant-observation component of this study.

21. This statement was made during a presentation at the ARF's 2008 Audience Measurement 3.0 conference, attended by the author as part of the participant-observation component of this study.

22. The term "dark matter" is borrowed from astronomy, where researchers have determined that there is a substantial amount of matter in the universe that is undetectable, but the existence of which can be inferred from its apparent gravitational effects on visible matter.

23. For an overview of the multiplying of radio platforms that has been taking place, see Rose and Lenski 2007.

24. For a detailed overview of the various methodological approaches to measuring Web audiences, see Media Rating Council 2007.

25. This statement comes from a promotional flyer obtained during participant-observation data-gathering at the IAB's MIXX 2008 conference.

26. The current competitive landscape for firms providing television set-top box audience measurement systems has recently been described as one in which "there are several well-positioned companies jockeying for dominance

with their varying methodologies, data footprints, and sources" (Weisler 2009:1).

27. As one television researcher has noted, "There may be millions upon millions of set top boxes, allowing measurement of tiny networks without significant 'statistical error,' but what are they representative of? Certainly not all or even most viewers in the U.S. or even viewers in homes that have STB (since most of them do not have a two-way box on every set)" (Oscar 2008:3). These issues were the focus of the 2009 Changing Face of Viewer Analytics Webinar (hosted by *MultiChannel News*), attended by the author as part of the participant-observation data-gathering conducted for this study.

28. This information comes from a presentation by an audience measurement industry executive at the ARF's 2009 Audience Measurement 4.0 conference, attended by the author as part of the participant-observation data-gathering conducted for this study.

29. A Slingbox is a device that allows users to remotely view their cable, satellite, or DVR programming from a computer with a broadband Internet connection (see http://www.slingmedia.com).

30. Springel refers to the "great transition . . . of the audience itself, which is evolving from passive consumer to active collaborator" (1999:155).

31. For a brief history of user-generated content, see IAB 2008a.

32. In this regard it is important to emphasize that the concepts of interactivity and mass communication can to some extent intersect; although, as Bucy (2004) has noted, interactivity is rarely analyzed or discussed as a mass communication phenomenon.

33. For a discussion of the transition from "Web 1.0" to "Web 2.0," see Swisher 2007, and Beer and Burrows 2007. The defining characteristic of this transition is, of course, the Web's evolution from an environment in which "institutions would publish information and end users would consume it," to one that is "truly dynamic, user-driven and completely networked" and that "provides for live collaborations between the publisher and the audience" (Swisher 2007:33).

34. It should be noted, however, that according to some estimates, only about 2 percent of the online audience actively participates in any form of user-generated content production (Dovey 2008). Other studies suggest that the interest in, and enthusiasm for, taking advantage of the more participatory aspects of Web 2.0 is limited to a select few demographic segments (see, e.g., Bergstrom 2008).

35. As Knight notes within the context of an analysis of the motion picture and home video industries, "distribution has always been the least visible part of our film industry and culture; and it has been and remains the most under-researched" (2007:24).

36. As Croteau notes, "one key to the Internet's unique significance is that it provides the infrastructure necessary to facilitate the distribution of all forms

of self-produced media to a potentially far-flung audience" (2006:341). Such acknowledgments of the significance of distribution capacity are rare in the ongoing discussions of user-generated content and its implications.

37. Deuze labels this process the "corporate appropriation of participatory culture" (2008:27).

38. It should be noted that there are thousands of individuals and organizations contributing videos to YouTube who take part in the site's revenue sharing "partner program." These partners, however, represent a very small fraction overall of the contributors to the site (see Stelter 2008b).

39. See Dreyfuss 1990 for a discussion of the legal implications of the increasing use of brand imagery as a form of personal self-expression.

40. At the 2008 Digital Media Measurement and Pricing Summit, one advertising industry executive described an example in which three thousand user-generated ads were created in response to a contest sponsored by Doritos.

41. According to Artz, "although many of Smythe's concerns have been championed and popularized in international communication discourse, his observations regarding the function of audiences in the media process have been less visible. In fact, despite cogent argument and ample evidence, his perspective on the commodity audience has been institutionally shunned by academic departments across the U.S. for some fifty years" (2008:60). This point is further evidenced by the fact that some analyses of the "free labor" provided by media audiences in the form of the production of user-generated content have neglected to reference Smythe's work (see, e.g., Johnson 2007; Peterson 2008; Terranova 2000; van Dijk 2009).

42. Efforts to define interactivity have been extensive (see, e.g., Cover 2006; Kim and Sawhney 2002; van Dijk and de Vos 2001).

3. THE TRANSFORMATION OF AUDIENCE INFORMATION SYSTEMS

1. As one audience measurement firm executive recently noted in the context of television, "The advent of Return Path Data (RPD) has reshaped and forever changed the face of TV audience measurement in the United States and around the world" (Oscar 2008:2).

2. As Andrejevic notes, online forums where audiences discuss and critique media products do not "just add value to the product," they also "double as audience research" (2008:33).

3. In a study of "data collection events" on the Internet by fifteen of the largest media companies, comScore found that Yahoo led the way, with 400 billion data collection events in a month, followed by Time Warner with 100 billion, and Google with 91 billion (Story 2008a). For this research, a "data collection event" was defined as any of the following: (a) pages displayed; (b) search queries entered; (c) videos played; (d) advertising displayed; and (e) ads served on pages anywhere on the Web by advertising networks owned by the

media companies. The logic of these criteria is that each time one of these events occurs, "there is a conversation between the user's computer and the server of the company that owns the site or serves the ad" (Story 2008a:1). The study also suggested that "the rich troves of data at the fingertips of the biggest Internet companies are also creating a new kind of digital divide within the industry. Traditional media companies, which collect far less data about visitors to their sites, are increasingly at a disadvantage when they compete for ad dollars" (Story 2008b:2; see also Hong et al. 2005).

4. This is often but not always the case, given those instances of what have been termed "incidental exposure," in which an audience member unintentionally stumbles upon content of interest (see, e.g., Prior 2007; Sunstein 2007). Think, for example, of Web-surfing or channel-surfing behaviors that lead to an audience member discovering, and then consuming, a particular content option.

5. Hayes and Bing describe the "tracking" research used by the motion picture industry as "one of the most entrenched—and divisive—mechanisms studios use to plan their assault on the national consciousness. [Tracking] is the first public referendum on a film's prospects that carries the weight of empirical truth" (2004:238).

6. For a critical perspective on efforts by media organizations to monitor the expressive activities of their audiences, see Andrejevic 2007a, 2007b.

7. It is worth noting that some researchers who initially studied these issues utilizing the "involvement" terminology (e.g., Malthouse, Calder, and Tamhane 2007) have subsequently adopted the "engagement" terminology for essentially the same line of research (e.g., Malthouse et al. 2008), most likely in recognition of the popularization of the engagement terminology.

8. As one television industry trade press report noted, "While ratings remain the television industry's currency, advertisers are increasingly evaluating 'engagement' when they buy spots" (Albiniak 2007:16).

9. This statement was made during a presentation at the 2010 Online Media, Marketing, and Advertising Metrics and Measurement conference in New York, attended as part of the participant-observation data-gathering for this study.

10. That same year the *Journal of Advertising Research* for the first time devoted an entire issue to the concept of engagement; the editor noted that "judging from the interest that the topic has generated and the work that has yet to be done, I am confidently predicting that it won't be our last" (Woodard 2006:354).

11. The ARF's (2006a) efforts to organize the various definitional approaches to engagement organized the definitions according to three categories: (a) measures of brand impact; (b) measures of brand idea and surrounding context; and (c) measures of media context.

12. According to Holmes et al., engagement can be approached from either a "media-centric" perspective—which focuses on the media channel or content—or an audience- and context-centered perspective—which focuses on the behavior and experiences of the user (2006:1–2).

13. For a review of the engagement literature through 2006, see Magazine Publishers of America 2006.

14. There have been a number of studies, however, that demonstrate the opposite effect, in which greater audience engagement with a particular content option has resulted in diminished advertising effectiveness (for a review and methodological critique of this research, see Lloyd and Clancy 1991). The logic underlying such findings is that advertisements represent a more annoying intrusion into content in which audiences are highly engaged. Obviously, at this point the media, advertising, and audience measurement industries have embraced the "positive effects" hypothesis instead.

15. As one participant in the ARF's 2008 Re:Think conference noted, "Engagement is a real concept, but you have to define the engagement that's relevant to you." This conference was attended by the author as part of the participant-observation component of this study.

16. It is not surprising, therefore, that engagement has been described as "a catch-all term that covers everything from viewer attentiveness and recall to the somewhat fuzzier quality of emotional connection" (Crupi 2008a:10). One Internet audience measurement firm, in a presentation at the 2010 Online Media, Marketing, and Advertising Metrics and Measurement conference, touted providing one hundred and fifty *different* engagement metrics, suggesting that the term truly is becoming a generic catchall for virtually all audience metrics.

17. Danaher and Lawrie, for instance, proposed that audience appreciation (a commonly identified element of engagement) for individual television programs could be determined simply by using minute-by-minute People Meter data to calculate the average percentage of a program's minutes viewed by the program's audience. Thus, "if a person tunes into the entire 30 minutes duration of a comedy show then it is likely that they [*sic*] enjoy the comedy more than someone who watches just 15 minutes of the comedy plus 15 minutes of other programming in the same 30-minute period" (Danaher and Lawrie 1998:54).

18. The identified specific elements of such an expanded analytical approach include audience duplication, DVR usage, audience flow, and ad retention (i.e., the extent to which a program's audience is retained for the ad; see Dish Network/Rentrak Corporation 2009).

19. Gunter and Wober (1992) provide a detailed overview and history of industry efforts to assess audiences' reactions to television programming and to determine whether such reactions are related to advertising effectiveness. Their account addresses efforts in the U.S. (where such research initiatives gained very little traction) and throughout Europe, where a number of noncommercial broadcasters embraced such research to a much greater degree than ever took place in the U.S.

20. According to Micu, Plummer, and Cook, in terms of engagement, "emotional reactions come first. So, if we were to test to determine how engaging adver-

tising messages are, we would start by testing for and learning first about emotion, the reaction that impacts any further processing of the brand idea and motivation to purchase and/or use the brand" (2007:9).

21. For details on the NeuroFocus methodology, data, and applications, see http://www.neurofocus.com.

22. Other firms, such as NewMediaMetrics, have also begun offering emotional response metrics. NewMediaMetrics produces an "emotional attachment study" that examines audiences' emotional attachment to thirty broadcast television networks, individual television programs, and more than a a dozen new media properties (e.g., Google, Yahoo, YouTube) and sports properties (e.g., the Olympics, the NFL) (see NewMediaMetrics 2007).

23. Kathryn Montgomery describes similar instances of Web sites being established for the specific purpose of gathering data from the online conversations of teenagers. As she notes, "Market research became such an integral part of the online teen culture that it not only shaped the content, in many cases *it was* the content" (2007:117). As she notes, in many instances Web sites targeting teenagers found that the revenue generated from the data gathered about the sites' visitors exceed the revenue generated through more traditional streams such as advertising and subscriptions (Montgomery 2007).

24. Institutional resistance to such expressions of audience engagement is discussed in chap. 4.

25. These figures came from a presentation delivered at the 2008 Digital Media Measurement and Pricing Summit, attended by the author as part of the participant-observation data-gathering conducted for this study.

26. According to Nielsen Online, "73 percent of online U.S. adults actively participate in consumer-generated media (CGM) in some form" (2008:2). This level of online participation is obviously far larger than the levels indicated by other studies.

27. IAG Research was originally an independent audience research firm founded in 2000. The firm was purchased by, and integrated into, the Nielsen Company in 2008 for 225 million dollars ("Nielsen to Acquire," 2008). This acquisition is indicative of a common pattern in the audience measurement industry in which large, established audience measurement firms absorb upstart firms and consequently acquire whatever technological or methodological innovations these new firms have brought to the table.

28. For a discussion and critique of the IAG methodology, see Askwith 2007. The IAG web interface can be found at http://www.rewardtv.com.

29. For instance, one interactive marketing firm outlines "behavioral proofs of engagement," which include time spent with an advertisement or taking an action such as requesting more information, requesting a coupon or sample, or purchasing the product (ARF 2006a:3).

30. This statement came from field notes taken during a presentation at the ARF's 2007 Audience Measurement 2.0 conference, attended by the author

as part of the participant-observation component of this study. According to an industry white paper, moving beyond demographics has changed from an aspiration to an imperative within most sectors of the media and advertising industries (Maiville and Engel 2007).

31. There is a fairly compelling body of research indicating that audience demographics are a fairly poor predictor of consumers' product-purchasing behaviors (for a review of this research, see Napoli 2003a). Nonetheless, in the absence of a more effective alternative, demographics have remained the dominant standard.

32. In the U.K., there is a similar ongoing project, under the direction of the Institute of Practitioners in Advertising (IPA), called the IPA Touchpoints Initiative (see, e.g., Robinson 2009; Robinson and Turner 2007). In France a single-source audience measurement service for television called Marketing-Scan has been in operation since 1996 (Battais and Stehle 2007). These initiatives are still operational at the time of this writing.

33. Nielsen is engaged in a similar effort, though this one involves the fusion of consumer data and media consumption data from different panels (appropriately titled Nielsen Fusion; see Marich 2008). Nielsen's effort is notable in that it also fuses data from multiple media measurement systems (Internet, television, and billboards; see Doe and Connolly 2007). For a discussion of data fusion techniques, see Ephron 2008.

34. In this regard, the Internet has been described as "both blessed and cursed by the click. Blessed because it differentiated itself as more measurable than traditional media—and cursed because it has pigeonholed the medium as an engine of direct-response" (Morrissey 2009a:1).

35. For more details on deep-packet inspection, see Dykes 2008.

36. See Turow 2006 for a discussion of "mass customization" as a strategic outgrowth of interactive media.

37. Clifford (2009a), for instance, describes an initiative recently launched by cable multiple-system operator (MSO) Cablevision, which has begun testing a system that delivers targeted commercials to subscribers in New York and New Jersey. In this case the targeting is based on demographic characteristics such as income, ethnicity, and gender; however, the continuing development of set-top box applications that also facilitate product purchases and requests for product information (see Spangler 2009a) offers the opportunity for the delivery of targeted television advertisements that are based on behavioral responses in addition to media consumption.

38. For a discussion of the prominence of search-based advertising online, see IAB 2009.

39. According to Arango (2008), the cable television industry believes that Canoe Ventures will allow them to increase their annual advertising revenues from 5 billion annually to 15 billion annually. Progress on this venture, however, has been significantly slowed by technical problems (Hampp 2009b).

40. This engagement index is defined as follows: Σ (Ci + Di + Ri + Li + Bi + Fi +Ii), where C = click depth (page and event views); D = duration (time spent on site); R = recency (rate at which visitors return to the site over time); L = loyalty (the level of long-term interaction with the content); B = brand awareness; F = feedback (propensity to solicit information or supply direct feedback); I = interactions (visitor interaction with content or functionality designed to increase attention level) (see Peterson and Carrabis 2008).

41. The specific calculation for eGRPs would be as follows: (traditional GRPs) $\times$ (engagement index) = eGRPs (Eubank and Griffiths 2007).

42. In many ways this notion of eGRPs is an extension of much earlier efforts at computing a CPMI (cost per thousand involved) in place of traditional CPMs (cost per thousand) (see Lloyd and Clancy 1991). Like GRPs, CPMs are a common metric for assessing and comparing the costs of advertising within different media content options. To compute CPMIs, Lloyd and Clancy (1991) advocate integrating audience involvement data into the audience measurement process, and combining such data with traditional exposure data, in order to facilitate the calculation of the CPMI. Their research indicated that the utilization of CPMI data would lead to advertising-placement decisions significantly different from what would be reached via the utilization of traditional CPM data.

43. Today's situation has been described as one in which "many advertisers leap over conventional measurements like audience demos and CPMs" (Ephron 2009:1).

44. More recently ABC announced that although it has developed a performance metric for individual programs that can prove the level of advertising effectiveness, efforts at deploying it are being frustrated by marketers' unwillingness to share the product sales data necessary for the metric to be calculated (Goetzl 2009).

45. For an overview of the evolution of the pricing of online audiences, see Bermejo 2009.

46. This information came from a presentation by an online media executive at the ARF's 2009 Audience Measurement 4.0 conference, attended by the author as part of the participant-observation data-gathering conducted for this study.

47. Regarding the increased reliance on specialized knowledge, it is worth noting the recent spurt in books devoted specifically to analyzing those professionals involved in the increasingly complicated field of large-scale marketing database creation and analysis (see, e.g., Ayres 2007; Baker 2008; Turow 2006). A central underlying theme of these works is the extent to which the individuals working in these professions are becoming increasingly powerful in terms of the knowledge they are able to generate and, more important, increasingly valued and influential within the decision-making processes of various industry sectors—including media and communications.

4. CONTESTING AUDIENCES

1. For a review of the social shaping of technology literature, see Williams and Edge 1996.

2. There is a thematic consistency in many of the titles of the work in this vein (e.g., "Hollywood Versus the Internet" [Currah 2006]; *Hollywood Versus the Future* [Dekom and Sealey 2003]; *Hollywood's War Against the Digital Generation* [Lasica 2005]).

3. Another study, conducted at roughly the same time and using a comparable methodology, put the percentage of videos removed because of copyright violations at 5 percent (Cha et al. 2007).

4. According to this report, YouTube is focused on attracting more "professional" videos, because such videos "are more appealing to advertisers than videos uploaded by users" (Stelter 2009b:1). Obviously, if such advertiser preferences persist, this will represent a significant institutional pressure preserving a somewhat privileged position for traditional media content relative to user-generated content and thereby affecting the orientation of the growing array of platforms capable of distributing both forms of content.

5. For a detailed discussion of the factors contributing to the tendency toward the "massification" of new media, see Napoli 1998c, 2008.

6. Harvard University's Citizen Media Law Project monitored sixteen copyright infringement lawsuits directed at bloggers and other online publishers in 2007—up from three such lawsuits in 2004 and 2005 (Stelter 2009a).

7. This focus on news stories is a reflection of the very dire economic state of journalism (Downie and Schudson 2009; Knight Commission 2009)—a situation that is increasingly attracting the attention of policymakers (see, e.g., Joshi 2009).

8. As one advertising executive stated at the ARF's 2008 Audience Measurement 3.0 conference (attended as part of the participant-observation component of this study), "We're not a big fan of interactive television because we don't want to lose the audience." The implication here is that if the technological capacity for interactivity undermines desired business models, that capacity may go unrealized.

9. This may explain Ornebrink'smore recent conclusion that "traditional news organizations are unwilling to add features that give users more control and influence over the content," based on data indicating that "users are mostly empowered to create popular culture-oriented content and personal/everyday life-oriented content rather than news/informational content" (2008:783).

10. In the case of SoundScan, several major record labels withdrew their advertising support from *Billboard* magazine in an effort to discourage *Billboard* from relying upon SoundScan data for the compiling of the *Billboard* charts (Anand and Peterson 2000).

11. Andrews and Napoli (2006) document an early period of book publishing industry resistance to the BookScan system for measuring book sales, which employed a much more sophisticated methodology than that employed to calculate the *New York Times*' best-seller lists. This resistance arose mainly in response to the high costs associated with obtaining BookScan data, but also to concerns that the BookScan service would introduce the problem of information overload to the book publishing industry.

12. Some critics have asserted that the monopoly, or near-monopoly, status that many audience measurement services enjoy places them in a particularly powerful position to stifle innovations, particularly those developed by upstart, potentially competing, firms (see Mandese 2006). This argument was at the core of an unsuccessful antitrust lawsuit filed in the US by upstart television audience measurement firm erinMedia against incumbent Nielsen (Hinman 2008). For an alternative perspective on the monopoly issue, see Furchtgott-Roth, Hahn, and Layne-Farrar 2007.

13. History and mission of the MRC, available at: http://www.mediaratingcouncil .org/History.htm.

14. ARF's (2005) report summarizes a daylong meeting (attended by the author as part of the participant-observation data-gathering conducted for this study), held in Feb. 2005, in which media industry stakeholders came together to discuss concerns about the current state of audience measurement and possible alternative oversight structures for the audience measurement industry.

15. For a detailed discussion of a similar radio audience measurement dispute in the UK (though one lacking much of the diversity rhetoric that was intertwined with the US dispute), see Starkey 2002.

16. For a more theoretically oriented critique of the PPM, see Tudor 2009.

17. This information came from a presentation by an Arbitron executive at the Advances in Audience and Consumer Measurement seminar held at the University of Miami in March 2009, attended by the author as part of the participant-observation data-gathering conducted for this study.

18. This pattern is reflected in the fact that PPM data show that listeners listen to an average of 4.5 different stations per week, compared to the average of 2.7 stations per week that is reported under the diary system. Also, given that Hispanics and African Americans exhibit the highest levels of radio listening, the fact that the stations most popular among these audiences experienced larger than average ratings declines reflects the premise that habitual listening tended to be overrepresented in the diary method (this information came from a presentation by an Arbitron executive at the Advances in Audience and Consumer Measurement seminar held at the University of Miami in March 2009, which was attended by the author as part of the participant-observation data-gathering conducted for this study).

19. This information came from a presentation by an Arbitron executive at the Advances in Audience and Consumer Measurement seminar held at the

University of Miami in March of 2009, attended by the author as part of the participant-observation data-gathering conducted for this study.

20. This information came from a presentation by an Arbitron executive at the Advances in Audience and Consumer Measurement seminar held at the University of Miami in March of 2009, attended by the author as part of the participant-observation data-gathering conducted for this study.

21. For instance, according to the New York attorney general, "By imposing the flawed PPM methodology . . . Arbitron has deprived minority businesses of the equal opportunity to engage in contractual relationships and commercial activity free from discrimination, in violation of civil rights laws. It has also knowingly deprived minority communities of the right to diversity of programming and services on the airwaves" (*People of the State of New York v. Arbitron* 2008:11).

22. The Florida lawsuit is ongoing at the time of this writing (see *State of Florida, Office of the Attorney General v. Arbitron, Inc.* 2009).

23. For a useful overview of the tests that have been employed in the analysis of commercial speech, see Boedecker, Morgan, and Wright 1995.

24. As the court noted in this decision, "In the context of regulation of false or misleading advertising, this typically means that the speech consists of representations of fact about the business operations, products, or services of the speaker. . . . This is consistent with, and implicit in, the United States Supreme Court's commercial speech decisions" (*Kasky v. Nike* 2002:961). Also, as Earnhardt has noted, "The court concluded that because Nike was involved in commerce; because the intended audience was partially made up of potential or past customers of Nike; and because the statements were *factual representations* about its business operations and thus commercial in nature, the statements constituted commercial speech" (2004:802; emphasis added).

25. According to Arbitron, "The Arbitron Reports are original works of opinion that express the views of Arbitron based on its more than 40 years in the audience measurement field. Members of the radio industry, journalists, advertisers, academics and others seek out Arbitron's opinions and follow them regularly. It is clear that the Arbitron Reports are a matter of public interest and concern worthy of full First Amendment protection. Arbitron's ratings information is regularly and widely distributed in newspapers and other periodicals" (*Arbitron v. Andrew Cuomo* 2008b:4).

26. According to Arbitron, "Arbitron's works provide a form of news of significant concern to a great number of people far beyond Arbitron's subscribers, providing information about radio listening habits to various segments of the population as well as the performance of radio stations relative to one another in a given market. They do not provide information about Arbitron's own products or services—the classic definition of commercial speech" (*Arbitron v. Andrew Cuomo* 2008b:44).

27. In *Gertz v. Welch* (1974) the Supreme Court stated that "under the First Amendment there is no such thing as a false idea. However pernicious an opinion may seem, we depend for its correction not on the conscience of judges and juries but on the competition of other ideas. But there is no constitutional value in false statements of fact" (pp. 339–340).

28. Similar controversies have emerged in response to Nielsen's efforts to introduce television audience metrics at the local market level that account for time-shifted viewing. Unlike at the national level, these ratings do not include separate commercial ratings (see Friedman 2008, 2009a; Grillo 2009).

29. However, as the Congressional Research Service noted in its analysis of this issue, complications arise in terms of determining whether consent must be "affirmative" or can be "implied." That is, is an ISP subscriber, simply in subscribing to the service, giving implied consent to the interception of her communication with individual Web sites (see Ruane 2009:6)? Such ambiguities reflect the ongoing debate about the appropriateness of "opt in" versus "opt out" models of gathering information about media audiences.

30. For details regarding the Federal Trade Commission's history of involvement in online privacy issues, as well as details regarding its ongoing inquiry into online behavioral advertising, see Federal Trade Commission 2009.

31. Facebook Chief Privacy Officer Chris Kelly (2008) also was called to testify before Congress in connection with hearings held on the privacy implications of online advertising.

32. Another area where the boundaries of acceptable information gathering seem particularly unclear, and particularly ripe for stakeholder conflict, involves the gathering of television viewer information via cable set-top boxes (see, e.g., Spangler, Hartzel, and Gal-Or 2006). The Cable Communications Policy Act of 1984 places some rather ambiguous limits on how cable companies are allowed to use any data they gather from their subscribers (see Turow 2006). The act prohibits cable companies from gathering or disclosing "personally identifiable information" about their subscribers without subscribers' prior consent, although it includes an exception for when the information is necessary to conduct a "legitimate business activity related to a cable service or other service provided by the cable operator to the subscriber" (47 USCA §551(c)). Such an exception would seem to provide a substantial amount of leeway in terms of how cable companies can utilize the data they gather about their subscribers. It is also important to note that since the privacy provisions in the Cable Act were written specifically in reference to cable companies, a strict interpretation of the act would mean that these provisions are not applicable to newer multichannel video programming delivery services such as DBS and telecommunications companies (Tinic 2006), or to other set-top box service providers such as TiVo and Netflix (see, e.g., Chan 2004).

5. THE IMPLICATIONS OF AUDIENCE EVOLUTION

1. This statement was made at the ARF's Audience Measurement 4.0 conference, attended by the author as part of the participant-observation data-gathering conducted for this study.
2. For analyses of information overload problems within organizations, see Barr, Stimbert, and Huff 1992 and Edmunds and Morris 2000.
3. This issue was a frequent point of discussion at the March 2009 conference Advances in Audience and Consumer Measurement, held at the University of Miami, and at the IAB's MIXX 2008 conference, attended as part of the participant-observation component of this study.
4. This issue was a major point of discussion at the IAB's MIXX 2008 conference, attended as part of the participant-observation component of this study. According to one speaker, "The average media planner and sales person is going to have to look more like a management consultant."
5. The need for more intensive self-regulation of the ratings industry was the focus of a Sept. 29, 2005, meeting held by the ARF (and attended by the author as part of the participant-observation data-gathering conducted for this study) where the creation of the Audience Measurement Initiative was announced (see Mandese 2005).
6. *Feist Publications v. Rural Telephone Service Co.*, 499 U.S. 340, 347 (1991) ("facts do not owe their origin to an act of authorship. The distinction is one between creation and discovery: The first person to find and report a particular fact has not created the fact; he or she has merely discovered its existence").
7. As Sprague noted, "The pure researcher might say, 'After all, these are only estimates.' But the practical researcher knows that estimates are, in the real world, generally used as facts" (1981:44).
8. There are many individuals who still do not have access to the Internet. This, of course, represents a persistent access to the media problem.
9. For a discussion of these issues as they relate specifically to "public media," see Clark and Aufderheide 2009.

REFERENCES

Abbate, J. 2000. *Inventing the Internet.* Cambridge, MA: MIT Press.

Abels, J. E. 2008. I want my non-Nielsen TV. *Forbes,* Oct. 30. Retrieved Feb. 19, 2009, from: http://www.forbes.com/2008/10/30/media-television-ratings-biz-media-cx_jea_1030ratings.html.

Adams, W. B. 1953. A definition of motion-picture research. *Quarterly Journal of Film, Radio, and Television* 7.4:408–421.

Adams, W. J. 1994. Changes in ratings patterns for prime time before, during, and after the introduction of the people meter. *Journal of Media Economics* 7.2:15–28.

Ahlkvist, J. A. 2001. Programming philosophies and the rationalization of music radio. *Media, Culture, and Society* 23:339–358.

Ahlkvist, J. A., and R. Faulkner. 2002. "Will this record work for us?": Managing music formats in commercial radio. *Qualitative Sociology* 25.2:189–215.

Ahlkvist, J. A., and G. Fisher. 2000. And the hits just keep on coming: Music programming standardization in commercial radio. *Poetics* 27:301–325.

Aigrain, P. 2006. Diversity, attention, and symmetry in a many-to-many information society. *First Monday* 11.6. Retrieved Jan. 2, 2009, from: http://firstmonday.org/issues/issue11_6/aigrain/index.html.

Albiniak, P. 2007. Measuring "engagement": Beyond ratings, advertisers are after TV's hot new metric. *Broadcasting and Cable,* Oct. 1, 16.

Allen, C. 2005. Discovering "Joe Six Pack" content in television news: The hidden history of audience research, news consultants, and the Warner Class model. *Journal of Broadcasting and Electronic Media* 49.4:363–382.

——. 2007. News directors and consultants: RTNDA's endorsement of TV journalism's "greatest tool." *Journal of Broadcasting and Electronic Media* 51.3:424–437.

Allen, C. L. 1965. Photographing the TV audience. *Journal of Advertising Research* 5.1:2–8.

Allor, M. 1988. Relocating the site of the audience. *Critical Studies in Mass Communication* 5:217–233.

American Advertising Federation. 2008. Re: Online behavioral advertising proposed self-regulatory principles. Letter to Donald S. Clark, Secretary, Federal Trade Commission, April 9. Retrieved June 14, 2008, from: http://www.ftc.gov/os/comments/behavioraladprinciples/080409associations.pdf.

Anand, N., and R. A. Peterson. 2000. When market information constitutes fields: Sensemaking of markets in the commercial music field. *Organization Science* 11:270–284.

Anderson, C. 2004. The long tail. *Wired*, Oct. Retrieved Aug. 5, 2008, from http://www.wired.com/wired/archive/12.10/tail.html.

——. 2006. *The Long Tail: Why the Future of Business Is Selling Less of More.* New York: Hyperion.

——. 2009. Web production, news judgment, and merging categories of online newswork in metropolitan journalism. Paper presented at the International Symposium on Online Journalism, Austin, TX, April.

Andrejevic, M. 2002. The work of being watched: Interactive media and the exploitation of self-disclosure. *Critical Studies in Media Communication* 19.2:230–248.

——. 2007a. Surveillance in the digital enclosure. *Communication Review* 10:295–317.

——. 2007b. *iSpy: Surveillance and Power in the Interactive Era.* Lawrence: University Press of Kansas.

——. 2008. Watching television without pity: The productivity of online fans. *Television and New Media* 9.1:24–46.

Andrews, K., and P. M. Napoli. 2006. Changing market information regimes: A case study of the transition to the BookScan audience measurement system in the U.S. book publishing industry. *Journal of Media Economics* 19.1:33–54.

Ang, I. 1991. *Desperately Seeking the Audience.* London: Routledge.

Angus, I. 1994. Democracy and the constitution of audiences: A comparative media theory perspective. In J. Cruz and J. Lewis, eds., *Viewing, Reading, Listening: Audiences and Cultural Reception*, 233–252. Boulder, CO: Westview.

Anne Milgram v. Arbitron. 2009. Final consent judgment. Superior Court of New Jersey, Jan. 7. Retrieved March 22, 2009, from: http://www.nj.gov/oag/newsreleases08/pr20090107c-Arbitron-ConsentJudgment.pdf.

Appel, V. 1993. Anatomy of a magazine audience estimate: The ARF compatibility study revisited. *Journal of Advertising Research* 33.1:11–17.

Arango, T. 2008. Cable firms join forces to attract focused ads. *New York Times*, March 10. Retrieved March 4, 2009, from: http://www.nytimes.com/2008/03/10/business/media/10cable.html?_r=1.

Arbitron. 2006. The infinite dial: Radio's digital platforms. Retrieved March 1, 2009, from: http://www.daily-journal.com/podcast/arbitronstudy.pdf.

——. 2007a. Description of PPM methodology. New York: Author.

——. 2007b. Arbitron receives Media Rating Council accreditation for the Portable People Meter radio ratings data in Houston. News release. Retrieved Sept. 29, 2008, from: http://www.onlinepressroom.net/arbitron.

———. 2008. Planning and buying radio advertising in a PPM world. Retrieved July 25, 2008, from: http://www.arbitron.com/downloads/arbitron2008mediaplan. pdf.

———. 2010. Arbitron PPM commercialization schedule. Retrieved Feb. 20, 2010, from: http://www.arbitron.com/downloads/ppm_rollout.pdf.

Arbitron v. Andrew M. Cuomo. 2008a. Complaint. U.S. District Court, Southern District of New York (Oct. 6).

———. 2008b. Plaintiff's corrected memorandum of law in opposition to defendant's motion to dismiss and in further support of its motion for a preliminary injunction. U.S. District Court, Southern District of New York (Oct. 23).

———. 2008c. Plaintiff's proposed findings of fact and conclusions of law. U.S. District Court, Southern District of New York (Oct. 24).

———. 2008d. Defendant's memorandum of law in reply to plaintiff's opposition to motion to dismiss the complaint. U.S. District Court, Southern District of New York (Oct. 24).

ARF (Advertising Research Foundation). 2005. Accountability in audience measurement: A global examination. New York: Author.

———. 2006a. Engagement: Definitions and anatomy. New York: Author.

———. 2006b. Measures of engagement. New York: Author.

———. 2007. Measures of engagement, II. New York: Author.

Artz, L. 2008. Media relations and media product: Audience commodity. *Democratic Communiqué* 22.1:60–74.

Askwith, I. D. 2007. "Television 2.0: Reconceptualizing TV as an engagement medium." Unpublished Master's thesis, Massachusetts Institute of Technology.

Assael, H., and D. F. Poltrack. 2006. Using viewer attitudes to evaluate TV program effectiveness. *Journal of Advertising Research* 46.1:93–101.

Associated Press v. U.S. 326 U.S. 1 (1945).

Association of Hispanic Advertising Agencies. 2008. Association of Hispanic Advertising Agencies rallies industry leaders to tackle Portable People Meter challenges. News release, May 19.

Atkinson, C. 2008. How commercial ratings changed the $70B TV market. *Advertising Age*, Oct. 13. Retrieved March 13, 2009, from: http://adage.com/article?article_id=131426.

———. 2009. CIMM set to reveal details as MTV exec moves to forefront. *Broadcasting and Cable*, Oct. 26. Retrieved Nov. 3, 2009, from: http://www.broadcasting-cable.com/article/366478-CIMM_Set_To_Reveal_Details_As_MTV_Exec_Moves_To_Forefront.php.

Atlas Institute. 2008. Engagement mapping: A new measurement standard is emerging for advertisers. Retrieved Feb. 24, 2009, from: http://www.atlassolutions.com/uploadedFiles/Atlas/Atlas_Institute/Engagement_Mapping/eMapping-TP.pdf.

Auletta, K. 1992. *Three Blind Mice: How the TV Networks Lost Their Way.* New York: Vintage Books.

Austin, B. A. 1989. *Immediate Seating: A Look at Movie Audiences.* Belmont, CA: Wadsworth.

Ayres, I. 2007. *Super Crunchers.* New York: Bantam Dell.

Bachman, K. 2002a. Boston balks at Nielsen. *Mediaweek,* Feb. 4, 8.

——. 2002b. A sweeps without ratings. *Mediaweek,* April 22, 8.

——. 2004. "If I can make it there . . .," *Broadcasting and Cable,* April 5, 6.

——. 2009a. Univision refuses to encode signals in new PPM areas. *Mediaweek,* June 21. Retrieved Nov. 2, 2009, from: http://www.mediaweek.com/mw/content_display/esearch/e3i34e2ede5adb7e1e8832285a361a8cefe?pn=1.

——. 2009b. Cracking the set-top box code. *Adweek* (media insert), Aug. 17, 1–4.

Baker, S. 2008. *The Numerati.* New York: Houghton Mifflin.

Bakker, G. 2003. Building knowledge about the consumer: The emergence of market research in the motion picture industry. *Business History* 45.1:101–127.

Balkin, J. M. 2004. Digital speech and democratic culture: A theory of freedom of expression for the Information Society. *NYU Law Review* 79:1–55.

Balnaves, M., and T. O'Regan. 2002. The ratings in transition: The politics and technologies of counting. In *Mobilising the Audience,* ed. M. Balnaves, T. O'Regan, and J. Sternberg, 28–64. Queensland, Australia: University of Queensland Press.

——. 2008. Constructing an audience ratings convention. Paper presented at the ANZCA 08 conference, Power and Place, Wellington, New Zealand.

Banks, J. 2002. Gamers as co-creators: Enlisting the virtual audience—a report from the Net Face. In *Mobilising the Audience,* ed. M. Balnaves, T. O'Regan, and J. Sternberg, 188–212. Queensland, Australia: University of Queensland Press.

Banks, J., and S. Humphreys. 2008. The labour of user co-creators: Emergent social network markets? *Convergence* 14.4:401–418.

Banks, M. J. 1981. "A History of Broadcast Audience Research in the United States, 1920–1980, with an Emphasis on the Rating Services." Unpublished Ph.D. diss., University of Tennessee.

Barker, M. 1998. Film audience research: Making a virtue out of a necessity. *Iri* 26:131–147.

Barnes, B. E., and L. M. Thomson. 1988. The impact of audience information sources on media evolution. *Journal of Advertising Research* 28.5:RC9–RC14.

——. 1994. Power to the people (meter): Audience measurement technology and media specialization. In *Audiencemaking: How the Media Create the Audience,* ed. J. S. Ettema and D. C. Whitney, 75–94. Thousand Oaks, CA: Sage.

Barr, P. S., J. L. Stimpert, and A. S. Huff. 1992. Cognitive change, strategic action, and organizational behavior. *Strategic Management Journal* 13:15–36.

Barron, J. 1967. Access to the press: A new First Amendment right. *Harvard Law Review* 80:1641–1678.

——. 2007. Access to the media: A contemporary appraisal. *Hofstra Law Review* 35:937–953.

Barwise, P., and A. S. C. Ehrenberg. 1988. *Television and Its Audience.* Beverly Hills: Sage.

Barzel, Y. 1982. Measurement cost and the organization of markets. *Journal of Law and Economics* 25.1:27–48.

Battais, L., and J. Stehle. 2007. A powerful mix: Fusing audience data with consumer behaviour to measure advertising effects. Paper presented at the ESOMAR Worldwide Multi Media Measurement conference, Dublin, Ireland, June.

Baughman, J. L. 1997. *The Republic of Mass Culture: Journalism, Filmmaking, and Broadcasting in America Since 1941.* 2nd ed. Baltimore: Johns Hopkins University Press.

Baumann, S. 2007. *Hollywood Highbrow: From Entertainment to Art.* Princeton: Princeton University Press.

Beam, R. 1995. How newspapers use readership research. *Newspaper Research Journal* 16.2:28–38.

Beck, J. 2009. Tapping the wire: Audience response research in a non-linear age. Paper presented at the ESOMAR Worldwide Multi Media Measurement conference, Stockholm, Sweden, May.

Beer, D., and R. Burrows. 2007. Sociology and, of, and in Web 2.0: Some initial considerations. *Sociological Research Online* 12.5. Retrieved Aug. 21, 2008, from: http://www.socresonline.org.uk/12/5/17.html.

Beniger, J. 1987. *The Control Revolution: Technological and Economic Origins of the Information Society.* Cambridge, MA: Harvard University Press.

Benkler, Y. 2000. From consumers to users: Shifting the deeper structures of regulation toward sustainable commons and user access. *Federal Communications Law Journal* 52.3:561–579.

——. 2006. *The Wealth of Networks: How Social Production Transforms Markets and Freedom.* New Haven: Yale University Press.

Bergstrom, A. 2008. The reluctant audience: Online participation in the Swedish journalistic context. *Westminster Papers in Communication and Culture* 5.2:60–79.

Berkowitz, D., and C. Allen. 1996. Exploring newsroom views about consultants in local TV: The effect of work roles and socialization. *Journal of Broadcasting and Electronic Media* 40.4:447–459.

Berman, S. J., S. Abraham, B. Battino, L. Shipnuk, and A. Neus. 2007. Navigating the media divide: Innovating and enabling new business models. IBM Global Business Services. Retrieved March 16, 2009, from: http://www-935.ibm.com/services/us/index.wss/ibvstudy/gbs/a1026258.

Berman, S., B. Battino, and K. Feldman. 2009. Beyond advertising: Choosing a strategic path to the digital consumer. IBM Global Business Services. Retrieved April 2, 2009, from: ftp://ftp.software.ibm.com/common/ssi/pm/xb/n/gbe03189usen/GBE03189USEN.PDF.

Bermejo, F. 2007. *The Internet Audience: Constitution and Measurement.* New York: Lang.

——. 2009. Audience manufacture in historical perspective: From broadcasting to Google. *New Media and Society* 11.1/2:133–154.

Bernt, J. P., F. E. Fee, J. Gifford, and G. H. Stempel III. 2000. How well can editors predict reader interest in news? *Newspaper Research Journal* 21.2:2–10.

Berrios, R., and P. Moyano. 2005. Dealing with commercial avoidance. Paper presented at the ESOMAR Cross Media/Television conference, Montreal, June.

Berry, R. 2006. Will the iPod kill the radio star? Profiling podcasting as radio. *Convergence* 12.2:143–162.

Beville, H. M., Jr. 1940. The ABCD's of radio audiences. *Public Opinion Quarterly* 4.2:195–206.

——. 1988. *Audience Ratings: Radio, Television, Cable.* Hillsdale, NJ: Erlbaum.

Bhattacharjee, S., R. D. Gopal, K. Lertwachara, and J. R. Marsden. 2006. Impact of legal threats on online music sharing activity: An analysis of music industry legal actions. *Journal of Law and Economics* 49:91–113.

Bielby, D., and C. L. Harrington. 1994. Reach out and touch someone: Viewers, agency, and audiences in the televisual experience. In *Viewing, Reading, Listening: Audiences and Cultural Reception*, ed. J. Cruz and J. Lewis, 81–100. Boulder, CO: Westview.

Bielby, W. T., and D. D. Bielby. 1994. "All hits are flukes": Institutionalized decision-making and the rhetoric of network prime-time program development. *American Journal of Sociology* 99.5:1287–1313.

Billings, V. 1986. Culture by the millions: Audience as innovator. In *Media, Audience, and Social Structure*, ed. S. J. Ball-Rokeach and M. G. Cantor, 206–213. Beverly Hills: Sage.

Bimber, B. A. 1996. *The Politics of Expertise: The Rise and Fall of the Office of Technology Assessment.* Albany: State University of New York Press.

Black, L. 2005. Whose finger on the button? British television and the politics of cultural control. *Historical Journal of Film, Radio, and Television* 25.4:547–575.

Boczkowski, P. J. 2004a. The process of adopting multimedia and interactivity in three online newsrooms. *Journal of Communication* 54.2:197–213.

——. 2004b. *Digitizing the News: Innovation in Online Newspapers.* Cambridge, MA: MIT Press.

Boedecker, K. A., F. W. Morgan, and L. B. Wright. 1995. The evolving application of First Amendment protection for commercial speech. *Journal of Marketing* 59:39–47.

Bogart, L. 1956. Media research: A tool for effective advertising. *Journal of Marketing* 20.4:347–355.

——. 1957. Opinion research and marketing. *Public Opinion Quarterly* 27.1:129–140.

——. 1966. Is it time to discard the audience concept? *Journal of Marketing* 30.1:47–54.

——. 1969. Where does advertising research go from here? *Journal of Advertising Research* 9.1:3–12.

——. 1976. Mass advertising: The message, not the measure. *Harvard Business Review,* Sept./Oct., 107–116.

——. 1986a. What forces shape the future of advertising research? *Journal of Advertising Research* 26.1:99–104.

——. 1986b. Progress in advertising research? *Journal of Advertising Research* 26.3:11–15.

——. 1988/89. Advertising: Art, science, or business? *Journal of Advertising Research* 28.6:47–52.

Bolter, J. D., and R. Grusin. 2000. *Remediation: Understanding New Media.* Cambridge, MA: MIT Press.

Born, G. 2002. Reflexivity and ambivalence: Culture, creativity, and government in the BBC. *Cultural Values* 6.1:65–90.

Borneman, E. 1947. The public opinion myth. *Harper's*, July, 30–40.

Bracha, O., and F. Pasquale. 2008. Federal Search Commission? Access, fairness, and accountability in the law of search. *Cornell Law Review* 93:1149–1210.

Bratich, J. Z. 2005. Amassing the multitude: Revisiting early audience studies. *Communication Theory* 15.3:242–265.

Brill, S. A., M. Bloxham, M. Holmes, B. Moult, and J. Spaeth. 2007. Understanding audience consumption of media to further its measurement. Paper presented at ARF's Audience Measurement symposium, New York, June 29.

Brubaker, R. 1984. *The Limits of Rationality.* London: Allen and Unwin.

Bryant, J. 2008. *Media Effects: Advances in Theory and Research.* 3rd ed. New York: Routledge.

Brynjolfsson, E., Y. J. Hu, and D. Simester. 2007. Goodbye, Pareto principle, hello, long tail: The effect of search costs on the concentration of product sales. Retrieved Jan. 20, 2009, from http://ssrn.com/abstract=953587.

Brynjolfsson, E., Y. J. Hu, and M. D. Smith. 2006. From niches to riches: Anatomy of the long tail. *MIT Sloan Management Review* 47.4:67–71.

Buck, S. 1987. Television audience measurement research—yesterday, today, and tomorrow. *Journal of the Market Research Society* 29.3:265–278.

Bucy, E. P. 2004. Interactivity in society: Locating an elusive concept. *The Information Society* 20:373–383.

Bughin, J. R. 2007. How companies can make the most of user-generated content. *McKinsey Quarterly*, Aug. Retrieved April 10, 2009, from: http://www.mckinsey-quarterly.com/How_companies_can_make_the_most_of_user-generated_content_2041.

Burns, C. 2004. Letter to Deborah Platt Majoras, chairman, Federal Trade Commission, Oct. 7. Retrieved April 26, 2005, from: http://www.dontcountusout.com/resources/100704Burnsltr.pdf.

Butche, R. 2007. Beware new media metrics. *Newsroom Magazine*, Dec. 26. Retrieved Jan. 10, 2008, from: http://newsroom.lookie.us/?p=305&print=1.

Butsch, R. 2000. *The Making of American Audiences: From Stage to Television, 1750–1990.* New York: Cambridge University Press.

——. 2008. *The Citizen Audience: Crowds, Publics, and Individuals.* New York: Routledge.

Buxton, W. J. 1994. The political economy of communications research. In *Information and Communication in Economics*, ed. R. E. Babe, 147–175. Norwell, Ma: Kluwer Academic.

Buzzard, K. S. 1990. *Chains of Gold: Marketing the Ratings and Rating the Markets.* Metuchen, NJ: Scarecrow Press.

——. 2002. The peoplemeter wars: A case study of technological innovation and diffusion in the ratings industry. *Journal of Media Economics* 15.4:273–291.

——. 2003a. James W. Seiler of the American Research Bureau. *Journal of Radio Studies* 10.2:186–201.

——. 2003b. Net ratings: Defining a new medium by the old, measuring Internet audiences. In *New Media: Theories and Practices of Digitextuality*, ed. J. T. Caldwell and A. Everett, 197–208. New York: Routledge.

Cable Communications Policy Act. 1984. 47 USC §551.

Calder, B. J., and E. C. Malthause. 2005. Managing media and advertising change with integrated marketing. *Journal of Advertising Research* 45.4:356–361.

Caldwell, J. T. 2006. Critical industrial practice: Branding, repurposing, and the migratory patterns of industrial texts. *Television and New Media* 7.2:99–134.

Callius, P., A. Lithner, and S. Svanfeldt. 2005. Changing the Internet audience measurement standard. Paper presented at the ESOMAR Cross Media Measurement conference, Montreal.

Campbell, J. E., and M. Carlson. 2002. Panopticon.com: Online surveillance and the commodification of privacy. *Journal of Broadcasting and Electronic Media* 46.4:586–606.

Cantor, M. G., and J. M. Cantor. 1986. Audience composition and television content: The mass audience revisited. In *Media, Audience, and Social Structure*, ed. S. J. Ball-Rokeach and M. G. Cantor, 214–225. Beverly Hills: Sage.

Cappo, J. 2003. *The Future of Advertising: New Media, New Clients, New Consumers in the Post-Television Age.* New York: McGraw-Hill.

Carey, J. W. 1980. Changing communications technology and the nature of the audience. *Journal of Advertising* 9.2:3–43.

Carlson, M. 2006. Tapping into TiVo: Digital video recorders and the transition from schedules to surveillance in television. *New Media and Society* 8.1:97–115.

Carr, D. 2008a. Newspapers' new owners turn grim. *New York Times*, March 24. Retrieved April 27, 2009, from: http://www.nytimes.com/2008/03/24/business/media/24carr.html?_r=1&scp=1&sq=Newspapers'%20new%20owners%20turn%20grim&st=cse.

——. 2008b. Now on the endangered species list: Movie critics in print. *New York Times*, April 1. Retrieved April 27, 2009, from: http://www.nytimes.com/2008/04/01/movies/01crit.html?scp=1&sq=Now+on+the+endangered+species+list%3A+Movie+critics+in+print&st=nyt.

Carter, B. 2009. Comedy Central tries to gauge passion of its viewers. *New York Times*, Aug. 26. Retrieved Nov. 2, 2009, from: http://www.nytimes.com/2009/08/26/business/media/26adco.html.

Caves, R. E. 2000. *Creative Industries: Contracts Between Art and Commerce.* Cambridge, MA: Harvard University Press.

Central Hudson v. Public Service Commission of New York. 1980. 447 U.S. 557, 562–563.

Cha, M., H. Kwak, P. Rodriguez, Y. Ahn, and S. Moon. 2007. I tube, you tube, everybody tubes: Analyzing the world's largest user-generated content video system. Paper presented at the Internet Measurement conference, San Diego, Oct.

Chaffee, S. H. 2000. George Gallup and Ralph Nafziger: Pioneers of audience research. *Mass Communication and Society* 3.2/3:317–327.

Chagrin, C. 2005. Testimony before the United States Senate Committee on Commerce, Science, and Transportation on the FAIR Ratings Act (S. 1372), July 27.

Chambers, R. W. 1947. Need for statistical research. *Annals of the American Academy of Political and Social Science* 254:169–172.

Chan, T. W. 2004. A traitor in our midst: Is it your TiVo? *Vanderbilt Journal of Entertainment Law and Practice* 7:166–181.

Chandler, J. A. 2007. A right to reach an audience: An approach to intermediary bias on the Internet. *Hofstra Law Review* 35.3:1095–1138.

Chandler-Pepelnjak, J. 2008. *Measuring ROI Beyond the Last Ad.* Seattle: Atlas Institute.

Chappell, M. N., and C. E. Hooper. 1944. *Radio Audience Measurement.* New York: Daye.

Cheong, Y., and J. D. Leckenby. 2003. The media type interaction cycle. Center for Interactive Advertising working paper. Retrieved Feb. 4, 2009, from http://www.ciadvertising.org/studies/reports/presentation/AAA_2004_Cheong_Leckenby_MediaTypeInteraction.pdf.

Cheong, H. J. and M. A. Morrison. 2008. Consumers' reliance on product information and recommendations found in UGC. *Journal of Interactive Advertising* 8.2. Retrieved April 29, 2009, from: http://www.jiad.org/article103.

Chester, G. 1949. The press-radio war: 1933–1935. *Public Opinion Quarterly* 13.2:252–264.

Chozick, A. 2009. Making Ugly Betty prettier: To gauge viewer reaction, ABC turns to online focus groups to test its star. *Wall Street Journal*, Oct. 16. Retrieved Oct. 18, 2009, from: http://online.wsj.com/article/SB100014240527487041072045744 69733432844964.html.

Chris, C. 2006. Can you repeat that? Patterns of media ownership and the "repurposing" trend. *Communication Review* 9:63–84.

Chung, D. S. 2007. Profits and perils: Online news producers' perceptions of interactivity and uses of interactive features. *Convergence* 13.1:43–61.

Cirlin, B. D., and J. N. Peterman. 1947. Pre-testing a motion picture: A case history. *Journal of Social Issues* 3.3:39–41.

Clancey, M. 1993. To be or not to be (counted)? *Journal of Advertising Research* 33.3:RC3–RC5.

Clark, J., and P. Aufderheide. 2009. Public media 2.0: Dynamic, engaged publics. Center for Social Media white paper. Retrieved March 14, 2009, from: http://www.centerforsocialmedia.org/resources/publications/public_media_2_0_dynamic_engaged_publics.

Clarke, D. 2000. The active pursuit of active viewers: Directions in audience research. *Canadian Journal of Communication* 25.1. Retrieved Jan. 20, 2009, from http://www.cjc-online.ca/viewarticle.php?id=561.

Clifford, S. 2008. Web privacy on the radar in Congress. *New York Times*, Aug. 11. Retrieved April 27, 2009, from: http://www.nytimes.com/2008/08/11/technology/11privacy.html?_r=1&scp=1&sq=Web%20privacy%20on%20the%20radar%20in%20Congress&st=cse.

——. 2009a. Cable companies target commercials to audience. *New York Times*, March 4. Retrieved March 5, 2009, from: http://www.nytimes.com/2009/03/04/business/04cable.html?scp=1&sq=%22cable+companies+target+commercials+to+audience%22&st=nyt.

——. 2009b. Advertisers get a trove of clues in smartphones. *New York Times*, March 11. Retrieved April 27, 2009, from: http://tech2.nytimes.com/technology/personaltech/gps/overview.html?scp=1&sq=Advertisers%20get%20a%20trove%20of%20clues%20in%20smartphones&st=Search.

Coffey, S. 2001. Internet audience measurement: A practitioner's view. *Journal of Interactive Advertising* 1.2. Retrieved March 15, 2008, from: http://www.jiad.org/vol1/no2/coffey/index.htm.

Cohen, A. J.-J. 2001. Virtual Hollywood and the genealogy of its hyper-spectator. In *Hollywood Spectatorship: Changing Perceptions of Cinema Audiences*, ed. M. Stokes and R. Maltby, 152–163. London: British Film Institute.

Cohen, J. E. 1996. A right to read anonymously: A closer look at "copyright management" in cyberspace. *Connecticut Law Review* 28:981–1039.

——. 2000. Examined lives: Informational privacy and the subject as object. *Stanford Law Review* 52:1373–1437.

——. 2005. The place of the user in copyright law. *Fordham Law Review* 74:347–374.

Cohen, N. S. 2008. The valorization of surveillance: Towards a political economy of Facebook. *Democratic Communique* 22.1:5–22.

Collins, S. 2009. Television is starting to look beyond the 18–49-year-old demographic. *Los Angeles Times*, Jan. 11. Retrieved Jan. 11, 2009, from: http://www.latimes.com/entertainment/news/business/la-et-demographic11-2009jan11,0,5034868.story.

"ComScore Announces New Digital Audience Measurement Tool, Media Metrix 360." 2009. June 1. Retrieved Nov. 2, 2009, from: http://www.medianewsline.com/news/121/ARTICLE/4614/2009-06-01.html.

Consumer Federation of America. 2008. Re: Behavioral marketing principles. Letter to Donald S. Clark, Secretary, Federal Trade Commission, April 11. Retrieved June 14, 2008, from: http://www.ftc.gov/os/comments/behavioraladprinciples/080411cfacu.pdf.

Cook, T. E. 2005. *Governing with the News: The News Media as a Political Institution.* Chicago: University of Chicago Press.

Cooper, A. C., and D. Schendel. 1976. Strategic responses to technological threats. *Business Horizons* 19.1:61–69.

Cooper, A. C., and C. G. Smith. 1992. How established firms respond to threatening technologies. *Academy of Management Executive* 6.2:55–70.

Cooper, M., S. Grant, and C. Murray. 2008. Letter from the Consumer Federation of America to Donald S. Clark, Secretary, Federal Trade Commission, re: Behavioral marketing principles, April 11. On file with author.

Costello, V., and B. Moore. 2007. Cultural outlaws: An examination of audience activity and online television fandom. *Television and New Media* 8.2:124–143.

Couldry, N. 2004. The productive "consumer" and the dispersed "citizen." *International Journal of Cultural Studies* 7.1:21–32.

Council for Research Excellence. 2006. Report of the marketplace practices committee, Dec. 1. On file with author.

Coutant, F. R. 1939. Determining the appeal of special features of a radio program. *Journal of Applied Psychology* 23.1:54–57.

Cover, R. 2004. New media theory: Electronic games, democracy and reconfiguring the author-audience relationship. *Social Semiotics* 14.2:173–191.

——. 2006. Audience inter/active: Interactive media, narrative control, and reconceiving audience history. *New Media and Society* 8.1:139–158.

Croteau, D. 2006. The growth of self-produced media content and the challenge to media studies. *Critical Studies in Media Communication* 23.4:340–344.

Crupi, A. 2008a. It pays to be gay: Logo tops key demos in Simmons engagement study. *Mediaweek*, April 28, 10–11.

Currah, A. 2006. Hollywood versus the Internet: The media and entertainment industries in a digital networked economy. *Journal of Economic Geography* 6.4:439–468.

Dahlberg, L. 2004. Cyberpublics and the corporate control of online communication. *Javnos–The Public* 11.3:77–92.

——. 2005. The corporate colonization of online attention and the marginalization of critical communication? *Journal of Communication Inquiry* 29.2:160–180.

Dahlgren, P. 1998. Critique: Elusive audiences. In *Approaches to Audiences: A Reader*, ed. R. Dickinson, R. Harindranath, and O. Linne, 298–310. London: Arnold.

Danaher, P. J., and J. M. Lawrie. 1998. Behavioral measures of television audience appreciation. *Journal of Advertising Research* 38.1:54–65.

Daneels, E. 2004. Disruptive technology reconsidered: A critique and research agenda. *Journal of Product Innovation Management* 21:246–258.

Davenport, T. H., and J. C. Beck. 2002. *The Attention Economy: Understanding the New Currency of Business.* Cambridge, MA: Harvard Business School Press.

Davenport, T. H., and J. G. Hassis. 2009. What people want (and how to predict it). *MIT Sloan Management Review* 50.2:23–31.

Davies, C. L., and J. Sternberg. 2007. The spaces and places of audience research in Australian television. *Media International Australia Incorporating Culture and Policy* 122:28–42.

Dekom, P., and P. Sealey. 2003. *Not on My Watch: Hollywood Versus the Future.* Beverly Hills: New Millennium.

Dellarocas, C., and R. Narayan. 2007. Tall heads vs. long tails: Do consumer reviews increase the informational inequality between hit and niche products? Retrieved April 29, 2009, from: http://papers.ssrn.com/sol3/papers.cfm?abstract_id=1105956.

Desilva and Phillips, LLC. 2008. Online ad networks: Monetizing the long tail. March. New York: Author.

Deuze, M. 2003. The Web and its journalisms: Considering the consequences of different types of newsmedia online. *New Media and Society* 5.2:203–230.

——. 2006. Participation, remediation, bricolage: Considering principal components of a digital culture. *Information Society* 22.2:63–75.

——. 2007. Convergence culture in the creative industries. *International Journal of Cultural Studies* 10.2:243–263.

——. 2008. Corporate appropriation of participatory culture. In *Participation and Media Production: Critical Reflections on Content Creation*, ed. N. Carpentier and B. De Cleen, 27–40. Newcastle, UK: Cambridge Scholars Publishing.

De Vany, A. 2004. *Hollywood Economics: How Extreme Uncertainty Shapes the Film Industry.* New York: Routledge.

DeWerth-Pallmeyer, D. 1997. *The Audience in the News.* Mahwah, NJ: Erlbaum.

DiMaggio, P., and M. Useem. 1979. Decentralized applied research: Factors affecting the use of audience research by arts organizations. *Journal of Applied Behavioral Science* 15.1:79–94.

Dimling, J. 1985. Measuring future electronic media audiences. *Journal of Advertising Research* 25:RC3–RC7.

Dimmick, J. 2002. *Media Competition and Coexistence: The Theory of the Niche.* Mahwah, NJ: Erlbaum.

Dish Network/Rentrak Corporation. 2009. Size does matter: Measuring the fragmenting media marketplace. Paper presented at ARF's Audience Measurement 4.0 conference, New York, June.

Doe, P., and J. Connolly. 2007. Billboards, buses, and malls (and other media, too). Paper presented at ARF's Audience Measurement 2.0 conference, New York, June.

Donaton, S. 2004. *Madison and Vine: Why the Entertainment and Advertising Industries Must Converge to Survive.* New York: McGraw-Hill.

Don't Count Us Out Coalition. 2004. Leading New York state lawmakers committed to stop Nielsen from undercounting minority and young adult viewers. Press release, March 28. Retrieved June 15, 2004, from: http://www.dontcountusout.com/pr032804/.

Doscher, L. 1947. The significance of audience measurement in motion pictures. *Journal of Social Issues* 33.3:51–57.

Dovey, J. 2008. Dinosaurs and butterflies—media practice research in new media ecologies. *Journal of Media Practice* 9.3:243–256.

Downey, K. 2008. Arbitron: The PPM rollout will proceed. *Media Life*, Oct. 3. Retrieved Oct. 3, 2008, from: http://www.medialifemagazine.com/artman2/publish/Radio_46/Arbitron_The_PPM_rollout_will_proceed.asp.

Downie, L. R., and M. Schudson. 2009. The reconstruction of American journalism. Retrieved Nov. 3, 2009, from: http://www.journalism.columbia.edu/cs/ContentServer?pagename=JRN/Render/DocURL&binaryid=1212611716626.

Downing, J. D. H. 2003. Audiences and readers of alternative media: The absent lure of the virtually unknown. *Media, Culture, and Society* 25:625–645.

Dreyfuss, R. C. 1990. Expressive genericity: Trademarks as language in the Pepsi Generation. *Notre Dame Law Review* 65:397–424.

Duarte, L. G., and J. P. Beauchamp. 2007. Single-source audience and consumption measurement in a non-linear world: A case study. Paper presented at ARF's Audience Measurement 2.0 conference, New York, June.

Dykes, B. 2009. Testimony of Bob Dykes, CEO NebuAd, Inc., before the Senate Committee on Commerce, Science, and Transportation. July 9. Retrieved April 2, 2009, from: http://commerce.senate.gov/public/_files/RobertDykesNebuAdOnlinePrivacyTestimony.pdf.

Eadie, W. 2007. Return on engagement: Quantifying the impact of reader engagement on ad effectiveness. Paper presented at ARF's Audience Measurement 2.0 conference, New York, June.

Eaman, R. 1994. *Channels of Influence: CBC Audience Research and the Canadian Public.* Toronto: University of Toronto Press.

Earnheardt, J. W. 2004. *Nike, Inc. v. Kasky*: A golden opportunity to define commercial speech—why wouldn't the Supreme Court finally "Just Do It"? *North Carolina Law Review* 82:797–810.

Eastman, S. T. 1998. Programming theory under stress: The active industry and the active audience. *Communication Yearbook* 21:323–378.

Edmunds, A., and A. Morris. 2000. The problem of information overload in business organisations: A review of the literature. *International Journal of Information Management* 20.1:17–28.

Ehrenberg, A. 1996. Measuring TV audiences: Reinventing the wheel again. *Journal of the Market Research Society* 38.4:549–551.

Ehrenberg, A. S. C. 1968. The time and the place for readership panels. *Journal of Advertising Research* 8.2:19–22.

Elberse, A. 2008. Should you invest in the long tail? *Harvard Business Review,* July/Aug., 88–96.

Elberse, A., and F. Oberholzer-Gee. 2008. Superstars and underdogs: An examination of the long-tail phenomenon in video sales. July. Retrieved Jan. 29, 2008, from: http://www.people.hbs.edu/aelberse/papers/hbs_07-015.pdf.

Electronic Communications Privacy Act. 1986, Pub. L. 99-508, Oct. 21, 1986, 100 Stat. 1848, 18 U.S.C. §2510.

Electronic Privacy Information Center. 2009. Facebook privacy. Retrieved April 4, 2009, from: http://epic.org/privacy/facebook/default.html.

Elms, S. 2007. The long media tail: Are you wagging it or is it wagging you? Paper presented at the ESOMAR Worldwide Multi Media Measurement conference, Dublin, Ireland, June.

Elsbach, K. D., and R. M. Kramer. 1996. Members' responses to organizational identity threats: Encountering the *Business Week* rankings. *Administrative Science Quarterly* 41:442–476.

Emmett, B. P. 1968. A new role for research in broadcasting. *Public Opinion Quarterly* 32.4:654–665.

Ephron, E. 2008. A blast from the past: Nielsen's new fused data may be a better way to target television. *The Ephron Letter*, June. Retrieved April 27, 2009, from: http://www.ephrononmedia.com/article_archive/article_pdf/blast_06_08.pdf.

——. 2009. How PPM could rescue radio. *The Ephron Letter*, March. Retrieved March 29, 2009, from: http://www.ephrononmedia.com/article_archive/article_pdf/arbitron_03_09.pdf.

Ephron, E., and J. C. Philport. 2005. Creative heresy in audience measurement. Paper presented at the ESOMAR Worldwide Audience Measurement conference, Montreal, June.

Erichson, S. 2009. OnDemand Online, TV Everywhere, and what it means for audience measurement. *Nielsenwire*, Sept. 8. Retrieved Nov. 2, 2009, from: http://blog.nielsen.com/nielsenwire/online_mobile/ondemand-online-tv-everywhere-and-what-it-means-for-audience-measurement/.

Espeland, W. N., and M. Sauder. 2007. Rankings and reactivity: How public measures recreate social worlds. *American Journal of Sociology* 113.1:1–40.

Ettema, J. S., and D. C. Whitney. 1994. The money arrow: An introduction to audiencemaking. In *Audiencemaking: How the Media Create the Audience*, ed. J. S. Ettema and D. C. Whitney, 1–18. Thousand Oaks, CA: Sage.

Eubank, S., and H. Griffiths. 2007a. Linking media engagement to sales. Presentation at ARF's Audience Measurement 2.0 conference, New York, June.

——. 2007b. Exploring media engagement. Paper presented at ARF's Audience Measurement 2.0 conference, New York, June.

Faasse, J. 2007. This could be heaven: How to measure media in a fragmented universe. Paper presented at the ESOMAR Worldwide Multi Media Measurement conference, Dublin, Ireland, June.

Fairness and Accuracy in Ratings Act. 2005. S. 1372. 109th Congress, 1st Session, July 1. Retrieved Oct. 14, 2005, from: http://thomas.loc.gov/cgi-bin/query/z?c109:S.1372.

Federal Communications Commission. 2008. PPM coalition files petition seeking Commission inquiry pursuant to Section 403 of the Communications Act of 1934. Media Bureau Action, MB docket no. 08-187, Sept. 4.

Federal Trade Commission. 2007. Online behavioral advertising: Moving the discussion forward to possible self-regulatory principles. Dec. 20. Retrieved June 14, 2008, from: http://www.ftc.gov/os/2007/12/P859900stmt.pdf.

———. 2009. Self-regulatory principles for online behavioral advertising. FTC staff report, Feb. Retrieved March 5, 2009, from: http://www.ftc.gov/opa/2009/02/behavad.shtm.

Feldman, M. S., and J. G. March. 1981. Information in organizations as signal and symbol. *Administrative Science Quarterly* 26:171–186.

Ferrier, L. 2002. Bring out the "backroom boys": The role of media planners and buyers in the knowledge economy. *Media International Australia Incorporating Culture and Policy* 105:66–76.

Finin, T., A. Joshi, P. Kolari, A. Java, A. Kale, and A. Karandikar. 2008. The information ecology of social media and online communities. *AI Magazine* 28.3:77–92.

Finkelstein, S. 2008. Google, links, and popularity versus authority. In *The Hyperlinked Society: Questioning Connections in the Digital Age*, ed. J. Turow and L. Tsui, 104–120. Ann Arbor: University of Michigan Press.

Fiske, M., and L. Handel. 1946. Motion picture research: Content and audience analysis. *Journal of Marketing* 11.2:129–134.

———. 1947a. Motion picture research: Response analysis. *Journal of Marketing* 11.3:273–280.

———. 1947b. New techniques for studying the effectiveness of films. *Journal of Marketing* 11.4:390–393.

Fitzgerald, T. 2007. In fall, Nielsen will deliver the bar set. *Media Life*, April 13. Retrieved Jan. 20, 2009, from http://www.medialifemagazine.com/artman/publish/printer_11409.asp.

———. 2009a. "Gossip" effect: Real value of web buzz. *Media Life*, Feb. 13. Retrieved Feb. 16, 2009, from: http://www.medialifemagazine.com/artman2/publish/New_media_23/Gossip_effect_Real_value_of_web_buzz.asp.

———. 2009b. Cable recap: Another year and cable's bite deepens. *Media Life*, April 1. Retrieved April 1, 2009, from: http://www.medialifemagazine.com/artman2/publish/Cable_65recap/Another_year_and_cable_s_bite_deepens.asp.

Fleder, D., and K. Hosanagar. 2009. Blockbuster culture's next rise or fall: The impact of recommender systems on sales diversity. *Management Science* 55.5:697–712.

Fligstein, N. 1996. Markets as politics: A political-cultural approach to market institutions. *American Sociological Review* 61.4:656–673.

Fonio, C., et al. 2007. Eyes on you: Analyzing user-generated content for social science. Paper presented at the Towards a Social Science of Web 2.0 conference, York, UK, May.

Foote, J. 2002. Cultural consumption and participation. *Canadian Journal of Communication* 27.2. Retrieved May 2, 2009, from: http://www.cjc-online.ca/viewarticle.php?id=718.

"For Nielsen, Fear and Loathing in LA." 2004. *Media Life*, May 11. Retrieved May 11, 2004, from: http://69.20.6.242/news2004/may04/may10/2_tues/news1tuesday.html.

Fox, S., and G. Livingston. 2007. Latinos online. Pew Internet and American Life Project, March. Retrieved March 1, 2009, from: http://www.pewinternet.org/pdfs/Latinos_Online_March_14_2007.pdf.

Freidson, E. 1953. Communications research and the concept of the mass. *American Sociological Review* 18.3:313–317.

Friedman, W. 2008. Station victory: TVB endorses L3 ratings. *Media Daily News*, Nov. 14. Retrieved Nov. 15, 2008, from: http://www.mediapost.com/publications/index.cfm?fa=Articles.showArticle&art_aid=94849.

——. 2009a. L3 sounds like C3—but advertisers' ears hear the difference. *Media-Post's TVWatch*, Jan. 8. Retrieved Jan. 8, 2009, from: http://www.mediapost.com/publications/index.cfm?fa=Articles.showArticle&art_aid=97939.

——. 2009b. Which Web-based TV shows are up, down—or out? *MediaPost's TVWatch*, Jan. 20. Retrieved Jan. 21, 2009, from: http://www.mediapost.com/publications/?fa=Articles.showArticle&art_aid=98706.

——. 2009c. Ad-on: "Q" score may suggest better TV performance, Jan. 21. *Media Daily News*. Retrieved Jan. 21, 2009, from http://www.mediapost.com/publications/?fa=Articles.printFriendly&art_aid=98834.

——. 2009d. Show me: Reality outpaces scripted fare in key engagement categories. *Media Daily News*, June 2. Retrieved June 25, 2009, from: http://www.mediapost.com/index.cfm?fa=Articles.showArticle&art_aid=107213.

——. 2009e. Group M's Scanzoni slams Nielsen live-plus. *Media Daily News*, Sept. 11. Retrieved Oct. 18, 2009, from: http://www.mediapost.com/publications/?fa=Articles.showArticle&art_aid=113370.

——. 2009f. Nielsen Catalina Ventures creates TV ROI measurement. *Media Daily News*, Dec. 14. Retrieved Feb. 25, 2010, from: http://www.mediapost.com/publications/?fa=Articles.showArticle&art_aid=119077.

——. 2010. Rentrak's "stickiness" mines TV value on a granular level. *Media Daily News*, Jan. 27. Retrieved Jan. 27, 2010, from: http://www.mediapost.com/publications/?fa=Articles.showArticle&art_aid=121389.

Furchtgott-Roth, H., R. W. Hahn, and A. Layne-Farrar. 2007. Regulating the raters: The law and economics of ratings firms. *Journal of Competition Law and Economics* 3.1:49–96.

Furhof, L. 1973. Some reflections on newspaper concentration. *Scandinavian Economic History Review* 21.1:1–27.

Gabler, N. 2003. The tyranny of 18–49: American culture held hostage. Retrieved Aug. 5, 2008, from: http://www.learcenter.org/pdf/18to49.pdf.

Gallup, G. 1928. "A New Technique for Objective Methods for Measuring Reader Interest in Newspapers." Unpublished Ph.D. diss., University of Iowa.

Galperin, H. 2004. *New Television, Old Politics: The Transition to Digital TV in the United States and Britain.* New York: Cambridge University Press.

Gandy, O. H., Jr. 1996. Legitimate business interest: No end in sight? An inquiry into the status of privacy in cyberspace. *University of Chicago Legal Forum*, 1996, 77–137.

——. 2000. Exploring identity and identification in cyberspace. *Notre Dame Journal of Law, Ethics, and Public Policy* 14:1085–1110.

——. 2002. The real digital divide: Citizens v. consumers. In *The Handbook of New Media*, ed. L. Lievrow and S. Livingstone, 448–460. Thousand Oaks, CA: Sage.

Gans, H. J. 1979/2005. *Deciding What's News: A Study of CBS Evening News, NBC Nightly News, Newsweek, and Time.* Evanston, IL: Northwestern University Press.

Garfield, B. 2005. Bob Garfield's chaos scenario. *Advertising Age*, April 13. Retrieved April 29, 2009, from: http://adage.com/article?article_id=45561.

——. 2007. Bob Garfield's chaos scenario 2.0: The post advertising age. *Advertising Age*, April 24. Retrieved April 29, 2009, from: http://www.jingleman.com/clients/ChaosScenario2.0.pdf.

——. 2008. Your data with destiny. *Advertising Age*, Sept. 15. Retrieved April 29, 2009, from: http://adage.com/digital/article?article_id=130969.

Garfield, B. 2009. *The Chaos Scenario.* New York: Stielstra.

Garrison, L. C. 1972. The needs of motion picture audiences. *California Management Review* 15.2:144–152.

Gertner, J. 2005. Our ratings, ourselves. *New York Times Magazine*, April 10. Retrieved April 27, 2009, from: http://www.nytimes.com/2005/04/10/magazine/10NIELSENS.html?_r=1&scp=1&sq=Our%20ratings,%20ourselves&st=cse.

Gertz v. Robert Welch, Inc. 1974. 418 U.S. 323.

Gillmor, D. 2004. *We the Media: Grassroots Journalism by the People, for the People.* Sebastopol, CA: O'Reilly Media.

Gitlin, T. 1983/2000. *Inside Prime Time.* Berkeley: University of California Press.

Glickman, L. B. 2006. The consumer and the citizen in Personal Influence. *Annals of the American Academy of Political and Social Science* 608:205–212.

Gluck, M., and M. R. Sales. 2008. The future of television? Advertising, technology, and the pursuit of audiences. The Norman Lear Center, University of Southern California, Sept. Retrieved Feb. 27, 2009, from: http://www.learcenter.org/pdf/FutureofTV.pdf.

Goetzl, D. 2008. On eve of TV upfront, Nielsen ratings remain unaccredited. *Media Daily News*, May 12. Retrieved March 25, 2009, from: http://www.mediapost/com/publications/?fa=Articles.printFriendly&art_aid82374.

——. 2009. ABC has ad metric to prove effectiveness, but marketers won't share data. *Media Daily News*, April 23. Retrieved April 23, 2009, from: http://www.mediapost.com/publications/?fa=Articles.showArticle&art_aid=104746.

Goldberg, M. A. 1989. Broadcast ratings and ethics. *Review of Business* 11:19–20, 27.

Goldhaber, M. H. 1997. The attention economy and the Net. *First Monday.* Retrieved April 29, 2009, from: http://firstmonday.org/htbin/cgiwrap/bin/ojs/index.php/fm/article/viewArticle/519/440.

Goldman, W. 1983. *Adventures in the Screen Trade.* New York: Warner Books.

Gomes, L. 2006. It may be a long time before the long tail is wagging the Web. *Wall Street Journal*, July 26. Retrieved April 29, 2009, from: http://online.wsj.com/

public/article/SB115387606762117314-Wwm0ACNV7rjYDAvcwtpe8vMpMYs_20070725.html?mod=rss_free.

Goolsbee, A. 2007. "American Idol" is the price we pay for a menu of so many channels. *New York Times*, April 26. Retrieved April 28, 2009, from: http://www.nytimes.com/2007/04/26/business/26scene.html?scp=2&sq=).%20"American%20Idol"%20is%20the%20price%20we%20may%20for%20a%20menu%20of%20so%20many%20channels.%20New%20York%20Times&st=cse.

Goosey, R. W. 2005. Advanced techniques in panel and server data integration. Paper presented at the ESOMAR Worldwide Audience Measurement conference, Montreal, June.

Goran v. Atkins. 2006/2008. 464 F. Supp.2d 315 (S.D.N.Y. 2006), aff'd 279 Fed. Appx. 40WL 2164656 (2d Cir. 2008).

Gordon, W. J. 1992. Reality as artifact: From *Feist* to fair use. *Law and Contemporary Problems* 55:93–107.

Goss, J. 1995. "We know who you are and we know where you live": The instrumental rationality of geodemographic systems. *Economic Geography* 71.2:171–198.

Green, K. 2002. Mobilising readers: Newspapers, copy-tasters, and readerships. In *Mobilising the Audience*, ed. M. Balnaves, T. O'Regan, and J. Sternberg, 213–234. Queensland, Australia: University of Queensland Press.

Greenberg, J. 2008. *From Betamax to Blockbuster: Video Stores and the Invention of Movies on Video.* Cambridge, MA: MIT Press.

Griffen-Foley, B. 2004. From Tit-Bits to Big Brother: A century of audience participation in the media. *Media, Culture, and Society* 26.4:533–548.

Grillo, J. 2009. Ad buyers opposed to local L3 ratings. *TV Newsday*, Jan. 7. Retrieved Jan. 8, 2009, from http://www.newsday.com/articles/2009/01/07/daily.1/.

Grimmelmann, J. 2009. Saving Facebook. *Iowa Law Review* 94:1137–1206.

Gunter, B., and M. Wober. 1992. *The Reactive Viewer: Review of Research on Audience Reaction Measurement.* Cornwall, UK: Libbey.

Gunzerath, D. 2001. An analysis of the proposed use of Arbitron data to define radio markets. Comments of the National Association of Broadcasters, Definition of Radio Markets, attachment B (MM docket 00-244), Feb. 26.

Hackenbruch, T. 2009. Cross-media measurement by the centralized collection of comparable data. Paper presented at the ESOMAR Worldwide Multi Media Measurement conference, Stockholm, Sweden, July.

Hackley, C. 2002. The panoptic role of advertising agencies in the production of consumer culture. *Consumption Markets and Culture* 5.3:211–229.

Hagen, I. 1999. Slaves of the ratings tyranny: Media images of the audience. In *Rethinking the Media Audience: The New Agenda*, ed. P. Alasuutari, 130–150. London: Sage.

Hampp, A. 2009a. Media, marketers, and agencies challenge Nielsen's ratings monopoly. *Advertising Age*, Sept. 10.

——. 2009b. Addressable advertising: Still in the pipe-cleaning stage. *Advertising Age.* Retrieved Nov. 3, 2009, from: http://adage.com/mediaworks/article?article_id=140094.

Handel, L. 1950. *Hollywood Looks at Its Audience: A Report of Film Audience Research.* Urbana: University of Illinois Press.

——. 1953. Hollywood market research. *Quarterly Journal of Film, Radio, and Television* 7.3:304–310.

Hannan, M. T., and J. Freeman. 1984. Structural inertia and organizational change. *American Sociological Review* 49.2:149–164.

Hansell, S. 2006. As Internet TV aims at niche audiences, the slivercast is born. *New York Times*, March 12. Retrieved April 29, 2009, from: http://www.nytimes.com/2006/03/12/business/yourmoney/12sliver.html.

Hargittai, E., and G. Walejko. 2008. The participation divide: Content creation and sharing in the digital age. *Information, Communication, and Society* 11.2: 239–256.

Harris, C. D., and J. Chasin. 2006. The impact of technological innovation on media exposure tracking: In search of "the new traditional." Paper presented at ARF's Audience Measurement Symposium, New York, June.

Harris, L. 2008. Statement of Leslie Harris, president/CEO, Center for Democracy and Technology, before the Senate Commerce, Science, and Transportation Committee, July 9. Retrieved March 31, 2009, from: http://www.cdt.org/testimony/20080709harris.pdf.

Harrison, T. M., and B. Barthel. 2009. Wielding new media in Web 2.0: Exploring the history of engagement with the collaborative construction of media products. *New Media and Society* 11.1/2:155–178.

Hartley, J. 1988. Critical response: The real world of audiences. *Critical Studies in Mass Communication* 5:234–238.

Harvey, B. 2009. Flight to accountability. *Adweek*, Jan. 7. Retrieved Feb. 18, 2009, from: http://www.adweek.com/aw/content_display/community/columns/other-columns/e3i7e37e50c920eaa55f076ab3a63c1ecc4.

Haven, B., and S. Vittal. 2008. Five tools and technologies to measure engagement. April 22. New York: Forrester Research.

Hayes, D., and J. Bing. 2006. *Open Wide: How Hollywood Box Office Became a National Obsession.* New York: Miramax.

Heath, R. 2007. How do we predict attention and engagement? Paper presented at ARF's annual convention, New York, June. Retrieved March 1, 2009, from: http://opus.bath.ac.uk/286/1/2007-09.pdf.

Helft, M. 2008. Is Google a media company? *New York Times*, Aug. 10. Retrieved April 29, 2009, from: http://www.nytimes.com/2008/08/11/technology/11google.html?_r=1&em.

Helft, M. 2009. YouTube's quest to suggest more. *New York Times*, Dec. 30. Retrieved Jan. 4, 2010, from: http://www.nytimes.com/2009/12/31/technology/internet/31tube.html.

Herbig, P. A., and H. Kramer. 1994. The effect of information overload on the innovation choice process. *Journal of Consumer Marketing* 11.2:45–54.

Herbst, S. 1995. *Numbered Voices: How Opinion Polling Has Shaped American Politics.* Chicago: University of Chicago Press.

Herbst, S., and J. R. Beniger. 1994. The changing infrastructure of public opinion. In *Audiencemaking: How the Media Create the Audience*, ed. J. G. Ettema and D. C. Whitney, 95–114. Thousand Oaks, CA: Sage.

Hernandez, R., and S. Elliott. 2004a. Planned Nielsen changes criticized. *New York Times*, March 31, C3.

——. 2004b. The odd couple vs. Nielsen. *New York Times*, June 14, C1.

Hesbacher, P., R. Downing, and D. G. Berger. 1975. Record roulette: What makes it spin? *Journal of Communication* 25:74–85.

Hesmondhalgh, D. 2007. *The Cultural Industries.* 2nd ed. Los Angeles: Sage.

Hilderbrand, L. 2007. YouTube: Where cultural memory and copyright converge. *Film Quarterly* 61.1:48–57.

Hillesund, T. 2007. Reading *Books in the Digital Age* subsequent to Amazon, Google, and the long tail. *First Monday* 12.9. Retrieved Feb. 13, 2008, from http://firstmonday.org/issues/issue12_9/hillesund/index.html.

Hindman, M. 2009. *The Myth of Digital Democracy.* Princeton: Princeton University Press.

Hinman, M. 2008. Nielsen, erinMedia settle antitrust suit. *Tampa Bay Business Journal*, April 1. Retrieved April 3, 2009, from: http://www.bizjournals.com/tampabay/stories/2008/03/31/daily16.html.

Hirsch, P. M. 1972. Processing fads and fashions: An organization-set analysis of cultural industry systems. *American Journal of Sociology* 77.4:639–659.

Hodgkinson, G. P. 1997. Cognitive inertia in a turbulent market: The case of UK residential estate agents. *Journal of Management Studies* 34.6:921–945.

Hoffman, D. L., and R. Batra. 1991. Viewer response to programs: Dimensionality and concurrent behavior. *Journal of Advertising Research* 31.4:46–56.

Hoheb, M. 2004. So what's the Don't Count Us Out Coalition anyhow? *Media Life*, June 17. Retrieved June 17, 2004, from: http://69.20.6.242/news2004/june04/june14/4_thurs/news1thursday.html.

Holden, J., and N. North. 2008. Audience value across media: Beyond a measure of exposure. Paper presented at the ESOMAR Worldwide Multi Media Measurement conference, Budapest, Hungary, June.

Holmes, M. E., R. A. Papper, M. N. Popovich, and M. Bloxham. 2006. Engaging the ad-supported media. Middletown Media Studies white paper, Ball State University.

Hong, T., M. L. McLaughlin, L. Pryor, C. E. Beaudoin, and P. Grabowicz. 2005. Internet privacy practices of news media and implications for online journalism. *Journalism Studies* 6.1:15–28.

Hughes, J. 2007. Created facts and the flawed ontology of copyright law. *Notre Dame Law Review* 83:43–108.

Hujanen, J. 2008. RISC monitor audience rating and its implications for journalistic practice. *Journalism* 9.2:182–199.

Hurwitz, D. 1983. "Broadcast 'Ratings': The Rise and Development of Commercial Audience Research and Measurement in American Broadcasting." Unpublished Ph.D. diss., University of Illinois at Urbana-Champaign.

——. 1984. Broadcasting ratings: The missing dimension. *Critical Studies in Mass Communication* 1.2:205–215.

——. 1988. Market research and the study of the U.S. radio audience. *Communication* 10:223–241.

IBM Global Business Services. 2008. The end of advertising as we know it. Retrieved Jan. 22, 2009, from http://www-03.ibm.com/industries/global/files/media_ibv_advertisingv2.pdf?re=media&sa_message=title=download_complete_ibm_institute_for_business_value_study.

Igo, S. E. 2007. *The Averaged American: Surveys, Citizens, and the Making of a Mass Public.* Cambridge, MA: Harvard University Press.

Integrated Media Measurement, Inc. 2008. Understanding the true value of multi-platform advertising. June. New York: Author.

IAB (Interactive Advertising Bureau). 2008a. User-generated content, social media, and advertising—an overview. April. New York: Author.

——. 2008b. Use of "ad networks" surges six-fold as media companies step up monetization of unsold online advertising inventory. News release, Aug. 11.

——. 2008c. Interactive Advertising Bureau audience reach measurement guidelines, version 1.0. New York: Author.

——. 2009. IAB Internet advertising revenue report. New York: Author.

Jackaway, G. 1995. *Media at War: Radio's Challenge to Newspapers, 1924–1939.* Westport, CT: Praeger.

Jackson, S. E., and J. E. Dutton. 1988. Discerning threats and opportunities. *Administrative Science Quarterly* 33.3:370–387.

Jaffe, J. 2005. *Life After the 30-Second Spot: Energize Your Brand with a Bold Mix of Alternatives to Traditional Advertising.* Hoboken, NJ: Wiley.

James, E. P. H. 1937. The development of research in broadcast advertising. *Journal of Marketing* 2.2:141–145.

James, M. 2008. Charter to sell L.A. TV viewing data. *Los Angeles Times*, March 13. Retrieved Feb. 3, 2009, from http://www.latimes.com/business/la-fi-nielsen-13mar13,1,6670886.story.

Jealous, B. T. 2008. Letter to Kevin Martin, chairman, Federal Communications Commission, Oct. 3. On file with author.

Jeffrey, L. 1994. Rethinking audiences for cultural industries: Implications for Canadian research. *Canadian Journal of Communication* 19.3. Retrieved Jan. 19, 2008, from: http://www.cjc-online.ca/viewarticle.php?id=253.

Jenkins, H. 2006. *Convergence Culture: Where Old and New Media Collide.* New York: New York University Press.

Jenkins, H., R. Purushotma, K. Clinton, M. Weigel, and A. J. Robinson. 2006. *Confronting the Challenges of Participatory Culture: Media Education for the Twenty-first Century.* Chicago: John D. and Catherine T. MacArthur Foundation.

Jesdanun, A. 2006. Imbalance in Net speeds impedes sharing. *Washington Post*, Dec. 18. Retrieved Sept. 18, 2008, from: http://www.washingtonpost.com/wp-dyn/content/article/2006/12/18/AR2006121800610.html.

Jhally, S. 1982. Probing the blindspot: The audience commodity. *Canadian Journal of Political and Social Theory* 6.1/2:204–210.

Jhally, S., and B. Livant. 1986. Watching as working: The valorization of audience consciousness. *Journal of Communication* 36:124–143.

Johnson, D. 2007. Inviting audiences in: The spatial reorganization of production and consumption in "TVIII." *New Review of Film and Television Studies* 5.1:61–80.

Joshi, P. 2009. FTC to assess business of news. *New York Times*, Aug. 23. Retrieved Aug. 23, 2009, from: http://www.nytimes.com/2009/08/24/business/media/24ftc.html?ref=media.

Kanaracus, C. 2008. Service aims to mine social networks for consumer insight. *Washington Post*, March 27. Retrieved Feb. 21, 2009, from: http://www.washingtonpost.com/wp-dyn/content/article/2008/03/27/AR2008032701427_pf.html.

Kang, S. 2008a. TNS aims to take bite out of Nielsen. *Wall Street Journal*, Jan. 31.

——. 2008b. Ad firm tracks consumers across media. *Wall Street Journal*, Oct. 14. Retrieved Oct. 14, 2008, from http://onlne.wsj.com/article/SB122394454320231201.html?mod=dis_smartbrief.

Kang, S., and S. Vranica. 2008. New ABC show: Ad dollars at work; marketers get a tool to target viewership. *Wall Street Journal*, May 13, B6.

Kaplan, D. 2008. Interview: Canoe Ventures' Verklin: Google TV Ads is a potential partner. *Paidcontent*, Sept. 24. Retrieved March 10, 2009, from: http://www.paidcontent.org/entry/419-interview-canoe-ventures-verklin-google-tv-ads-is-a-potential-partner/.

Karol, J. J. 1938. Analyzing the radio market. *Journal of Marketing* 2.4:309–313.

Kasky v. Nike. 2002. 27 Cal. 4th 939, 961.

Keegan, C. A. V. 1980. Qualitative audience research in public television. *Journal of Communication* 30.3:164–172.

Keller, P. 1966. Patterns of media-audience accumulation. *Journal of Marketing* 30.2:32–37.

Kelly, C. 2008. Testimony before the United States Senate Committee on Commerce, Science, and Transportation, hearing on the Privacy Implications of Online Advertising, July 9. Retrieved March 22, 2009, from: http://www.microsoft.com/presspass/exec/hintze/testimony070908.mspx.

Kennedy, R., C. Driesener, G. Goodhardt, C. McDonald, and L. Wood. 2008. How does advertising affect loyalty? Using Project Apollo data to investigate the relationship in a new way. Paper presented at the ESOMAR Worldwide Multi Media Measurement conference, Budapest, Hungary, June.

Kent, R., ed. 1994. *Measuring Media Audiences.* London: Routledge.

Kent, R. J. 2002. Second-by-second looks at the television commercial audience. *Journal of Advertising Research*, Jan./Feb., 71–78.

Kilger, M. 2008. Media engagement: Developing consistent measures across multiple media channels. Paper presented at the ESOMAR Worldwide Multi Media Measurement conference, Budapest, Hungary, June.

Kilger, M., and E. Romer. 2007. Do measures of media engagement correlate with product purchase likelihood? *Journal of Advertising Research* 47.3:313–325.

Kilkki, K. 2007. A practical model for analyzing long tails. *First Monday* 12.5. Retrieved Jan. 2, 2009, from http://firstmonday.org/issues/issue12_5/kilkki/index.html.

Kim, P., and H. Sawhney. 2002. A machine-like new medium—theoretical examination of interactive TV. *Media, Culture, and Society* 24:217–233.

Kingson, W. K. 1953. Measuring the broadcast audience. *Quarterly Journal of Film, Radio, and Television* 7.3:291–303.

Kinsley, M. 2006. Do newspapers have a future? *Time*, Sept. 25. Retrieved April 28, 2009, from: http://www.time.com/time/magazine/article/0,9171,1538652,00 .html.

Kirkham, M. 1996. Measuring the fragmenting television audience. *Journal of the Market Research Society* 38.3:219–226.

Klaassen, A. 2006a. TiVo: An advertiser's best friend? *Advertising Age*, Aug. 30. Retrieved Aug. 31, 2006, from http://adage.com/print?article_id=111572.

——. 2006b. The short tail: How the "democratized" medium ended up in the hands of the few—at least in terms of ad dollars. *Advertising Age*, Nov. 27, 1.

——. 2007. Economics 101: Web giants rule "democratized" medium. *Advertising Age*, April 8. Retrieved April 29, 2009, from: http://adage.com/digital/article?article_id=115986.

Klopfenstein, B. 1990. Audience measurement in the VCR environment: An examination of ratings methodologies. In *Social and Cultural Aspects of VCR Use*, ed. J. Dobrow, 45–72. Hillsdale, NJ: Erlbaum.

Knee, J., B. Greenwald, and A. Seave. 2009. *The Curse of the Mogul: What's Wrong with the World's Leading Media Companies*. New York: Portfolio.

Knight, J. 2007. DVD, video, and reaching audiences: Experiments in moving-image distribution. *Convergence* 13.1:19–41.

Knight Commission (Knight Commission on the Information Needs of Communities in a Democracy). 2009. *Informing Communities: Sustaining Democracy in the Digital Age*. Washington, DC: Aspen Institute.

Kok, F., and B. de Vos. 2005. Appreciation scores! Paper presented at the ESOMAR Worldwide Audience Measurement conference, Montreal, Canada, June.

Korda, M. 2001. *Making the List: A Cultural History of the American Bestseller, 1900–1999*. New York: Barnes and Noble.

Koretz, D. 2009. CPM pricing is doomed. *Online Publishing Insider*, Dec. 11. Retrieved Feb. 25, 2010, from: http://www.mediapost.com/publications/?fa=Articles.showArticle&art_aid=118991.

Kramer, S. D. 2002. Content's king. *Cable World*, April 29, 24, 32.

Kreshel, P. J. 1990. John B. Watson at J. Walter Thompson: The legitimation of "science" in advertising. *Journal of Advertising* 19.2:45–59.

——. 1993. Advertising research in the pre-depression years: A cultural history. *Journal of Current Issues and Research in Advertising* 15.1:59–75.

Kung, M. 2008. The marketing of *Cloverfield* has been as mysterious as the movie itself. *Boston Globe*, Jan. 13. Retrieved April 27, 2009, from: http://www.boston.com/ae/movies/articles/2008/01/12/the_marketing_of_cloverfield_has_been_as_mysterious_as_the_movie_itself.

Kuttner, R. 2007. The race: Newspapers have a bright future as print-digital hybrids after all—but they'd better hurry. *Columbia Journalism Review* 45.6:24–32.

Lafayette, J. 2006. How ads are measuring up: Broadcast nets grow angry over commercial ratings. *Television Week*, Oct. 30.

——. 2008a. "Cracking the code" to put online dollars where they belong. *TV Week*, Oct. 29. Retrieved Feb. 21, 2009, from http://www.tvweek.com/news/2008/10/cracking_the_code_to_put_online.php.

——. 2008b. Chart: Most watched vs. most discussed: Measuring engagement. *TV Week*, Dec. 9. Retrieved April 10, 2009, from: http://www.tvweek.com/news/2008/12/chart_most_watched_vs_most_dis.php.

Laird, P. W. 1998. *Advertising Progress: American Business and the Rise of Consumer Marketing*. Baltimore: Johns Hopkins University Press.

Lang, K., and G. E. Lang. 2009. Mass society, mass culture, and mass communication: The meaning of mass. *International Journal of Communication*3:998–1024.

Lanham, R. A. 2006. *Economics of Attention: Style and Substance in the Age of Information*. Chicago: University of Chicago Press.

Lardner, J. 1987. *Fast Forward: Hollywood, the Japanese, and the Onslaught of the VCR*. New York: Norton.

Lasica, J. D. 2005. *Darknet: Hollywood's War Against the Digital Generation*. Hoboken, NJ: Wiley.

Lazarsfeld, P. F. 1939. Radio research and applied psychology: Introduction by the guest editor. *Journal of Applied Psychology* 23.1:1–7.

——. 1947. Audience research in the movie field. *Annals of the American Academy of Political and Social Science* 254:160–168.

Lazarsfeld, P. F., and H. Field. 1946. *The People Look at Radio*. Chapel Hill: University of North Carolina Press.

Learmonth, M. 2007. Rentrak hopes to crack ratings: Digital information offers more detailed info. *Variety*, Oct. 19. Retrieved Nov. 19, 2008, from: http://www.variety.com/index.asp?layout=print_story&articleid=VR1117974343&categoryid=1019.

Leblebici, H., G. R. Slancik, A. Copay, and T. King. 1991. Institutional change and the transformation of interorganizational fields: An organizational history of the U.S. radio broadcasting industry. *Administrative Science Quarterly* 36:333–363.

Lee, G. 1972. The needs of motion picture audiences. *California Management Review* 15:144–152.

Lee, H. C., D. H. Ma, and T. K Lee. 2007. Program quality evaluation: Experience of a new assessment tool. Paper presented at the ESOMAR Worldwide Multi Media Measurement conference, Dublin, Ireland, June.

Lehman-Wilzig, S., and N. Cohen-Avigdor. 2004. The natural life cycle of new media evolution. *New Media and Society* 6.6:707–730.

Lenert, E. 2004. A social-shaping perspective on the development of the World Wide Web: The case of iCraveTV. *New Media and Society* 6.2:235–258.

Lenthall, B. 2007. *Radio's America: The Great Depression and the Rise of Modern Mass Culture.* Chicago: University of Chicago Press.

Lessig, L. 2004. *Free Culture: How Big Media Uses Technology and the Law to Lock Down Culture and Control Creativity.* New York: Penguin.

———. 2008. *Remix: Making Art and Commerce Thrive in the Hybrid Economy.* New York: Penguin.

Levy, M. R. 1982. The Lazarsfeld-Stanton program analyzer: A historical note. *Journal of Communication* 32.4:30–38.

Li, K. 2007. Big media videos play small role on YouTube: study. Reuters, April 4. Retrieved March 18, 2009, from: http://www.reuters.com/articlePrint?articleID= USN0436270020070404.

Likert, R. 1936. A method for measuring the sales influence of a radio program. *Journal of Applied Psychology* 20.2:175–182.

Litman, B. R. 1983. U.S. TV networks response to new technology. *Telecommunications Policy* 7.2:163–177.

Livant, B. 1979. The audience commodity: On the blindspot debate. *Canadian Journal of Political and Social Theory* 3.1:91–106.

———. 1982. Working at watching: A reply to Sut Jhally. *Canadian Journal of Political and Social Theory* 6.1/2:211–215.

Livingstone, S. 1996. Rethinking audiences: Towards a new research agenda. Paper presented at the annual meeting of the International Communication Association, Chicago, IL, May.

———. 1998. Audience research at the crossroads: The "implied audience" in media and cultural theory. *European Journal of Cultural Studies* 1.2:193–217.

———. 1999. New media, new audiences? *New Media and Society* 1.1:59–66.

———. 2003. The changing nature of audiences: From the mass audience to the interactive media user. In *Companion to Media Studies*, ed. A. Valdivia, 337–359. Oxford, UK: Blackwell.

Livingstone, S., and P. Lunt. 2007. Representing citizens and consumers in media and communications regulation. *Annals of the American Academy of Political and Social Science* 611:51–65.

Livingstone, S., P. Lunt, and L. Miller. 2007a. Citizens, consumers, and the citizen-consumer: Articulating the citizen interest in media and communications regulation. *Discourse and Communication* 1.1:63–89.

———. 2007b. Citizens and consumers: Discursive debates during and after the Communications Act of 2003. *Media, Culture, and Society* 29.4:613–638.

Lloyd, D. W., and K. J. Clancy. 1991. CPMs versus CPMIs: Implications for media planning. *Journal of Advertising Research* 31.4:34–44.

Lo, B. W. N., and R. S. Sedhain. 2006. How reliable are Website rankings? Implications for e-business advertising and Internet search. *Issues in Information Systems* 7.2:233–238.

Longstaff, H. P. 1939. A method for determining the entertainment value of radio programs. *Journal of Applied Psychology* 23.1:46–54.

Lotoski, A. 2000. The Nielsen local people meter initiative: Implications for Boston and future local markets (unpublished manuscript, WCVB-TV).

Lotz, A. D. 2007. *The Television Will Be Revolutionized.* New York: New York University Press.

Lotz, A. D., and S. M. Ross. 2004. Toward ethical cyberspace audience research: Strategies for using the Internet for television audience studies. *Journal of Broadcasting and Electronic Media* 48.3:501–512.

Lowrey, W. 2006. Mapping the journalism-blogging relationship. *Journalism* 7.4:477–500.

Lu, X., and H. Lo. 2007. Television audience satisfaction: Antecedents and consequences. *Journal of Advertising Research* 47.3:354–363.

Lull, J. 1988. Critical response: The audience as nuisance. *Critical Studies in Mass Communication* 5:239–243.

Lyons, D. 2009. Old media strikes back. *Newsweek*, March 2. Retrieved April 21, 2009, from: http://www.newsweek.com/id/185790/output/print.

Mabillot, D. 2007. User-generated content: Web 2.0 taking the video sector by storm. *Communications and Strategies* 65:39–49.

MacGregor, P. 2007. Tracking the online audience: Metric data start a subtle revolution. *Journalism Studies* 8.2:280–298.

Madden, M., S. Fox, A. Smith, and J. Vitak. 2007. Digital footprints: Online identity management and search in the age of transparency. Pew Internet and American Life Project. Retrieved April 2, 2009, from: http://www.pewinternet.org/~/media//Files/Reports/2007/PIP_Digital_Footprints.pdf.pdf.

Magazine Marketing Coalition. 2007. New accountability guide helps you make the case for magazines. Oct. New York: Magazine Publishers of America.

Magazine Publishers of America. 2005. Accountability: A guide to measuring ROI and ROO across media. New York: Author.

——. 2006. Engagement: Understanding consumers' relationships with media. New York: Author.

Maiville, M. S., and B. Engel. 2007. A "thin-sliced world" requires new methods, models, and systems for media audience analysis. Paper presented at ARF's Audience Measurement symposium, New York, June.

Maltby, R. 1999. Sticks, hicks, and flaps: Classical Hollywood's generic conception of its audience. In *Identifying Hollywood's Audiences: Cultural Identity and the Movies*, ed. M. Stokes and R. Maltby, 24–41. London: British Film Institute.

Malthouse, E. C., and B. J. Calder. 2007. Measuring involvement with editorial content. Paper presented at the ESOMAR Worldwide Multi Media Measurement conference, Dublin, Ireland, June.

Malthouse, E. C., B. J. Calder, and W. P. Eadie. 2003. Conceptualizing and measuring magazine reader experiences. Dec. Retrieved Feb. 25, 2009, from: http://www.mediamanagementcenter.org/research/magazineconcept.pdf.

Malthouse, E. C., B. J. Calder, and A. Tamhane. 2007. The effects of media context experiences on advertising effectiveness. *Journal of Advertising* 36.3:7–18.

Malthouse, E. C., B. J. Calder, B. C. Ware, and J. Bahary. 2008. A day in the life . . .: Leveraging media-advertisement experiential congruence. Paper presented at the ESOMAR Worldwide Multi Media Measurement conference, Budapest, Hungary, June.

Mandese, J. 2005. Madison Avenue launches AMI, entity to oversee media accountability. *Media Daily News,* Sept. 29. Retrieved Feb. 20, 2010, from: http://www.mediapost.com/publications/index.cfm?fa=Articles.showArticle&art_aid=34657.

——. 2006. Nielsen extends its reach. *Broadcasting and Cable,* April 17. Retrieved April 28, 2009, from: http://www.broadcastingcable.com/article/103713-Nielsen_Extends_Its_Reach.php.

——. 2008a. Nielsen launches controversial "convergence" panel, tracks both TV and Internet usage. *Media Daily News,* Oct. 9. Retrieved April 29, 2009, from: http://www.mediapost.com/publications/?fa=Articles.showArticle&art_aid=92342.

——. 2008b. Nielsen makes hey, plans to shut it down: Replacing social network with new consumer site. *Online Media Daily,* Oct. 17. Retrieved Feb. 26, 2009, from: http://www.mediapost/com/publications/?fa=Articles.printFriendly&art_aid=92860.

——. 2008. Nielsen Media chief: We now control three-quarters of world's TV currency data. *Media Post,* Nov. 17. Retrieved Nov. 18, 2008, from: http://www.tvrd.org/showthread.php?t=932.

——. 2009. Rentrak launches local TV ratings servie, acquires part of Nielsen. *Media Daily News,* Dec. 15. Retrieved Feb. 25, 2010, from: http://www.mediapost.com/publications/?fa=Articles.showArticle&art_aid=119124.

Marich, R. 2008. New audience metrics aim to leapfrog Web buzz: Advancements attempt to connect measurements of viewing with purchasing. *Broadcasting and Cable,* June 9, 14.

Marriott, M. 2006. Digital divide closing as blacks turn to Internet. *New York Times,* March 31. Retrieved March 1, 2009, from: http://www.nytimes.com/2006/03/31/us/31divide.html.

Mast, F., and G. Zaltman. 2006. Anatomy of engagement. Paper presented at ARF's Re:Think conference, New York.

Mattelart, A. 1991. *Advertising International: The Privatization of Public Space.* London: Routledge.

Mattlin, J. 2008. Experiments with passive measurement of print. *Admap,* April 6–8.

Maxwell, R. 2000. Picturing the audience. *Television and New Media* 1.2:135–157.

Mayle, A. 2008. The Facebook economy: Deficits in data privacy. Center for Digital Democracy. Retrieved April 6, 2009, from: http://www.democraticmedia.org/files/Facebookwid.pdf.

McBride, S. 2007. New way to count listeners shakes up radio. *Wall Street Journal*, Sept. 6. Retrieved May 2, 2009, from: http://online.wsj.com/article/SB118903798218018792.html.

McChesney, R. 1993. *Telecommunications, Mass Media, and Democracy: The Battle for the Control of U.S. Broadcasting, 1928–1935*. New York: Oxford University Press.

McClellan, S. 2008a. Arbitron, Nielsen end Project Apollo. *Adweek*, Feb. 25. Retrieved April 29, 2009, from: http://www.adweek.com/aw/content_display/news/media/e3i3da710641ca059c5b688dba1db227bf9.

——. 2008b. MSOs look to capitalize on STB data: Cable and satellite boxes may hold the key to highly targeted, addressable ads. *Adweek*, May 19. Retrieved April 29, 2009, from: http://www.adweek.com/aw/content_display/news/media/e3idda2f1661c03a55f8d521201eabec4ed.

——. 2008c. Demo-based TV buys not enough: New research shows networks must tie in consumer-buying behavior. *Adweek*, Dec. 8. Retrieved Feb. 18, 2009, from: http://www.adweek.com/aw/content_display/news/media/e3ie8946c da1b3f6da2387093a22958dc54.

McCourt, T., and E. Rothenbuhler. 1997. SoundScan and the consolidation of control in the popular music industry. *Media, Culture, and Society* 19.2:201–218.

McDonald, S. 2008. The long tail and its implications for media audience measurement. *Journal of Advertising Research*, Sept., 313–319.

McDonald, S., and Collins, J. 2007. Internet site measurement developments and print. Paper presented at the Worldwide Readership Research Symposium, Vienna. Retrieved April 29, 2009, from: http://www.readershipsymposium.org/node/2299.

McKenna, W. J. 1988. The future of electronic measurement technology in U.S. media research. *Journal of Advertising Research* 28.3:RC3–RC7.

McManus, J. H. 1994. *Market-Driven Journalism: Let the Citizen Beware?* Thousand Oaks, CA: Sage.

McQuail, D. 1969. Uncertainty about the audience and the organization of mass communications. *Sociological Review Monograph* 13, *The Sociology of Mass Media Communicators*, 75–84.

Meadows, M. 2002. "Tell me what you want and I'll give you what you need": Perspectives on indigenous media audience research. In *Mobilising the Audience*, ed. M. Balnaves, T. O'Regan, and J. Sternberg, 253–265. Queensland, Australia: University of Queensland Press.

Media Rating Council. 2007. A guide to understanding Internet measurement alternatives. Aug. Retrieved Feb. 13, 2009, from: http://www.mediaratingcouncil.org/MRC%20POV%20General%20Internet%20080307.pdf.

Meehan, E. R. 1984. Ratings and the institutional approach: A third answer to the commodity question. *Critical Studies in Mass Communication* 1.2:216–225.

Meehan, E. 1993. Heads of households and ladies of the house: Gender, genre, and broadcast ratings, 1929–1990. In *Ruthless Criticism: New Perspectives in U.S. Communication History*, ed. W. S. Solomon and R. W. McChesney, 204–221. Minneapolis: University of Minnesota Press.

Menneer, P. 1987. Audience appreciation—a different story from audience numbers. Annual Review of BBC Broadcasting Research Findings 13.

Mermigas, D. 2008. Do the math: Broadcast, cable network parity play. *Diane Mermigas: On Media*, Sept. 24. Retrieved Sept. 25, 2008, from: http://www.mediapost.com/blogs/on_media/?p=262.

Merrill, J. C., and R. L. Lowenstein. 1971. *Media, Messages, and Men: New Perspectives in Communication.* New York: McKay.

Micu, A. C., J. T. Plummer, and W. A. Cook. 2007. On the road to a new effectiveness model: Measuring emotional responses to television advertising. ARF white paper, Jan.

Miller, J. S. 2008. Testimony before the New York City Council, Sept. 10. Retrieved March 24, 2009, from: www.mmtconline.org/filemanager/fileview/173.

Min, I. 2004. Perceptions of the audience by the alternative press producers: A case study of the Texas Observer. *Media, Culture, and Society* 26.3:450–458.

Mitgang, L. 2002. *Big Bird and Beyond: The New Media and the Markle Foundation.* New York: Fordham University Press.

Moe, H., and T. Syvertsen. 2007. Media institutions as a research field: Three phases of Norwegian broadcasting research. *Nordicom Review* 28:149–167.

Montgomery, K. C. 2007. *Generation Digital: Politics, Commerce, and Childhood in the Age of the Internet.* Cambridge, MA: MIT Press.

Moorman, M., P. C. Neijens, and E. G. Smit. 2007. The effects of program involvement on commercial exposure and recall in a naturalistic setting. *Journal of Advertising* 46.1:121–137.

Morrison, D. E. 1978. Kultur and culture: The case of Theodor W. Adorno and Paul F. Lazarsfeld. *Social Research* 45.2:331–355.

Morrisson, V., and P. Gomy. 2008. Should we forget advertising awareness? Measuring emotions and implicit attitudes. Paper presented at the ESOMAR Worldwide Multi Media Measurement conference, Budapest, Hungary, June.

Morrissey, B. 2009a. Most marketers ignore brand metrics online. *Adweek*, June 1. Retrieved June 25, 2009, from: http://www.adweek.com/aw/content_display/news/digital/e3i372a427229d39d58f8364a7a9cd54c66.

——. 2009b. Social net ads: Fewer clicks, more engagement. *Adweek*, Sept. 28. Retrieved Nov. 2, 2009, from: http://www.adweek.com/aw/content_display/news/digtal/e3i470b0d4b36272857b0815d951dd9d16.

Mosco, V., and L. Kaye. 2000. Questioning the concept of the audience. In *Consuming Audiences? Production and Reception in Media Research*, ed. I. Hagen and J. Wasko, 31–46. Cresskill, NJ: Hampton Press.

Mullarkey, G. W. 2004. Internet measurement data—practical and technical issues. *Marketing Intelligence and Planning* 22.1:42–58.

Mullen, M. 2003. *The Rise of Cable Programming in the United States: Revolution or Evolution?* Austin: University of Texas Press.

Murdock, G. 1978. Blindspots about Western Marxism: A reply to Dallas Smythe. *Canadian Journal of Political and Social Theory* 2.2:109–119.

Myers, J. 2007. Upfront perspective: Commercial ratings are an end run around the future. mediaVillage, May 30. Retrieved Nov. 29, 2007, from: http://www.mediavillage.com/jmr/2007/05/30/jmr-05-30-07.

Mytton, G. 2007. *Handbook on Radio and Television Audience Research.* Paris: UNICEF/UNESCO.

Nakashima, R. 2008. TV networks search for perfect formula for ad-supported shows online. *AP News*, April 12. Retrieved April 29, 2009, from: http://www.blnz.com/news/2008/04/11/networks_seek_formula_online_9179.html.

Naples, M. J. 1984. Electronic media research: An update and a look at the future. *Journal of Advertising Research* 24.4:39–46.

Napoli, P. M. 1998a. Evolutionary theories of media institutions and their responses to new technologies. In *Communication Theory: A Reader*, ed. L. Lederman, 315–329. Dubuque, IA: Kendall/Hunt.

——. 1998b. Government assessment of FCC performance: Recurring patterns and implications for recent reform efforts. *Telecommunications Policy* 22.4/5:409–418.

——. 1998c. The Internet and the forces of "massification." *Electronic Journal of Communication* 8.2. Retrieved Feb. 20, 2010, from: http://www.cios.org/EJC-PUBLIC/008/2/00828.HTML.

——. 2001. The unpredictable audience: An exploratory analysis of the determinants of forecasting error for new prime-time network television programs. *Journal of Advertising* 30.2:53–60.

——. 2003a. *Audience Economics: Media Institutions and the Audience Marketplace.* New York: Columbia University Press.

——. 2003b. Environmental assessment in a dual-product marketplace: A participant-observation perspective on the broadcast television industry. *International Journal on Media Management* 5.2:100–108.

——. 2005. Audience measurement and media policy: Audience economics, the diversity principle, and the Local People Meter. *Communication Law and Policy* 10.4:349–382.

——. 2008. Hyperlinking and the forces of massification. In *The Hyperlinked Society: Questioning Connections in the Digital Age*, ed. J. Turow and L. Tsui, 56–69. Ann Arbor: University of Michigan Press.

——. 2009. Audience measurement, the diversity principle, and the First Amendment right to construct the audience. *St. John's Journal of Legal Commentary* 24:359–385.

——. 2010. Revisiting "mass communication" and the "work" of the audience in the new media environment. *Media, Culture, and Society* 32.3:505–516.

Napoli, P. M., and N. Gillis. 2006. Reassessing the potential contribution of communications research to communications policy: The case of media ownership. *Journal of Broadcasting and Electronic Media* 50.4:671–691.

Napoli, P. M., and S. Sybblis. 2007. Access to audiences as a First Amendment right: Its relevance and implications for electronic media policy. *Virginia Journal of Law and Technology* 12.1:1–31.

National Cable and Telecommunications Association. 2008. Industry data. Retrieved May 2, 2009, from: http://www.ncta.com/Statistics.aspx.

Neely, D. 2008. The real value of engagement. *Online Media Daily*, Aug. 20. Retrieved Aug. 20, 2008, from: http://www.mediapost.com/publications/?fa= Articles.printfriendly&art_aid=8858.

Neff, J. 2007. NBC to guarantee audience engagement for its programming. *Advertising Age*, Feb. 28, 28.

Negus, K. 1999. *Music Genres and Corporate Cultures.* London: Routledge.

Nemirovsky, P. 2003. Redefining digital audience: Models and actions. In *Human-Computer Interaction*, ed. M. Rauterberg et al., 391–398. Amsterdam: IOS Press.

Netcraft. 2009. Dec. 2008 Web server survey. Retrieved Jan. 15, 2009, from: http:// news.netcraft.com/archives/web_server_survey.html.

Networked Insights. 2008. Measuring the social report #1: Network television ratings. Retrieved Feb. 21, 2009, from: http://www.socialsights.com/post/56628872/ measuring-the-social-tv.

Neuman, W. R. 1991. *The Future of the Mass Audience.* New York: Cambridge University Press.

Newman, K. M. 2004. *Radio Active: Advertising and Consumer Activism, 1935–1947.* Berkeley: University of California Press.

NewMediaMetrics. 2007. Emotional attachment study. New York: Author.

News Corp. 2004. Press release: Statement regarding "Don't Count Us Out" Coalition. June 20. Retrieved Sept. 8, 2004, from: http://www.newscorp.com/news/ news_210.html.

New York City Council. 2008. Resolution no. 1583-A. Sept. 24.

New York v. Arbitron. 2009. Stipulated order on consent. Supreme Court of the State of New York, County of New York, Jan. 7. Retrieved March 22, 2009, from: http:// www.oag.state.ny.us/bureaus/civil_rights/pdfs/Arbitron%20Consent%20 Order%2001–07–08.pdf.

Nielsen IAG. 2009. Solutions: IAG. Retrieved Feb. 26, 2009, from http://www.iagr. net/sln_iagprogramengage.jsp.

"Nielsen Makes Strategic Investment in NeuroFocus, an Innovative Leader in Neuromarketing Research." 2008. *PR Newswire*, Feb. 7. Retrieved Feb. 21, 2009, from: http://www.prnewswire.com.

Nielsen Media Research. 2006a. News release: Nielsen to offer integrated, all-electronic television measurement across multiple media platforms. June 14. Retrieved July 25, 2006, from: http://www.everyonecounts.tv/news/documents/ A2M2_061406.pdf.

——. 2006b. Anytime anywhere audience measurement. Retrieved July 25, 2006, from: http://www.everyonecounts.tv/news/documents/A2M2_newsre-lease_061406.pdf.

——. 2008. Average U.S. home now receives record 118.6 TV channels, according to Nielsen. News release, June 6. Retrieved May 2, 2009, from: http://www.nielsen-media.com/nc/portal/site/Public/menuitem.55dc65b4a7d5adff3f65936147a062a0/?vgnextoid=fa7e220af4e5a110VgnVCM100000acoa260aRCRD.

Nielsen Online. 2008. Listening to consumers 101: How marketers can leverage consumer-generated media. New York: Author.

——. 2009. BuzzMetrics: The global measurement standard in consumer-generated media. Retrieved Feb. 19, 2009, from http://www.nielsen-online.com/downloads/us/BuzzMetrics_7x11_Single_Final.pdf.

"Nielsen to Acquire IAG Research." 2008. News release, April 7. Retrieved Feb. 27, 2009, from: http://www.nielsenmedia.com/nc/portal/site/Public/menuitem.55dc65b4a7d5adff3f65936147a062a0/?vgnextoid=ed599cfb65829110VgnVCM100000acoa260aRCRD.

"Nielsen Unveils Hey! Nielsen, Online Social Network for Popular Culture." 2007. News release, Sept. 24. Retrieved Feb. 26, 2009, from: http://www.prnewswire.com/cgi-bin/stories.pl?ACCT=109&STORY=/www/story/09-24-2007/0004668548&EDATE=.

Nightingale, V. 1996. *Studying Audiences: The Shock of the Real.* New York: Routledge.

Nightingale, V., and T. Dwyer. 2006. The audience politics of "enhanced" television formats. *International Journal of Media and Cultural Politics* 2.1:25–42.

Noll, A. M. 2006. *The Evolution of Media.* Lanham, MD: Rowman and Littlefield.

Norris, P. 2001. *Digital Divide: Civil Engagement, Information Poverty, and the Internet Worldwide.* New York: Cambridge University Press.

Notkin, E. O. 2006. Television remixed: The controversy over commercial-skipping. *Fordham Intellectual Property, Media, and Entertainment Law Journal* 16:899–938.

Ohmer, S. 1999. The science of pleasure: George Gallup and audience research in Hollywood. In *Identifying Hollywood Audiences: Cultural Identity and the Movies,* ed. M. Stokes and R. Maltby, 61–80. London: British Film Institute.

——. 2006. *George Gallup in Hollywood.* New York: Columbia University Press.

O'Malley, G. 2008. Networked Insight's music chart challenges traditional. *Online Media Daily,* Nov. 19. Retrieved Feb. 21, 2009, from http://www.mediapost.com/publications/?fa=Articles.printFriendly&art_aid=95034.

"Optimedia U.S. Launches Content Power Ratings Report." 2008. PR Newswire, March 4. Retrieved June 12, 2008, from: http://www.prnewswire.com/cgi-bin/stories.pl?ACCT=104&STORY=/www/story/03-04-2008/0004767600&EDATE=.

O'Regan, T. 2002. Arts audiences: Becoming audience-minded. In *Mobilising the Audience,* ed. M. Balnaves, T. O'Regan, and J. Sternberg, 104–130. Queensland, Australia: University of Queensland Press.

Ornebrink, H. 2008. The consumer as producer—of what? *Journalism Studies* 9.5:771–785.

Oscar, M. 2008. A set-top box set-up. *TV Board*, Dec. 23. Retrieved Feb. 3, 2009, from: http://www.mediapost.com/publications/?fa=Articles.showArticle&art_aid=97247.

Oswell, D. 2002. *Television, Childhood, and the Home: A History of the Making of the Child Television Audience in Britain.* Oxford: Oxford University Press.

Owen, B. M., and S. S. Wildman. 1992. *Video Economics.* Cambridge, MA: Harvard University Press.

Pace, M., and L. S. Moores. 2008. FaceTime: Measuring emerging media effectiveness. Presentation at ARF's Audience Measurement 3.0 conference, New York, June.

Pappachen, G., and K. Manatt. 2008. The mobile brand: Measuring advertising effectiveness on the mobile web. Paper presented at the ESOMAR World Wide Multimedia Measurement conference, Budapest, Hungary, June.

Paramount Pictures Corp v. ReplayTV. 2004. 298 F. Supp. 2d 921 (C.D. Cal.).

Pascu, C., D. Osimo, M. Ulbrich, G. Turlea, and J. C. Burgelman. 2007. The potential disruptive impact of Internet 2–based technologies. *First Monday* 12.3. Retrieved Aug. 26, 2008, from: http://firstmonday.org/issues/issue12_3/pascu/index.html.

Passikoff, R., and D. E. Schultz. 2007. C-MEEs: Cross-media engagement evaluations. Paper presented at ARF's Audience Measurement 2.0 conference, New York, June.

Passikoff, R., and C. Weisler. 2006. Engagement of the future: Brand bonding as predictor of future purchases. Paper presented at the ESOMAR Latin America conference, Rio de Janeiro, Brazil, Oct. Retrieved March 1, 2009, from: http://www.brandkeys.com/news/press/ESOMAR.2006.Rio.pdf.

Paulussen, S., A. Heinonen, D. Domingo, and T. Quandt. 2007. Doing it together: Citizen participation in the professional news making process. *Observatorio (OBS*) Journal* 1.3:131–154.

Paulussen, S., and P. Ugille. 2008. User-generated content in the newsroom: Professional and organizational constraints on participatory journalism. *Westminster Papers in Communication and Culture* 5.2:24–41.

Peacock, J., S. Purvis, and R. Hazlett. 2007. Radio and TV ad engagement—in context. Paper presented at ARF's Audience Measurement 2.0 conference, New York, June.

Peer, L., E. Malthouse, M. Nesbitt, and B. Calder. 2007. The local TV news experience: How to win viewers by focusing on engagement. Retrieved Feb. 23, 2009, from http://www.mediamanagementcenter.org/localTV/localTV.pdf.

Pekurny, R. 1982. Coping with television production. In *Individuals in Mass Media Organizations: Creativity and Constraint*, ed. J. S. Ettema and D. C. Whitney, 131–144. Beverly Hills: Sage.

Pellegrini, P. 2009. Panel-centric hybrid measurement: Successfully integrating traditional Web analytics approaches to enrich panel-centric measurement. Paper presented at the ESOMAR Worldwide Multi Media Measurement conference, Stockholm, Sweden, July.

Pellegrini, P., and A. Gluck. 2007. All possible worlds: Advancing passive electronic measurement of readership. Paper presented at the Worldwide Readership Research Symposium, Vienna, Austria, Oct.

People of the State of New York v. Arbitron. 2008. Notice of verified petition. Supreme Court of the State of New York, County of New York, 11 (Oct. 10).

Pérez-Peña, R. 2009. A.P. seeks to rein in sites using its content. *New York Times*, April 7. Retrieved April 7, 2009, from: http://www.nytimes.com/2009/04/07/business/media/07paper.html?_r=2&ref=technology.

Peters, J. D. 1996. The uncanniness of mass communication in interwar social thought. *Journal of Communication* 46.3:108–123.

Peterson, E. T., and M. Berger. 2008. Measuring multimedia content in a Web 2.0 world. Retrieved Jan. 10, 2009, from: http://www.nedstat.nl/uk/publications/measuring_multimedia_content.pdf.

Peterson, E. T., and J. Carrabis. 2008. Measuring the immeasurable: Visitor engagement. Retrieved Jan. 15, 2009, from: http://www.webanalyticsdemystified.com/sample/Web_Analytics_Demystified_and_NextStage_Global_-_Measuring_the_Immeasurable_-_Visitor_Engagement.pdf.

Peterson, R. A. 1994. Measured markets and unknown audiences: Case studies from the production and consumption of music. In *Audiencemaking: How the Media Create the Audience*, ed. J. S. Ettema and D. C. Whitney, 171–185. Thousand Oaks, CA: Sage.

Peterson, R. A., and N. Anand. 2004. The production of culture perspective. *Annual Review of Sociology* 30:311–334.

Peterson, S. M. 2008. Loser-generated content: From participation to exploitation. *First Monday* 13.3. Retrieved May 26, 2009, from: http://firstmonday.org/htbin/cgiwrap/bin/ojs/index.php/fm/article/viewArticle/2141/1948.

Pfanner, E. 2009. Germany looks at ways to protect online journalism. *New York Times*, Oct. 28. Retrieved Oct. 29, 2009, from: http://www.nytimes/com/2009/10/29/business/global/29copy.html.

Phalen, P. F. 1996. "Information and Markets and the Market for Information: An Analysis of the Market for Television Audiences." Unpublished Ph.D. diss., Northwestern University, Evanston, IL.

Philport, J. C. 1993. New insights into reader quality measures. *Journal of Advertising Research* 35.5:RC5–RC12.

Piccalo, G. 2004. TiVo will no longer skip past advertisers. *Los Angeles Times*, Nov. 17, A1.

Picker, R. C. 2004. The digital video recorder: Unbundling of advertising and content. *University of Chicago Law Review* 71.1:205–222.

Pilotta, J. J. 2008. Why ratings no longer matter. Radio Business Report/Television Business Report Intelligence Brief, Feb. 15.

Plunkett, L. 2008. Top-sellers? Bah, let's look at the 10 most "engaging" games. *Kotaku*, Dec. 17. Retrieved Feb. 21, 2009, from http://kotaku.com/5112876/top+sellers-bah-lets-look-at-the-10-most-engaging-games.

Politz, A. 1943. Family versus individual in measurement of audiences. *Journal of the American Statistical Association* 38:233–237.

Poovey, M. 1998. *A History of the Modern Fact: Problems of Knowledge in the Sciences of Wealth and Society.* Chicago: University of Chicago Press.

Porac, J. F., and H. Thomas. 1994. Cognitive categorization and subjective rivalry among retailers in a small city. *Journal of Applied Psychology* 79.1:54–66.

——. 1995. Recuperating First Amendment doctrine. *Stanford Law Review* 47:1269–1374.

Post, R. 2000. The constitutional status of commercial speech. *UCLA Law Review* 48:1–57.

Powell, W. W. 1978. Publishers' decision-making: What criteria do they use in deciding which books to publish? *Social Research* 45.2:227–252.

Pratt, A. 2004. The cultural economy: A call for spatialized "production of culture" perspectives. *International Journal of Cultural Studies* 7.1:117–128.

Prescott, L. 2006. Hitwise US consumer generated media report. Nov. New York: Author.

Prior, M. 2007. *Post-Broadcast Democracy: How Media Choice Increases Inequality in Political Involvement and Polarizes Elections.* New York: Cambridge University Press.

PR Newswire. 2007. Media industry's first multi-media ratings report measures total value of television shows across all platforms, reveals surprise winners. March 4. Retrieved June 12, 2008, from: http://www.prnewswire.com/cgi-bin/stories.pl?ACCT=104&STORY=/www/story/03-04-2008/0004767600&EDATE.

——. 2009. Broadcasters, advertisers and ad agency leaders partner with Arbitron to define radio affinity metric. Sept. 17. Retrieved Nov. 2, 2009, from: http://www.prnewswire.com/news-releases/broadcasters-advertisers-and-ad-agency-leaders-partner-with-arbitron-to-define-radio-affinity-metric-62203037.html.

Project for Excellence in Journalism. 2008. The changing newsroom. Retrieved May 2, 2009, from: http://www.journalism.org/node/11961.

Quantcast. 2008. Quantcast methodology overview: Delivering an actionable audience service. San Francisco: Author.

Raboy, M., B. D. Abramson, S. Proulx, and R. Welters. 2001. Media policy, audiences, and social demand: Research at the interface of policy studies and audience studies. *Television and New Media* 2.2:95–115.

Radio Business Report. 2008. Arbitron exec bonuses tied to PPM. Jan. 31. Retrieved March 27, 2009, from: http://www.rbr.com/epaper/issue21-08-dpf.html.

Rasmussen, A., C. Ude, and E. Landry. 2007. HD marketing 2010: Sharpening the conversation. Booz Allen Hamilton. Retrieved Feb. 4, 2009, from: http://www.boozallen.com/media/file/HD_Marketing_2010.pdf.

Razlogova, E. 1995. "The Voice of the Listener: Americans and the Radio Industry, 1920–1950." Unpublished Ph.D. diss., George Mason University.

Reese, R. M., and W. W. Stanton. 1980. "Home-grown" audience research for small radio stations. *Journal of Small Business Management* 18:24–30.

Reese, S. D., L. Rutigliano, K. Hyun, and J. Jeong. 2007. Mapping the blogosphere: The professional and citizen-based media in the global news arena. *Journalism* 8:235–261.

Reinhard, C. L. 2008. The Internet's role transforming the relationship between media producers and consumers: The collecting and co-opting of audience activity. Paper presented at the annual meeting of the International Association for Media and Communications Research, Stockholm, Sweden, July.

Reynolds, M. 2000. Repurposing with a purpose. *Cable World*, May 8. Retrieved April 29, 2009, from: http://www.highbeam.com/doc/1G1-62400615.html.

Richards, N. M. 2004. Reconciling data protection and the First Amendment. *UCLA Law Review* 52:1149–1222.

Robinson, L. 2002. Radio research in transition. *International Journal of Market Research* 42.4:381–394.

——. 2009. The IPA Touchpoints Initiative: Its effects on the marketplace and its future plans. Paper presented at the ESOMAR Worldwide Multi Media Measurement conference, Stockholm, Sweden, July.

Robinson, L., and D. Turner. 2007. Delivering the dream: The IPA Touchpoints Initiative. Paper presented at the ESOMAR Worldwide Multi Media Measurement conference, Dublin, Ireland, June.

Robinson, W. S. 1947. Radio audience measurement, and its limitations. *Journal of Social Issues* 3.3:42–50.

Rochet, L. R. 2006/2007. The "data slant": Why lack of media generated by minority users online is an offline problem. *Harvard Journal of Hispanic Policy* 19:39–49.

Rohle, T. 2007. Desperately seeking the consumer: Personalized search engines and the commercial exploitation of user data. *First Monday* 12.9. Retrieved May 1, 2009, from: http://firstmonday.org/htbin/cgiwrap/bin/ojs/index.php/fm/article/view/2008/1883.

Roscoe, T. 1999. The construction of the World Wide Web audience. *Media, Culture, and Society* 21:673–684.

Rose, B., and J. Lenski. 2007. The infinite dial, 2007: Radio's digital platforms. New York: Arbitron.

Roslo, L. 1989. Audience research: Pragmatism at work. *Review of Business* 11.1:15–18.

Ross, K., and V. Nightingale. 2003. *Media and Audiences: New Perspectives*. Berkshire, UK: Open University Press.

Ross, S. J. 1999. The revolt of the audience: Reconsidering audiences and reception during the silent era. In *American Movie Audiences: From the Turn of the Century to the Early Sound Era*, ed. M. Stokes and R. Maltby, 92–111. London: British Film Institute.

Ross, S. M. 2008. *Beyond the Box: Television and the Internet*. Malden, MA: Blackwell.

Rosse, J. N. 1980. The decline of direct newspaper competition. *Journal of Competition* 30:65–71.

Rossman, G. 2008. By the numbers: Lessons from radio. In *Engaging Art: The Next Great Transformation of America's Cultural Life*, ed. S. J. Tepper and B. Ivey, 257–270. New York: Routledge.

Rowson, J. A., R. Gossweiler, and K. MacDonald. 2005. PHIZ: Discovering TV's long tail through a channel-centric model. Paper presented at the 3rd European Conference on Interactive Television, Aalborg University, Denmark, March/April. Retrieved May 2, 2009, from: http://www.hpl.hp.com/techreports/2005/HPL-2005-84.pdf.

Ruane, K. A. 2009. Privacy law and online advertising: Legal analysis of data gathering by online advertisers such as Double Click and NebuAd. Congressional Research Service Report for Congress.

Rubens, W. S. 1984. High-tech audience measurement for new-tech audiences. *Critical Studies in Mass Communication* 1.2:195–205.

Russell, C. A., and C. P. Puto. 1999. Rethinking television audience measures: An exploration into the construct of audience connectedness. *Marketing Letters* 10.4:393–407.

Salganik, M. J., and Watts, D. J. 2008. Leading the herd astray: An experimental study of self-fulfilling prophecies in an artificial cultural market. *Social Psychology Quarterly* 71.4:338–355.

Sandoval, G. 2008. Could peace be near for YouTube and Hollywood? *CNET News*, July 23. Retrieved July 23, 2008, from: http://news.cnet.com/8301-1023_3-9996905-93.html.

Saphir, A. 2008. *Trib* buries news in redesign test. *Crain's Chicago Business*, July 21. Retrieved April 29, 2009, from: http://www.chicagobusiness.com/cgi-bin/news.pl?id=30261&seenIt=1.

Sass, E. 2009a. Nielsen, Arbitron battle for radio ratings. *Media Daily News*, Sept. 23. Retrieved Oct. 18, 2009, from: http://www.mediapost.com/publications/?fa=Articles.showArticle&art_aid=114188.

Saas, E. 2009b. Google will limit viewing of paid content. *Media Daily News,* Dec. 2. Retrieved Feb. 25, 2010, from: http://www.mediapost.com/publications/?fa=Articles.showArticle&art_aid=118377.

Savage, P. 2006. The audience massage: Audience research and Canadian public broadcasting. Paper presented at the RIPE@2006 conference, Amsterdam, Oct.

Schauer, F. 1988. Commercial speech and the architecture of the First Amendment. *University of Cincinnati Law Review* 56:1181–1203.

Schiavone, N. P. 1988. Lessons from the radio research experience for all electronic media. *Journal of Advertising Research* 28.3:RC11–RC15.

Schley, S. 2007. New ratings era may be out of the box: Researchers look to set-tops for clearer picture. *Multichannel News*, May 7. Retrieved April 22, 2009, from: http://www.multichannel.com/article/128890-New_Ratings_Era_May_Be_Out_of_the_Box.php.

Schudson, M. 2006. The troubling equivalence of citizen and consumer. *Annals of the American Academy of Political and Social Science* 608:193–204.

Schultz, D. E. 1979. Media research users want. *Journal of Advertising Research* 19.6:13–17.

Schultz, T. 2000. Mass media and the concept of interactivity: An exploratory study of online forums and reader email. *Media, Culture, and Society* 22.2:205–222.

Schwoch, J. 1990. Selling the sight/site of sound: Broadcast advertising and the transition form radio to television. *Cinema Journal* 30.1:55–66.

Scott, A. J. 2005. *On Hollywood: The Place, the Industry.* Princeton: Princeton University Press.

Searle, J. R. 1995. *The Construction of Social Reality.* New York: Free Press.

Seldes, G. V. 1950. *The Great Audience.* New York: Viking.

Sen, S., B. Padmanabhan, A. Tuzhilin, N. H. White, and R. Stein. 1998. The identification and satisfaction of consumer analysis-driven information needs of marketers on the WWW. *European Journal of Marketing* 32.7/8:688–702.

Shapo, M. S. 1997. Fact/opinion = evidence/argument. *Northwestern University Law Review* 91:1108–1113.

Shields, M. 2008a. Death of display? *Mediaweek*, Nov. 24.

———. 2008b. Quantcast heats up online video metrics space. *Mediaweek*, Dec. 15, 7.

———. 2009. YouTube plays partner. *Mediaweek*, March 16, 7.

Shimpach, S. 2005. Working watching: The creative and cultural labor of the media audience. *Social Semiotics* 15.3:343–360.

Siapera, E. 2004. From couch potatoes to cybernauts? The expanding notion of the audience on TV channels' Websites. *New Media and Society* 6.2:155–172.

Silver, B. n.d. Collective intelligence: Understanding the mindset of the online consumer through predictive insight. Retrieved Feb. 19, 2009, from http://www .brandintel.com/resources/Collective%20Intelligence%20Whitepaper%20 Feb%202008.pdf.

Silvey, R. 1944. Methods of listener research employed by the British Broadcasting Corporation. *Journal of the Royal Statistical Society* 107.3/4:190–230.

———. 1951. Methods of viewer research employed by the British Broadcasting Corporation. *Public Opinion Quarterly* 15.1:89–94.

———. 1974. *Who's Listening? The Story of BBC Audience Research.* London: Allen and Unwin.

Simmons Market Research Bureau. 2007. Multi-media engagement study. New York: Author.

Singer, J. B. 2004. Strange bedfellows? The diffusion of convergence in four news organizations. *Journalism Studies* 5.1:3–18.

Slot, M., and V. Frissen. 2007. Users in the "golden" age of the Information Society. *Observatorio Journal* 3:201–224.

Smillie, D. 2009. Murdoch wants a Google rebellion. *Forbes*, April 3. Retrieved Nov. 3, 2009, from: http://www.forbes.com/2009/04/03/rupert-murdoch-google-business-media-murdoch.html.

Smith, R. L. 1972. *The Wired Nation.* New York: Harper and Row.

Smith, S., and N. North. 2006. Finger on the pulse: How the BBC is revolutionising audience relationships. Paper presented at the ESOMAR Worldwide Multi Media Measurement conference, Shanghai, China, June.

Smith-Shomade, B. E. 2004. Narrowcasting in the new world information order: A space for the audience? *Television and New Media* 5.1:69–81.

Smythe, D. 1977. Communications: Blindspot of Western Marxism. *Canadian Journal of Political and Social Theory* 1.3:1–27.

——. 1978. A rejoinder to Graham Murdock. *Canadian Journal of Political and Social Theory* 2.2:120–129.

Smythe, T. C. 1986. The advertisers' war to verify newspaper circulation, 1870–1914. *American Journalism* 3.3:167–180.

Socolow, M. 2004. Psyche and society: Radio advertising and social psychology in America, 1923–1936. *Historical Journal of Film, Radio, and Television* 24.4:517–534.

de Sola Pool, I., and Shulman, I. 1959. Newsmen's fantasies, audiences, and newswriting. *Public Opinion Quarterly* 23.2:145–158.

Solove, D. J. 2004. *The Digital Person: Technology and Privacy in the Information Age*. New York: New York University Press.

Sorce, P., and A. Dewitz. 2006. The case for print media advertising in the Internet age. Research Monograph of the Printing Industry Center, Rochester Institute of Technology. Retrieved Jan. 20, 2009, from: http://print.rit.edu/pubs/ picrm200602-ch2.pdf.

Spangler, T. 2009a. Comcast "TV Warehouse" to collect STB clicks. *Multichannel News*, Jan. 9. Retrieved Jan. 9, 2009, from: http://www.multichannel.com/ article/161894-Comcast_TV_Warehouse_To_Collect_STB_Clicks.php.

——. 2009b. Interactive TV begins to bloom. *Multichannel News*, March 1. Retrieved March 5, 2009, from: http://www.multichannel.com/article/print/18294-Interactive_TV_Begins_To_Bloom.php.

Spangler, W. E., M. Gal-Or, and J. May. 2003. Using data mining to profile TV viewers. *Communications of the ACM* 46.12:67–83.

Spangler, W. E., K. S. Hartzel, and M. Gal-Or. 2006. Exploring the privacy implications of addressable advertising and viewer profiling. *Communications of the ACM* 49.5:119–123.

Spanish Radio Association. 2008. Leading Spanish-language radio broadcasters join forces to express concerns about Arbitron's flawed Portable People Meter. News release, June 11.

Spence v. Washington. 1974. 418 U.S. 405.

Spencer, S. 2007. Google deems cost-per-action as the "Holy Grail." *CNET News*, Aug. 27. Retrieved May 6, 2009, from: http://news.cnet.com/8301-13530_ 3-9764601-28.html.

Sprague, J. D. 1981. Exaggerated and understated newspaper reach. *Journal of Advertising Research* 21.6:39–44.

Springel, S. 1999. The new media paradigm: Users as creators of content. *Personal Technologies* 3:153–159.

Spurgeon, C. 2008. *Advertising and New Media*. London: Routledge.

Starkey, G. 2002. Radio audience research: Challenging the "gold standard." *Cultural Trends* 45:45–68.

——. 2004. Estimating audiences: Sampling in television and radio audience research. *Cultural Trends* 49:3–25.

Starr, P. 1987. The sociology of official statistics. In *The Politics of Numbers*, ed. W. Alonso and P. Starr. New York: Russell Sage Foundation.

——. 2009. Goodbye to the age of newspapers (hello to a new era of corruption). *New Republic*, March 4. Retrieved April 29, 2009, from: http://www.tnr.com/politics/story.html?id=a4e2aafc-cc92-4e79-90d1-db3946a6d119.

Starr, P., and R. Corson. 1987. Who will have the numbers? The rise of the statistical services industry and the politics of public data. In *The Politics of Numbers*, ed. W. Alonso and P. Starr, 415–447. New York: Russell Sage Foundation.

State of Florida, Office of the Attorney General v. Arbitron, Inc. 2009. Circuit Court of the Eleventh Judicial Circuit in and for Miami-Dade County, Florida.

Stavitsky, A. G. 1993. Listening for listeners: Educational radio and audience research. *Journalism History* 19.1:11–18.

——. 1995. "Guys in suits with charts": Audience research in U.S. public radio. *Journal of Broadcasting and Electronic Media* 39.2:177–189.

——. 1998. Counting the house in public television: A history of ratings use, 1953–1980. *Journal of Broadcasting and Electronic Media* 42.4:520–534.

Steinberg, B. 2006. More cable networks decline commercial-ratings system. *Wall Street Journal*, Oct. 25, B3.

——. 2007a. C3 ratings show 3% decline between ads and program audience. *Advertising Age*, Oct. 16. Retrieved May 2, 2009, from: http://adage.com/print?article_id=121186.

——. 2007b. ESPN, Nielsen take step toward "total audience" measurement. *Advertising Age*, Oct. 17. Retrieved Oct. 17, 2007, from: http://adage.com/print?article_id=121219.

——. 2008a. Olympics give NBC Universal first crack at cross-media metric. *Advertising Age*, Aug. 13. Retrieved Aug. 14, 2008, from: http://adage.com/mediaworks/article?article_id=130314.

——. 2008b. The broadcast ad model is broken. Now what? *Advertising Age*, Oct. 27. Retrieved May 2, 2009, from: http://adage.com/mediaworks/article?article_id=132006.

Steiner, G. A. 1963. *The People Look at Television: A Study of Audience Attitudes*. New York: Knopf.

Stelter, B. 2008a. Some media companies choose to profit from pirated YouTube clips. *New York Times*, Aug. 16. Retrieved April 29, 2009, from: http://www.nytimes.com/2008/08/16/technology/16tube.html?scp=1&sq=Some%20media%20companies%20choose%20to%20profit%20from%20pirated%20YouTube%20clips&st=cse.

——. 2008b. YouTube videos pull in real money. *New York Times*, Dec. 11. Retrieved April 29, 2009, from: http://www.nytimes.com/2008/12/11/business/media/11youtube.html?scp=1&sq=YouTube%20videos%20pull%20in%20real%20money&st=cse.

——. 2009a. Copyright challenges for sites that excerpt. *New York Times*, March 2. Retrieved April 29, 2009, from: http://www.nytimes.com/2009/03/02/business/media/02scrape.html?_r=1&8dpc.

——. 2009b. Disney's TV unit will make short videos available on YouTube. *New York Times*, March 31. Retrieved March 31, 2009, from: http://www.nytimes.com/2009/03/31/business/media/31youtube.html?scp=1&sq=Disney's%20TV%20unit%20will%20make%20short%20videos%20available%20on%20YouTube&st=cse.

——. 2009c. PBS finally signs up for Nielsen ratings. *New York Times*, December 21. Retrieved Dec. 21, 2009, from: http://www.nytimes/com/2009/12/21/business/media/21pbs.html.

Stern, M. 2010. Music radio where listeners are the DJs. *Media Life,* Feb. 11. Retrieved Feb. 25, 2010, from: http://www.medialifemagazine.com/artman2/publish/Radio_46/Music_radio_where_listeners_are_the_DJs.asp.

Stewart, D. W., and P. A. Pavlou. 2002. From consumer response to active consumer: Measuring the effectiveness of interactive media. *Academy of Marketing Science Journal* 30.4:376–396.

Stober, R. 2004. What media evolution is: A theoretical approach to the history of new media. *European Journal of Communication* 19.4:483–505.

Stone, D. 2001. *Policy Paradox: The Art of Political Decision-Making.* 3rd ed. New York: Norton.

Story, L. 2008a. How do they track you? Let us count the ways. *New York Times*, March 9. Retrieved March 10, 2008, from: http://bits.blogs.nytimes.com/2008/03/09/how-do-they-track-you-let-us-count-the-ways/.

——. 2008b. To aim ads, Web is keeping closer eye on you. *New York Times*, March 10. Retrieved March 10, 2008, from: http://www.nytimes.com/2008/03/10/technology/10privacy.html.

Strasser, S. 1989. *Satisfaction Guaranteed: The Making of the American Mass Market.* Washington, DC: Smithsonian Books.

Sullivan, L. 2010. Armchair CDs speak out on Super Bowl spots. *Online Media Daily*, Feb. 8. Retrieved Feb. 25, 2010, from: http://www.mediapost.com/publications/?fa=Articles.showArticle&art_aid=122062.

Sumpter, R. S. 2000. Daily newspaper editors' audience construction routines: A case study. *Critical Studies in Media Communication* 17.3:334–346.

Sunstein, C. 2007. *Republic.com 2.0.* Princeton: Princeton University Press.

Svoen, B. 2007. Consumers, participants, and creators: Young people's diverse use of television and new media. *ACM Computers in Entertainment* 5.2:1–16.

Swisher, P. S. 2007. The managed Web: A look at the impact of Web 2.0 on media asset management for the enterprise. *Journal of Digital Asset Management* 3.1:32–42.

Syvertsen, T. 2004. Citizens, audiences, customers, and players: A conceptual discussion of the relationship between broadcasters and their publics. *European Journal of Cultural Studies* 7.3:363–380.

Terranova, T. 2000. Producing culture for the digital economy. *Social Text* 18.2:33–58.

Thompson, C. 2008. If you liked this, you're sure to love that. *New York Times*, Nov. 23. Retrieved April 29, 2009, from: http://www.nytimes.com/2008/11/23/magazine/23Netflix-t.html?scp=1&sq=If%20you%20liked%20this,%20you're%20sure%20to%20love%20that&st=Search.

Thorson, E. 2008. Changing patterns of news consumption and participation: News recommendation engines. *Information, Communication, and Society* 11.4:473–489.

Thurman, N. 2008. Forums for citizen journalists? Adoption of user-generated content initiatives by online news media. *New Media and Society* 10.1:139–157.

Tinic, S. 2006. (En)visioning the televisual audience: Revisiting questions of power in the age of interactive television. In *The New Politics of Surveillance and Visibility*, ed. K. D. Haggerty and R. V. Ericson, 308–326. Toronto: University of Toronto Press.

TNS Media Research. 2008. The largest national audience measurement service in the United States: DirecTV and TNS Media Research unveil DirecTView. *Audience Matters*, spring. New York: Author.

Townely, B., D. J. Cooper, and L. Oakes. 1999. Performance measures and the dialectic of rationalization. Paper presented at the Critical Management Studies conference, Manchester, England.

Towns, A. 2009. Letter to Michael J. Copps, acting chairman, Federal Communications Commission, June 24. On file with author.

"Towns Opens Investigation Into Minority Owned Radio Stations' Ratings Decline." 2009. News release, June 29. Committee on Oversight and Government Reform, U.S. House of Representatives. Retrieved Oct. 8, 2009, from: http://oversight.house/gov/story.asp?ID=2521.

"Towns Subpoenas Media Ratings Council for Arbitron Documents." 2009. News release, Sept. 22. Committee on Oversight and Government Reform, U.S. House of Representatives. Retrieved Oct. 8, 2009, from: http://oversight.house/gov/story.asp?ID=2603.

TRA. 2008. 2008 TRA fact sheet. Retrieved Feb. 15, 2009, from: http://www.tra-global.com/Brochures/TRAGlobalBrochure.pdf.

Tucker, C., and J. Zhang. 2007. Long tail or steep tail? A field investigation into how online popularity information affects the distribution of customer choices. MIT Sloan School working paper 4655-07. Retrieved Jan. 20, 2009, from http://ssrn.com/abstract=1003286.

Tudor, D. 2009. Who counts? Who is being counted? How audience measurement embeds neoliberalism into urban space. *Media, Culture, and Society* 31.5:833–840.

Turow, J. 1977–78. Another view of "citizen feedback" to the mass media. *Public Opinion Quarterly* 41.4:534–543.

——. 1997. *Breaking Up America: Advertisers and the New Media World.* Chicago: University of Chicago Press.

——. 2006. *Niche Envy: Marketing Discrimination in the Digital Age.* Cambridge, MA: MIT Press.

Tushman, M. L., and P. Anderson. 1986. Technological discontinuities and organizational environments. *Administrative Science Quarterly* 31.3:439–465.

Univision Communications, Inc. v. Nielsen Media Research, Inc. 2004. No. BC 316833, 2004 WL 30507099 (Ca. Super., July 7).

Uricchio, W. 2004. Beyond the great divide: Collaborative networks and the challenge to dominant conceptions of creative industries. *International Journal of Cultural Studies* 7.1:79–90.

Uricchio, W., and R. Pearson. 1994. Constructing the audience: Competing discourses of morality and rationalization during the Nickelodeon period. *Iris* 17:43–54.

U.S. House of Representatives. 2008. Committee on Energy and Commerce: Hearing on what your broadband provider knows about your Web use: Deep-packet inspection and communications laws and policies, July 17. Retrieved April 2, 2009, from: http://energycommerce.house/gov/cmte_mtgs/110-ti-hrg.071708. DeepPacket.shtml.

U.S. Senate. 2004. Committee on Commerce, Science, and Transportation: Hearing on the implementation of Nielsen Local People Meter TV rating system, July 15. Retrieved Oct. 15, 2005, from: http://commerce.senate.gov/hearings/witnesslist. cfm?id=1269.

——. 2008a. Committee on Commerce, Science, and Transportation: Hearing on the privacy implications of online advertising, July 9. Retrieved April 2, 2009, from: http://commerce.senate.gov/public/index.cfm?FuseAction=Hearings. Hearing&Hearing_ID=e46b0d9f-562e-41a6-b460-a714bf37017.

——. 2008b. Committee on Commerce, Science, and Transportation: Hearing on broadband providers and consumer privacy, Sept. 25. Retrieved April 2, 2009, from: http://commerce.senate.gov/public/index.cfm?FuseAction=Hearings. Hearing&Hearing_ID=778594fe-a171-4906-a585-15fl9e2d602a.

van Dijk, J. 2009. Users like you? Theorizing agency in user-generated content. *Media, Culture, and Society* 31.1:41–58.

van Dijk, J., and L. de Vos. 2001. Searching for the Holy Grail: Images of interactive television. *New Media and Society* 3.4:443–465.

van Dijk, J., and K. Hacker. 2003. The digital divide as a complex and dynamic phenomenon. *The Information Society* 19:315–326.

Vasquez, D. 2007. What shows are getting the Web buzz. *Media Life*, Sept. 6. Retrieved Sept. 6, 2008, from: http://www.medialifemagazine.com/artman2/publish/Research_25/What_shows_are_getting_the_web_buzz.asp.

———. 2008a. Ranking TV shows by their buzz factor. *Media Life*, March 11. Retrieved March 11, 2008, from: http://www.medialifemagazine.com/artman2/publish/Research_25/Ranking_TV_shows_by_their_buzz_factor.asp.

———. 2008b. Why folks love the TV shows they do. *Media Life*, Sept. 25. Retrieved April 29, 2009, from: http://www.medialifemagazine.com/artman2/publish/Research_25/Why_folks_love_the_TV_shows_they_do.asp.

Verhaeghe, A., N. Schillewaert, S. Van Bellegham, C. Vergult, and D. Claus. 2007. A new approach for measuring "buzz": Word of mouth and word of mouse. Paper presented at the ESOMAR Worldwide Multi Media Measurement conference, Dublin, Ireland, June.

Viacom v. YouTube. 2007. Complaint for declaratory and injunctive relief and damages. U.S. District Court for the Southern District of New York.

Vidmeter.com. 2007. Analysis of copyrighted videos on YouTube.com. Retrieved March 19, 2009, from: http://www.vidmeter.com/i/vidmeter_copyright_report.pdf.

Virginia State Board of Pharmacy v. Virginia Citizen's Consumer Council, Inc. 1976. 425 U.S. 748, 762.

Vogt, C., and S. Knapman. 2007. Personal Web spaces and social networks: Understanding what it means for marketers. Paper presented at the ESOMAR Wordwide Multi Media Measurement conference, Dublin, Ireland, June.

Wang, A. 2006. Advertising engagement: A driver of message involvement on message effects. *Journal of Advertising Research* 46.4:355–368.

Ward, D. B. 1996. "Tracking the Culture of Consumption: Curtis Publishing Company, Charles Coolidge Parlin, and the Origins of Market Research, 1911–1930." Unpublished Ph.D. diss., University of Maryland.

Wasserman, E. 2008. Journalism becoming a consumer product. *Miami Herald*, Jan. 7. Retrieved Jan. 8, 2009, from: http://www.miamiherald.com/430/v-print/story/369434.html.

Waterman, D. 2004. Business models and program content. In *Internet Television*, ed. E. Noam, J. Groebel, and D. Gerbarg, 61–80. Mahwah, NJ: Erlbaum.

Waterman, D., S. W. Ji, and L. R. Rochet. 2007. Enforcement and control of piracy, copying, and sharing in the movie industry. *Review of Industrial Organization* 30:255–289.

Weaver, D. H., R. A. Beam, B. J. Brownlee, P. S. Voakes, and G. C. Wilhoit. 2006. *The American Journalist in the Twenty-first Century: U.S. News People at the Dawn of a New Millennium.* Mahwah, NJ: Erlbaum.

Weber, M. 1978. *Economy and Society.* Berkeley: University of California Press.

Webster, J. G. 1998. The audience. *Journal of Broadcasting and Electronic Media* 42.2:190–208.

———. 2006. Beneath the veneer of fragmentation: Television audience polarization in a multichannel world. *Journal of Communication* 55.2:366–382.

———. 2008. Developments in audience measurement and research. In *Kellogg on Advertising and Media*, ed. B. Calder, 123–138. New York: Wiley.

Webster, J. G., and S. F. Lin. 2002. The Internet audience: Web use as mass behavior. *Journal of Broadcasting and Electronic Media* 46.1:1–12.

Webster, J. G., and P. F. Phalen. 1997. *The Mass Audience: Rediscovering the Dominant Model.* Mahwah, NJ: Erlbaum.

——. 1994. Victim, consumer, or commodity? Audience models in communication policy. In *Audiencemaking: How the Media Create the Audience*, ed. J. S. Ettema and D. C. Whitney, 19–37. Thousand Oaks, CA: Sage.

Webster, J. G., P. F. Phalen, and L. L. Lichty. 2006. *Ratings Analysis: The Theory and Practice of Audience Research.* 3rd ed. Mahwah, NJ: Erlbaum.

Wehner, P. 2002. No place like home? Media audience research and its social imaginaries. Working paper, the Emory Center for Myth and Ritual in American Life. Retrieved Sept. 30, 2008, from: http://www.marial.emory.edu/pdfs/wp015_02.pdf.

Weinstein, J. 2002. Database protection and the First Amendment. *Dayton Law Review* 28:305–350.

Weisler, C. 2009. Set-top-box data: Next steps. *TV Board*, Feb. 4. Retrieved Feb. 9, 2009, from: http://www.mediapost.com/publications/?fa=Articles.showArticle& art_aid=99745.

Wenthe, J. F., and L. S. Wenthe. 2001. Who is surfing the Net? An analysis of Web measurement, rating, and auditing services. *Journal of Promotion Management* 6.1/2:19–30.

White, T. R. 1990. Hollywood's attempt at appropriating television: The case of Paramount Pictures. In *Hollywood in the Age of Television*, ed. T. Balio, 145–163. Boston: Unwin Hyman.

Wiebe, G. D. 1939. A comparison of various rating scales used in judging the merits of popular songs. *Journal of Applied Psychology* 23.1:18–22.

Wilbur, K. C. 2008. How the digital video recorder (DVR) changes traditional television advertising. *Journal of Advertising* 37.1:143–149.

Wilcox, S. 2000. Sampling and controlling a TV audience measurement panel. *International Journal of Market Research* 42.4:413–430.

Williams, R., and D. Edge. 1996. The social shaping of technology. *Research Policy* 25:865–899.

Winfield, B. H., ed. 2008. *Journalism, 1908: Birth of a Profession.* Columbia: University of Missouri Press.

Winseck, D. 2002. Netscapes of power: Convergence, consolidation, and power in the Canadian mediascape. *Media, Culture, and Society* 24:795–819.

Winston, B. 1999. *Media Technology and Society: A History from the Telegraph to the Internet.* New York: Routledge.

Wood, J. P. 1962. George Gallup. *Journal of Marketing* 26.4:78–80.

Wood, L., and D. C. Gloeckler. 2007. Project Apollo: Consumer-centric insights. Paper presented at the ESOMAR Worldwide Multi Media Measurement conference, Dublin, Ireland, June.

Wood, L., and J. Spaeth. 2008. Scoring media for ROI potential. Paper presented at the ESOMAR Worldwide Multi Media Measurement conference, Budapest, Hungary, June.

Wood, O. 2008. Measuring emotional engagement in advertising. Paper presented at ARF's Re:Think conference, New York, June.

Woodard, B. 2006. Building "engagement," one brick at a time. *Journal of Advertising Research* 46.4:353–354.

Wunsch-Vincent, S., and G. Vickery. 2007. Participative Web: User-created content. Report prepared for the OECD Committee for Information, Computer, and Communications Policy.

Wurtzel, A. 2009. Now or never: An urgent call to action for consensus on new media metrics. *Journal of Advertising Research* 49.3:263–265.

Yim, J. 2003. Audience concentration in the media: Cross-media comparisons and the introduction of the uncertainty measure. *Communication Monographs* 70.2:114–128.

Young, A. 2008. Beyond Nielsen: A new rating for TV shows. *Advertising Age*, March 4. Retrieved March 5, 2008, from: http://adage.com/print?article_id=125466.

Zittrain, J. 2008. *The Future of the Internet: And How to Stop It.* New Haven: Yale University Press.

Zornow, D. 2008. Nielsen to measure 50 radio markets next spring. *Media News and Views*, Nov. 18. Retrieved March 31, 2009, from: http://www.medianewsandviews.com/2008/11/nielsenradiocumulu/.

INDEX

ABC, 94; advertising value index, 114
access: to audiences, 166–68; to the
    media, 165, 166
accuracy, 161, 163
ad-supported media, 66; audience
    fragmentation, impact of, 67, 69–
    70; consumer-supported media
    versus, 71; "magazine model" of,
    70
advertising: audience control over
    exposure to, 84; "behavioral," 16–17;
    engagement and, 96–99, 114; expo-
    sure, product loyalty and, 110; Great
    Depression and, 35; impression-
    based to impact-based, shift from,
    150; newspapers and, 56–57; online
    behavioral, 145–46; radio and, 33–35;
    rates, 70, 114; rationalization of
    audience understanding and, 41–42;
    social media sites and, 156; targeted,
    111–12, 145
Advertising Age, 149
Advertising Research Foundation:
    emotional response, publications
    on, 104; white papers, 96, 99
"affinity metric", 103–104
Amazon, 59, 60, 65, 86
American Association of Advertising
    Agencies, 95
Anderson, Chris, 58

"Anytime Anywhere Media Measure-
    ment" program, 76
"appreciation index," 49
appropriated content, 126
Arbitron, 73, 103–104; competition, 141;
    lawsuits, 137, 138–41. *See also* Por-
    table People Meter (PPM) initiative
Associated Press (AP), 128
Association of Hispanic Advertising
    Agencies, 136
asymmetrical bandwidth, 129
attention economy, 6
attentiveness, 90; audience value, as
    part of, 103
attitude, 91, 108
audience: active versus passive, 78, 152;
    actual versus potential, 34; as citizen
    versus consumer, 47; content pro-
    vider, distinction from, 11–13; "former
    audience," 78; information flows, 87f;
    as institution, 2; pacification of, 13; as
    product, 66; work of the, 82–84
audience appreciation, 90–91; assess-
    ment of, 102–104
audience attention: distribution,
    change in, 61–62; "long tail" of, mea-
    suring the, 71–72; monetization of,
    70, 73–74, 77; "power law distribu-
    tion" of, 60
audience autonomy, 5, 77–84

audience marketplace and, 84–87; components of, 79t; content production and, 154–55; defined, 8, 55; effects of, 7–8; overview, 77–78; resistance to, 123–30

audience behavior: deconstructing, 89–91; dimensions of, 94; integrated approaches to, 112–13; model of, 91f; online, monitoring of, 145–47; representation and transformation of, 118–19. *See also* behavioral responses

audience conceptualization. *See* audience understanding

audience engagement. *See* engagement

audience evolution, 4, 5, 12; audience information systems and, 113–16; broader implications of, 18–19; content production and, 154–59; factors driving, 118, 122, 150; media policy and, 165–69; necessary conditions for, 28; political economy of, 153–54; process of, 149–52; resistance to, 15–17

audience fragmentation, 57–58, 152; ad-supported media, impact on, 67, 69–70; resistance to, 123–30

audience information systems, 9–11, 113–16; audience conceptualization and, 150–51; innovation in, 121; motion picture industry and, 39; privacy and, 144–47; qualitative, failed attempts at, 47–48; rationalization of audience understanding and, 157; resistance to, 16–17, 131–48; for user-generated content, 92–93

"audience intellectuals," 36–37

audience marketplace: audience autonomy and, 84–87; "crisis of confidence" in, 76; "long tail" phenomenon of the, 66–77

audience measurement, 10; competition in, 141–42; data sources, 19–21; electronic versus paper, 74; initiatives, 74; legislation, 134; panel-based, 72–73, 74–75; regulation of, 160–65; sample-based, 72; single source systems, 109–110; site-centric, 74–75; state of, 149. *See also* audience information systems; People Meters

audience research: market research, connection with, 53; methodological developments, 37–39; resistance to, 43; uncertainty of, 50–51

audience understanding, xi–xii, 1–2, 5–6; alternative, rise of, 151f; audience information systems and, 150–51; challenges, 7, 8; importance of, 18; intuitive model, 32–33; passive, 13; politics of, 17; stakeholder negotiations and, 15; traditional model of, 13. *See also* audience research; rationalization of audience understanding

audience value, 103

Auletta, Ken, 120

awareness, 89–90, 92–93

"bandwagon effect," 64; review systems and, 65

BBC, 34–35; audience appreciation, assessment of, 103; audience research, resistance to, 44; behavioral responses, 108–112, 114

"behavioral advertising," 16–17

Benkler, Yochai, 122

"Big 3" broadcast networks: innovation, ineffective response to, 120. *See also* ABC; CBS; NBC Universal

Blockbuster, 63

blogs, xi, 9, 80; data from, 93, 105; news-related, 128, 129–30; resistance to, 126

Bogart, Leo, 45–46, 48

Bookscan system, 131–32

box office figures, 33

brainwave research, 104

BrandIntel, 92

broadcast industry. *See* broadcast television; radio

broadcast television, 55; advertising rates, 70; environmental change, slow response to, 120; ratings under LPM initiative, 133–34

Broadcast Rating Council. *See* Media Rating Council (MRC)

bundling of media content, 128–29

Bureau of Applied Research, 177n6, 177n10

buzz data, 91–94, 112

BuzzMetrics, 92, 105

C3 ratings system, 142–44

Cable Communications Policy Act of 1984, 191n32

cable television, 55; advertising rates, 70; audience measurement, 72–73; evolution of, 30; industry response to, 120; ratings under LPM initiative, 133–34. *See also* set-top boxes, television

Cablevision, 186n37

"calibrated journalism," 157

Canoe Ventures, 111–12

Catalina Marketing, 110

CBS, 127

cell phones, 55; as measurement systems, 76

Center for Digital Democracy, 147

"channel surfing," 60

chatrooms, 93

"chatter," 9–10, 92

"Chicago school" of sociology, 37

Cirlin Reactograph, 39

civil rights violations, 137

classified services, 56

click-through rates, 85, 110

Cloverfield (film), 155

Coalition for Innovative Media Measurement, 143

comments systems, consumer-generated, 82

commercial audiences, 142–43

commercial versus noncommercial speech, 138–41

commercial viewership index (CVI), 101

communication, reciprocal, 31, 42

competition, emergence of, 141–42

"competitive displacement," 27

computers, rise of, 40

comScore, 72, 73; "data collection events" assessment, 88–89

congressional hearings, 134

consumer empowerment, 77

consumer-generated media (CGM). *See* user-generated content

consumer-generated review systems, 65

consumer-supported media, 71

consumption, media. *See* media consumption

consumption culture, 35

content. *See* media content

content exposure: in audience behavior, 90; "dark matter" of, 73; data, 72; duration of, 101–102; maximizing, 6; measuring, 7, 9; precursors to, 91–94

"content power ratings," 112

content production, 154–59. *See also* user-generated content

content providers, 11–13, 16, 33

content storage capacity: of the Internet, 60; "long tail" phenomenon and, 62

content-delivery platforms, types of, 1

control: over audience unpredictability, 51–52. *See also* audience autonomy

cookies, 111

copyright issues, 16, 106; user-generated content and, 126–27

"cost-per-engagement" pricing model for online advertising, 114

costs: distribution capacity and, 58–59; programming, 67–68; user-generated content to reduce, 69

CPMI, 187n42

Craigslist, 56

"created facts," 162

"crisis of confidence" in audience marketplace, 76

culture: consumption, 35; content and, 18, 154, 155, 159; democratic, 166
currency: audience as, 163; ratings, 135, 143

"dark matter" of content exposure, 73
data: collection events, 88–89; DVR viewing, 101; exposure, 72; as non-speech, 163–65; qualitative, 94; search activities as, 86; server log, 75; shopping, 110; as "social facts," 160–62; sources, 19–21; symbolic value of, 52. *See also* buzz data; ratings data
decision-making: audience perspective and, 18; data analysis and, 158–59; formulation versus justification, 52
deep-packet inspection, 111, 146
delivery platforms, media, 55
democratic culture, 166
diaries, paper: listening, 38, 135, 136, 141; viewing, 40, 74, 132, 134
digital: fingerprinting, 127; footprints, 88, 144
"digital divide," 107
digital video recorders (DVRs). *See* DVRs
direct-broadcast satellite (DBS) television, 75
disaggregation of traditional media content, 56–57
discursive construct, audience as, 163
discussion boards, 9
distribution capacity, 58–59; "long tail" phenomenon and, 62
Don't Count Us Out Coalition, 134
DoubleClick, 145, 160
"double jeopardy effect," 175n3
DVRs, xi, 1, 55; capacity versus functionality, 17; fast-forwarding features, 8, 17; introduction and diffusion of, 142–44; legal challenges to, 125; recommendation features, 60; resistance to, 16; stakeholder conflict and, 124–25; viewing data, 101

economic(s): of media content, 58–59; recessions, xi
EDiaries, 141
eGRPs, 113
"80/20 rule," 58
electronic book readers, 55
Electronic Communications Privacy Act of 1986, 145
Electronic Privacy Information Center (EPIC), 147
"elite to popular/mass" stage of media evolution, 26
emotional bonding Q scores, 104
emotional response, 90–91; assessment of, 104
empowerment, consumer, 77
engagement, 90; in advertising and content, 96–99; components of, 91, 100; definitions of, varying, 96, 97–98t, 101; effects of, 100; exposure-derived approaches to, 100–102; history of, 95; magazines and, 101
Engagement: Definitions and Anatomy, 96
"enjoyment index," 48
environment, new media, 123
environmental change, organizational responses to, 118–22
E-Poll Market Research, 92
"evaluative facts," 162

Facebook, 160; core business model for, 81–82; privacy and, 146–47, 191n31
facial recognition technologies, 104
Fairness and Accuracy in Ratings Act, 160
"fan fiction," 126
fan mail, 33
fast-forwarding features, 8, 17, 101; for online videos, 127

Federal Communications Commission (FCC), 137
Federal Trade Commission (FTC), 134; investigations, 16–17, 145–46
film industry. *See* motion pictures
First Amendment protection. *See* free speech protection
"former audience," 78
"formula thinking," 45–46
Forrester Research, 77
FOX, 127, 134
fragmentation of the media environment, 55–66; audience autonomy and, 78–79, 123–30; contributing factors, 1; defined, 54–55; effects of, 4–7, 42. *See also* audience fragmentation; media fragmentation
fraud, 137
free speech protection: privacy and, 144; ratings data, 137–41, 163–65
frequent shopper cards, 110
FTC. *See* Federal Trade Commission (FTC)

Gallup, George, 37, 178n17
Gitlin, Todd, 161
Google, 82, 128
Great Depression, impact of, 35

hand-held devices, xi, 1
hearings, congressional, 134
heart rate monitoring, 104
Hey! Nielsen, 105
Hidden, The (film), 62–63
"hits" on audience attention, 58; ad-supported media and, 70
Homescan, 110
households as units of analysis, 41
Hughes, Justin, 162
Hulu, 127

IAG (Nielsen service), 108, 185n28
IMDB.com (Internet Movie Database, online), 86

impact-based advertising, 150
impression-based advertising, 150
impressions, 114
"incidental exposure," 183n4
income, per capita, 26
individuals as units of analysis, 152
industry sectors, media: blurred boundaries between, 56. *See also* magazines; newspapers; radio; television
information overload, 158–59
innovation: convergence with established media, 127–28; organizational responses to, 117–22; as threat, 119–20
"institutionalized audience," 2, 3
"institutionally effective audience," 2, 3, 7
institutions, definitions of, 2–3
Integrated Media Measurement (IMMI), 76
interactivity, 8, 144–47
interest, 90, 92–93
inter-media fragmentation, 55
Internet: access statistics for U.S., 107; advertising, 41–42, 70, 114; audience measurement, 72–73, 74–75; "chatter," 9–10, 92; conversations, analysis of, 104–106; interactivity of, 145; media fragmentation, apex of, 78–79; news, 55, 56; "stickiness" of Web sites, 90; streams, 55; "time spent," 90; "too measurable," 10, 86; websites, estimated number of, 56
intra-media fragmentation, 56
investigative journalism, 57
IPA Touchpoints Initiative, 186n32
iPad, xi
iPhone, xi
iPod, 55
iTunes, 60, 62–63

Jhally, Sut, 83
Journal of Advertising Research, 183n10

Journal of Marketing, 35
journalism: audience research, resistance to, 43–44; "calibrated," 157; "community funded," 157–58; investigative, 57; participatory, 129–30

Kazaa, 128
Kellner, Jamie, 125
Kelly, Chris, 191n31
Kindle, xi, 55
King Kong (film), 68–69

"law of the suppression of radical potential," 29–30
lawsuits. *See* legal challenges
Lazarsfeld, Paul, 37, 39, 46, 177n6
Lazarsfeld's Radio Research Project, 46
Lazarsfeld-Stanton Program Analyzer, 37, 39
legal challenges, 29; for copyright violation, 126–27; to DVR technology, 125; Local People Meter initiative and, 134; Portable People Meter initiative and, 137
legislation, audience measurement, 134
letters, audience, 33, 34–35
listener mail, 34–35
literacy, media evolution and, 26
Livant, Bill, 83
Local People Meter (LPM) initiative, 74, 160; resistance to, 132–35
Logos, 113–14
"long tail" of media consumption, 5, 21–22, 58–66; of the audience marketplace, 66–77; lengthening, 62; thickening, 62–65
Lost, 155
loyalty, 90, 110
LPM system. *See* Local People Meter (LPM) initiative
"lurkers," 106

"magazine model" of ad-supported media, 70

magazines, 37, 73; diversification, 28; engagement and, 101
mail: fan, 33; listener, 34–35
market information regimes, 155, 175n4
market research, 53
Marketing Evaluations, 104
Marketing-Scan, 186n32
"mash-ups," 126
mass communication, egalitarianism of, 80
Measures of Engagement, 99
media audience. *See* audience
media consumption: dynamics of, 122–31, 151–52; predictions of, 92; as wageless labor, 83. *See also* "long tail" of media consumption
media content: abundance, overstated, 68; bundling of, 128–29; copied, 126; influence of, 18; navigation tools, 59–60; "pure public good" model of, 58; "repurposing," 68–69; retail providers of, 22; traditional, disaggregation of, 56–57. *See also* content exposure; content production
media effects, 18
media evolution, 25, 26–30; resistance to, 28–30; stages of, 26–27
media fragmentation: content abundance and, 68; defined, 55; intermedia fragmentation, 55; intramedia fragmentation, 56; resistance to, 128
media organizations, 2, 3
media policy, 19, 23, 165–69; public interest and, 46–47
Media Rating Council (MRC), 133, 136, 143
media scholarship, 19, 23, 169–73
media strategy, changing, 5–6
message boards, online, 106
methodology, 19–21
Minority Media and Telecommunications Council, 136
minority populations: audience measurement systems, underrep-

resented by, 134, 136, 137; Internet access, 107

monetization: of audience attention, 70, 73–74, 77; of user-generated content, 81

Monster.com, 56

motion pictures: audience research, 38–39, 50, 93; audience understanding and, 32–33, 36, 51; content production, 155; industry resistance, 29, 43; symbolic value of data, 52; VCR as extension of, 30

MRI, 73

Murdoch, Rupert, 128

music: audience research and, 37; charts, 37; data sources, reliance on, 40; downloads, 56; industry lawsuits, 29

MySpace, core business model for, 81–82

NAACP, 136

"narrowcasting," 57

National Association of Black-Owned Broadcasters, 136

navigability of media, 59–60; "long tail" phenomenon and, 62

NBC Universal, 76, 127, 149; DVR technology, investment in, 125; engagement, guaranteed, 114

NebuAd, 145, 160

Netflix, 60, 62–63, 65, 82, 86

Networked Insights, 104–105

NeuroFocus, 104

"new economy of free labor," 82

"new managerialism," 44

new media environment, layers of, 123

NewMediaMetrics, 185n22

news: consulting, 37; piracy, 128

News Corp., 134

newspapers: advertising content, diminishing, 56–57; audience measurement, 73; audience understanding and, 32; blogs and, 128; "circulation spiral," 178n2; delivery platforms, 55; diversification, 27–28;

online publishing, response to, 120; rationalization of audience understanding and, 40–41; resistance to radio news, 29, 128

niche content, 63–64; production of, 65–66; "repurposing," 68–69

Nielsen Company, 73, 104; competition, 141; initiatives, 74, 76, 110, 132–35; lawsuits, 139. *See also* Local People Meter (LPM) initiative

Nielsen Fusion, 186n33

Nielsen NetRatings, 73

Nielsen Online, 75, 92, 104–105

1984 (radio program), 35

noncommercial versus commercial speech, 138–41

non-speech, audience data as, 163–65

objectivity, 163

on-demand service, cable, 55

online: activities as measure of engagement, 105–106; ad networks, 71; behavioral advertising, 16–17, 111–12, 145–46; conversations, analysis of, 104–108; forums, 80; participation, asymmetry of, 106; privacy (*see* privacy); surveys, 108

online television, 78

online videos: measurement systems, 75. *See also* YouTube

opinions: audience as, 163; defining elements of, 161; ratings data as, 140

Optimedia, 92, 112

panel-based methods of audience measurement, 72–73; site-centric methods, merged with, 74–75

paper diaries: listening, 38, 135, 136, 141; viewing, 40, 74, 132, 134

Pareto Principle, 58

"participation gap," 107

"participatory journalism," 129–30

People Meters, 103. *See also* Local People Meter (LPM) initiative; Portable People Meter (PPM) initiative

piracy: news, 128; user-generated content and, 129

podcasts, usage estimates for, 80

policy, media. *See* media policy

political economy of audience evolution, 153–54

Politics of Numbers, The, 153–54

popularity, product, 64–65

Portable People Meter (PPM) initiative, 74, 110, 141, 160; resistance to, 132, 135–37

post-exposure audience marketplace, 15, 149

"power law distribution" of audience attention, 60

PPM system. *See* Portable People Meter (PPM) initiative

privacy, 145–47

private goods used to distribute public goods, 58–59

privatization of media, 44–45

product: loyalty, 90, 110; purchasing behavior, 109–110

"produsage," 79

"program engagement score," 108

program guides, television, 60

programming costs, 67–68

Project Apollo, 110

Project Canoe, 111–12

"prosumers," 79, 82

psychology, audience research and, 37

public goods, 58–59

Public Opinion Quarterly, 35

public service media, 44–45

Q scores, emotional bonding, 104

qualitative research, 48–49

"quality evaluation index," 103

radio, 12–13; appreciation assessment, 103–104; "audience intellectuals" and, 36–37; audience measurement, 73; audience understanding and, 33–35, 36; newspapers, resistance from, 29, 128; programming philosophies, 49–50; qualitative research, failed attempts at, 48; ratings data, free speech protection of, 138–41; syndicated ratings services, 37–39; "time spent listening," 90. *See also* paper diaries

Radio Act of 1927, 36

ratings data, 112–13; content exposure and, 170; free speech protection and, 137–41; as opinion, 140

ratings systems, consumer-generated, 48, 82, 86

rationalization of audience understanding, 11, 26, 152; audience information systems and, 157; contributing factors, 35–36, 41–42; critiques, 45–50; elements of, 30; motivations for, 50–53; newspapers and, 40–41; radio, accelerated in, 38; reciprocal communication and, 31, 42; resistance to, 15, 42–45; television and, 40

reality television, 79, 156

recall, 91; engagement and, 100, 108

recommendation systems, consumer-generated, 60, 62–63, 86; media consumption and, 64–65

regulation of audience measurement, 160–65

Rentrak, 75

ReplayTV, 124

"repurposing" of media content, 68–69

resistance and negotiation, stakeholder, 15–17, 117–131; to audience evolution, 15–17; to audience information systems, 131–48; to media evolution, 28–30; to media fragmentation, 128; to rationalization of audience understanding, 15, 42–45; to user-generated content, 125–30. *See also* innovation

retail industry, 22

"return path data," 88

revenue-sharing agreements, 127

review systems, consumer-generated, 65, 82

"right to read anonymously," 144
RottenTomatoes.com, 86
Roy Morgan International, 108
royalties, 128

samples, audience, 72
Scarborough, 73
Schauer, Frederick, 163
scholarship, media, 19, 23
search activities as data source, 86
search engines, 128, 168–69
searchability of media, 60; media consumption and, 62–65
Searle, John, 162
self-regulatory principles for online behavioral advertising, 145–46
server log data, 75
set-top boxes, television, 41, 110, 143; as data source, 75, 101, 111–12. *See also* People Meters
Showtime, 127
"silent majority," 106
"slivercasting," 57
single source audience measurement systems, 109–110
site-centric methods of audience measurement, 74–75
skin conductance analysis, 104
Slingbox, 78
smartphones, 89
Smythe, Dallas, 83
"social facts," audience data as, 160–62
social media, 80; advertising and, 156. *See also* social networking sites
social networking sites, 80, 106–107; as data source, 105; privacy and, 146–47; rise of, xi
socioeconomic status, online participation and, 107
sociology, 37
Soundscan system, 131–32
Spanish Radio Association, 136
"specialized" stage of media evolution, 27
speech: audience data as non-, 163–65;

commercial versus noncommercial, 138–41
Spence v. Washington, 164
Spot.us, 157–58
stakeholders. *See* resistance and negotiation, stakeholder
Starr, Paul, 153–54
"statistical system," 153–54
"stickiness," 90, 156
Stop‖Watch ratings service, 101
storage capacity. *See* content storage capacity
streaming media. *See* online television; online videos
"suppression of radical potential," 124
surveys, 104; online, 108; telephone, 93
symbolic value of data, 52

"talent gap" in the media industry, 159
technology: audience evolution compelled by, 13–14, 27, 118, 122; fragmentation and, 5, 41; resistance to, 16. *See also* innovation
telephone surveys, 93
television: appreciation assessment, 103; buzz data and, 93–94; clips, 56; content abundance and, 67; content production, 155; delivery platforms, 55; direct-broadcast satellite (DBS), 75; electronic guides, 60; emotional response assessment, 104; engagement assessment, 105–106, 108; measurement systems, 76; minority viewers, 134; qualitative research, failed attempts at, 48; ratings data, 112–13; rationalization of audience understanding and, 40; "surplus watching time," 83; video clips, online, 105–106; viewers, minority, 134. *See also* broadcast television; cable television; online television; paper diaries; reality television
theater, interactive, 12, 13
"threat bias," 120
"time spent listening," 90

Time Warner, 182n3

TiVo, 101; data from, 110; DVR technology, introduction of, 124–25; FTC investigation of, 16; recommendation features, 60, 86

TNS Media Intelligence, 92

TNS Media Research, 75

"Total Audience Measurement Index" (TAMI), 76

TRA Inc., 110

traditional exposure model: audience autonomy and, 85; challenges and strategies, 74; critique of, 46; decline of, 13–15, 76–77, 150, 151f; fragmentation of the media environment and, 72; reconceptualized media audience versus, 17

"triple jeopardy effect," 175n3

Turner Broadcasting, 125

TV Warehouse, 112

"Tyranny of More, The," 66–67

Ugly Betty, 94

Univision Communications Inc. v. Nielsen Media Research 2004, 134, 139

U.S. Federal Trade Commission. See FTC

user-generated content: advent of, 79; audience information systems for, 92–93; as budgetary strategy, 69; copyright issues, 126–27; creation and consumption estimates, 80; defined, 78; distribution capacity, changes in, 81; engagement and, 105; monetization of, 81; piracy and, 129; privacy and, 146–47; resistance to, 125–30; traditional media content versus, 1

VCR technology: ban of, attempted, 29; film industry, extension of, 30; industry response to, 120

Viacom, 29; lawsuits, 126–27

VideoCensus, 75

viewers, minority. See minority populations

Visible Technologies, 92

"walled gardens," 42

Wal-Mart, 107

Waterman, David, 70

Web 2.0, 80; consumer role in, changing, 81–82

Web Analytics Demystified, 112

Weber, Max, 30

Web-scraping software, 92

Web sites, estimated number of, 56

Webster, James G., 68

wikis, 80

"word of mouse," 92

word-of-mouth, 83, 92, 105

"worker film movement," 12

Wurtzel, Alan, 149

Yahoo, 182n3, 185n22

YouTube, 60, 185n22; copyright violation and, 126–27; core business model for, 81–82; lawsuits, 29. See also online videos